BUILDING AN AMERICAN IDENTITY

Pattern Book Homes and Communities, 1870–1900

Linda E. Smeins

AltaMira
PRESS

A Division of Sage Publications, Inc.
Walnut Creek • London • New Delhi

For information, address:

AltaMira Press
1630 North Main Street, Suite 367
Walnut Creek, CA 94596

SAGE Publications Ltd.
6 Bonhill Street
London EC2A 4PU
United Kingdom

SAGE Publications India Pvt. Ltd.
M-32 Market
Greater Kailash I
New Delhi 110 048 India

Printed in the United States of America

Library of Congress Cataloging-in-Publication Data
Building an American identity: pattern book homes and communities, 1870-1900 / Linda E. Smeins.
p. cm.
Includes bibliographical references (p. 310) and index.
ISBN 0-7619-8962-5 (cloth) — ISBN 0-7619-8963-3 (pbk.)
1. Suburban homes—United States. 2. Eclecticism in architecture—United States. 3. Nationalism and architecture—United States. 4. Architecture, Modern—19th century—United States. 5. Architecture, Domestic—United States—Designs and plans. I. Title.
NA7571 .S54 1999
728'.0973'09034—ddc21
98-40127

ISBN Cloth: 0-7619-8962-5
Paper: 0-76199-8963-3

99 00 01 02 03 04 8 7 6 5 4 3 2 1

Editorial Coordination: Pam Lucas
Production Management & Services: Virginia Alderson Hoffman
Typesetting and Layout: ibid, northwest, hamilton, mt
Cover Design: Joanna Ebenstein

To the memory of my father,
Egbert Smeins, a small-town carpenter

⌖ Contents ⌖

List of Figures

Acknowledgments

◿ List of Figures ◣

◿ Acknowledgments ◣

This book is the product of several stages of development. In each stage, I posed different questions about late-nineteenth-century houses and during each, I benefitted from the kindnesses of friends and colleagues who offered encouragement and critical input. I am most indebted to Joseph Krause, whose enthusiasm for California history and regional architecture turned my early research interests from the history of canonized individuals to homes and communities. When this first phase of study required touring the streets of Los Angeles County to locate and visually document some four hundred late-nineteenth-century houses, it was accomplished with the patience and photographic expertise of Vincent Fusco.

Faculty at the University of British Columbia were instrumental to the manuscript's expansion to its North American scope. Rhodri Windsor Liscombe deserves special consideration for his unflagging support as my advisor. With his insistence on thorough research and close reading, plus the uncountable hours he contributed to discussing, reading drafts, and editing, he set an example as a teacher and a scholar. Following the completion of my graduate thesis, many contributed to the manuscript's theoretical development. Conversations with Kay Dian Kriz, Toby Smith, Jane Lomholt, and Charles Dyke continually pushed the limits of my critical thinking. Barbara Rofkar and Leslie Nordtvedt receive heartfelt thanks for their encouragement, analytical critique, and draft readings. Without our shared hours of walking and talking, the manuscript surely would not have been completed. The editors at AltaMira Press deserve credit for bringing the book together conceptually, for they proposed that I develop my manuscript's considerations of community. Pam Lucas has since offered insightful suggestions that demonstrate a special eye for the relationship of detail to the larger project. Virginia Hoffman has calmly guided the manuscript through editing, skillfully balancing the readers' interests with my own.

I am indebted to many who have helped me through the years, for writing this book has been more a collaborative than an individual project. Both the University of British Columbia and Western

Washington University have provided research travel funds. Western's professional leave support and a Bureau for Faculty Research grant for production of the illustrations were invaluable. I have benefitted from the professional assistance of reference and special collections librarians at both institutions as well as from archival curators and community historians across the continent. They tracked down obscure information and kindly offered me access to their resources. Homeowners have invited me into their historic houses and have shared personal documents and photographs. Georgia Sentkowski and Pat Eley in the Department of Art were my source of stability as I worked through technical problems. Alan Sanders of Quicksilver Photo Lab often achieved the impossible as he prepared the prints for the book's illustrations. Finally, I wish to thank my students from these past several years who asked questions of their own research that prompted me daily to look anew at my work. They have given me no intellectual rest, and for this I am most grateful.

◣ *Introduction* ◢

> The nineteenth century may be known for many things in the future, but it cannot well escape one uncomfortable name, that of the Century of Ugliness (*Craftsman*, 1904).[1]

> The nineteenth century was an undisguised triumph of mechanics over aesthetics, and it is one of the most urgent of present tasks to again make civilization lovely . . . let us bring to our homes all the possible elements of culture (*Craftsman*, 1905).[2]

The objects of this harsh criticism were today's beloved, colorfully painted, and ornate nineteenth-century houses with their turrets, scalloped shingles, and bay windows (Fig. 1). They are found in most communities that experienced growth in the last quarter of the nineteenth century. Although the houses are known by many style names—Queen Anne, Eastlake, Stick, and others, we often place them under the aegis "Victorian" as a means of identifying houses that defy precise stylistic categorization. This designation was not commonly used in the nineteenth century, but despite its historical inaccuracy— or perhaps *because* of its imprecision—the word "Victorian" catches our imagination. It gives a name to a host of activities and values that have been attributed to life in the United States a century and more ago. Visions of a time long lost, when daily life was grounded in an untroubled community and a closely knit family, have joined with a need to identify physical, visual notations to feed our current historical memory. As the quotations above attest, twentieth-century Americans have not always loved these houses; it is a late-century phenomenon. With the entrance of classical, colonial, and bungalow fashions, homeowners removed their scroll-sawn decoration and painted the now-simplified buildings white, and at mid-century they modernized thousands of houses by cutting in picture windows and covering details with sheets of plywood. Exuberant examples of

Fig. 1. Robert Morse home, 1897, Bellingham, Wash., from George F. Barber's architectural pattern book, Cottage Souvenir, *No. 2, 1891, Knoxville, Tennessee. (Photograph courtesy of Galen Biery)*

late-nineteenth-century houses in numbers impossible to estimate were destroyed. But by the 1970s, with the coming bicentennial of the United States, popular interest in preserving the nation's late-nine-teenth-century architectural heritage grew, and since then, these houses have been the subject of innumerable private and civic pres-ervation efforts. Communities across the United States have published books and pamphlets that celebrate their "Victorian" homes. Popu-lar periodicals showing nineteenth-century houses and home life have proliferated, joining in the production of nostalgia for a less harried time, and books with lavish displays of colorful, gingerbread-en-crusted homes have helped to fuel a passion for seeing, refurbishing, and replicating these "Painted Ladies."[3]

For my study, I replace "Victorian" with the phrase "modern suburban home" as the operative designation for these houses. This is not done to introduce yet another style name, but to apply popular words of the nineteenth century. Although "Queen Anne" was a common designation through the last quarter of the century, houses more frequently were not categorized, and when style names were used, they were applied loosely. When Queen Anne was applied to buildings, it encompassed New England shingle-covered houses, small frame houses with little decoration, and those elaborate houses with complex massing and colorful detail that we call Queen Anne today. The late-nineteenth-century landscape of houses was characterized by variety. Nonetheless, a general type of house emerged as "modern" and the fashion of the time. Architectural pattern book author Robert Shoppell illustrated for his prospective clients a history of American domestic architecture that began with a log cabin and culminated in the "Modern House." In between, there was colonial, Greek Revival as his "classic mansion," "the nondescript," Gothic, Italian, and mansard roof houses (Fig. 2).[4] The modern conclusion was not a specific style in the architectural literature of the time but a genre of design having a picturesque silhouette that was inspired by nature and painted in its colors. Stemming from the confluence of suburban development and residential architectural fashion, Shoppell and other pattern book authors frequently attached the label "suburban" to their house designs as well, which meant a house graced by trees, lawns, and gardens. The houses were described as picturesque, cozy, and sometimes with old-fashioned touches, but they were above all modern and suburban.

Suburban development was seen as a prime example of progress. Pattern books and other contributors to the discourse on suburban homes perceived claiming rural space for housing as a production of American character and a process of American advancement, which encompassed suburbs within commuting distance of cities as well as autonomous towns. Expanding communities were conceptualized as large expanses of land that were retrieved for the national experience, as they were consumed for building detached houses. The nation's citizens were invited to relocate to a transformed geography exemplifying their very own dreams of Americanization and a more

Fig. 2. Illustrated "History of Domestic Architecture in America," culminating in the modern style of house. (Robert Shoppell, Modern Houses, *ca. 1887)*

cohesive social identity. Notions of suburban living were ever present in pictorial imagery that worked with the textual messages to enhance the authority of suburban space. Robert Shoppell made explicit the relation between geography and social identity with two illustrations arranged in a "before and after" format (Fig. 3). The first drawing, "The Virgin Tract," depicted a scene of rolling hills representing nature untouched by human hands. The second, with unmistakable contrast yet continuing to reveal the rural setting, demonstrated the

Fig. 3. The transformation of undeveloped land into suburbs and new communities was a sign of national progress. In this before-and-after pattern book illustration, a "virgin tract" becomes a "populous town" through "Enterprise and Improvement." (Robert Shoppell, Modern Houses, ca. 1887)

beauties of progress with hills and valley now covered with newly built houses in a "Populous Town." Through visual means he underscored the importance of new community development, then in the caption employed textual means to celebrate American "enterprise and improvement":

> In this country two good genii named Enterprise and Improvement perform feats as wonderful as those related in the Arabian Nights. They reclaim the wilderness literally, making it blossom as the rose. They build a few houses on a virgin tract; next year they build a few more; . . . the fifth year a still greater number, and establish a water supply, a sewage system and gas works, and so on, until a populous town extends through the valley and climbs up the sides of the hills. A distant mountain top, outlined against the sky, is all that is left of the virgin tract . . . "[5]

The ideal of a suburban house was not new, but it took more coherent shape for late-nineteenth-century Americans as an alternative to living in crowded cities. At a time when buildings were believed to exemplify, communicate, and influence the character of a nation's people, the subject of domestic architecture and its location became a site for negotiating traits of national identity. Among the most contested issues in the quest for a national style of building were what American houses would look like and who would determine their appearance. This came at a time when professionalism was becoming increasingly important to establishing public confidence in medical and law practices, university education, and appropriately trained architects. The design of houses for the United States was taken on as one of the issues on which members of the American Institute of Architects and contributors to their journal, the *American Architect and Building News,* defined parameters of their professional authority. In the late nineteenth century, anyone working in the building trades could call himself an architect, and in the estimation of those arguing professional status, local carpenters and builders who took advantage of the title, as well as homeowners who hired them, were too "uncultured" to recognize true art. The aspiring professionals found sufficient proof for this judgment in the eclectic mix of houses found in communities across the United States. At mid-century, houses with sharply pointed gables and heavily decorated barge boards stood next to houses with segmented bays and bulky corbels in the Italian fashion, representing in domestic form the traditional nineteenth-century architectural choices between medieval and classical. Both styles had supplanted the ubiquitous classic revival houses of the 1820s and 1830s and, with a multiplicity of fashionable alterations, remained viable choices for homeowners well into the last quarter of the century. Following the Civil War, and continuing until the end of the century, houses with Swiss broad eaves and brackets, Old English chimneys and half-timbering, French mansard roofs, and diverse details were added to the colorful mixture. Identifiable stylistic categories, such as gothic and what became known later as French Second Empire, gained relative serial popularity, but one style did not completely replace another. By 1876, the Centennial year, a house with a mansard roof in the modern French style could be built in the same community and at the same time as a Swiss or Italian gothic cottage. But during the last decades of the century, architectural features of style were frequently intermingled with a newly found freedom on single buildings, making any precise stylistic taxonomy an impossibility. However, these houses frequently were derived from and conceived by the general public under the umbrella stylistic term "Queen Anne," an architectural fashion first introduced in England. Many of the professional architects, some of whom were producers of pattern books, were fearful that the latest fashion import permitted too much architectural design freedom, and they recommended simplicity based on their perception of colonial historical foundations of American architecture. They presented their homes as dignified in contrast with the "barber-pole painting" and fancy "gew gaws" of popular homes.

Their message was directed primarily to an upper-middle-class audience, whose homes had the potential to symbolize the character of the American people. My use of the middle class as a category in this study recognizes that the plural—middle *classes*—is more accurate, for there are no distinct strata. Nineteenth-century middle-class status was attained through economic position, type of employment, and level of material goods consumption. In this way, it includes many from the working as well as the new managerial classes. I apply as well a broader definition of the middle class in terms of cultural hegemony. The dominant beliefs and values of the late nineteenth century supported the interests of the middle class and these became the unquestioned common sense of American identity. While economic and social differences were recognized, nineteenth-century texts defined Americans as a culturally homogenous group with similar goals. Values and beliefs that were considered American were predominantly a production of the middle classes, but became the status quo in spite of social contradictions, to be supported by lesser classes. The codification of an operative definition of the "American," whose beliefs were inherently middle class, was central to the cultural politics of the late nineteenth century.

At the same time, social distinctions were made, and these were evident in literature for the nation's home-building public. While architects with ties to the northeastern United States published articles in magazines reaching the more affluent among the middle classes, other popular magazines were directed elsewhere. Readers of *Scribner's* and *Harper's* found essays criticizing carpenter-built houses, but readers of *Godey's Lady's Book* looked at house designs that would be interpreted by local carpenters. Beginning in 1846, the magazine inserted monthly a small line drawing of an architect-designed house and its plan for interpretation by readers. Over 450 house designs were published between 1846 and 1892, and the editor of *Godey's*, Louis Antoine Godey, claimed in 1868 that more than 4,000 houses had been built with their plans.[6] Other popular periodicals that featured house designs with more or less frequency included, among others, *American Agriculturalist*, *American Farmer*, *New England Farmer and Horticultural Register*, and *Ladies Home Companion*. Building trade journals included such offerings as the *American Builder* and *Manufacturer and Builder*. Each was positioned in the spectrum of social distinctions. Among the publications, pattern books with house plans and descriptions that were marketed to prospective home owners in suburbs and small towns from coast to coast contributed most to the spread of fashions. The more entrepreneurial, and the most used, were harshly criticized by the architects who wrote from the urban perspective of the northeast.

The popularity of the modern suburban home grew commensurately with competitive entrepreneurship in pattern book production. Today's community architectural surveys show that pattern book designs and pattern-book-inspired houses were built up and down both coasts and across the North American continent, including Canada. Innovative pattern book authors explored means by which they could take advantage of the potential for increased sales of books and services. As participants in the nation's competitive entrepreneurial activity, which was encouraged by nineteenth-century theories of social evolution and capitalism, some vied with one another to introduce more services to their public. By the end of the century, architects and related companies provided architectural plans, specifications, loans, consulting services, even building materials, all of which could be ordered by mail. Pattern book architects were businessmen who participated in the prevailing credo of success by anticipating and responding to the professional architects and to the middle class public's practical and social building needs. At the same time, they promulgated middle-class home ownership as a vital affirmation of the prevailing ideology of progress as a moral imperative and social mobility. This became their most subtle and resourceful marketing technique. The pattern books were products of their time, and the language used in their introductory commentaries and house design descriptions adroitly supported those precepts which, according to the dominant perspective, were inherent to a democratic system. Hard work and success were moral imperatives and both became manifest in home ownership. From this belief, the virtue of the American people, thus of the nation, was founded in the home and held strong by the homeowner.

The discourses that converged in the search for American archi- ·tectural identity were structured on differences within the nation's mix of peoples—professional architects versus pattern book authors and untrained carpenters, a cultured public versus an uneducated public. But at the heart of these discourses was a difference between those who met the criteria of American character and those who through circumstance or belief lived dissimilarly. Through the last quarter of the nineteenth century, fears that dominant values were being eroded contributed to forging "American" attitudes and beliefs. Already living with economic fluctuations, the middle classes saw massive numbers of immigrants crowd into city tenements, labor riots spread across the states, trade unions grow in size and number, and socialism and communism proposed as alternatives to the current form of government. To many, the foundations of American life— Christian values, a work ethic based on a self-help conviction, a belief in social mobility, capitalism, and nuclear family structure—seemed to be at risk, and norms of cultural practice were sought to uphold the notion that there was a singular American character. Constructing an "American dream" narrative of financial, moral, and domestic security became a common enterprise, and the home surrounded by lawn and like-minded neighbors became its cultural symbol.

The following chapters are not a complete story of the late-nineteenth-century home; rather, they add to studies by others who have provided a foundation for this work. Clifford Clark, in *The American Family Home, 1800–1960* (1986), focuses on the ideal of the family home in the United States, with examinations of interior planning, the relationship between exterior architectural display and individual social needs, and changes in the home brought by technological developments in plumbing, heating, and lighting. David Handlin's *The American Home: Architecture and Society 1815–1915* (1979) is organized thematically to explain a home's location in community and landscape as well as exterior house design, interior planning, and new technologies. Gwendolyn Wright, in *Moralism and the Model Home: Domestic Architecture and Cultural Conflict in Chicago 1873–1913* (1980) and *Building the Dream: A Social History of Housing in America* (1981), examines the implications of establishing social norms for house, home, and community. In her accounts of the conflict stemming from differing interpretations of the model home and community among architects, builders, and pattern book authors, she introduces an important voice from reformers who sought ways to improve housing for the masses. Wright (*Building the Dream*, 1981), Ruth Schwartz Cowan (*More Work for Mother*, 1983), Susan Strasser (*Never Done*, 1982), and other authors take us into the private sphere of the home and the structuring of gender roles in the "cult of domesticity."[7] Essays in

The Women's West, edited by Susan Armitage and Elizabeth Jameson (1987), explore the ways in which women accepted or rejected this formation of female identity. More recent publications, for example, Ellen Gruber Garvey's *The Adman in the Parlor* (1996), have brought together the intersections of public and private domains in studies of women as nineteenth-century consumers.

These studies contribute greatly to our understanding of domestic architecture and the home in the late nineteenth century. To add to the work on meanings of home and community, I analyze the valences of cultural power that were articulated in the public discourses on identity. Because I am interested in the production of hegemony and its relationship to sites of cultural authority, I have paid close attention to debates on national style as they applied to domestic architecture. I have chosen to examine the first professional journal of the American Institute of Architects, which was published in Boston, because its editorial polemics on architecture were an attempt to set standards for the nation. Their efforts centered on establishing professional criteria for architectural practice and included definitions of a professional's credentials, buildings, and clients. That the standards were contested is evident in entrepreneurial pattern books and other trade publications. Yet, distinctions that were argued in the *American Architect* were interpreted for us. The *California Architect and Building News*, for example, gradually turned from having little interest in discriminating among carpenters, builders, and architects to appeals to standardize qualifications for the profession. The *Inland Architect*, serving the Midwest, published not-so-lightly veiled criticisms of the *American Architect*'s attempts to dictate national taste, but the *Inland Architect* also argued for professional standards.

From debates on national identity and architecture, I introduce the places where modern houses were built to explore the meanings of the suburban home as it applied to growing cities, suburbs and rural towns. Chapter Three explains the entrepreneurial expansion of architectural pattern books and their role in spreading the message of home building across the nation. The following chapter analyzes how the concept of home ownership, most notably a house in suburban nature, was articulated as a requirement of American identity. From the cultural mandate for individual home ownership, the question of who would design the homes and what they would look like introduces us to another feature of identity building. The middle-class home became a ground for contesting the cultural authority of builders and carpenters in debates as the self-proclaimed professional architects attempted to circumscribe access to meanings and designs in domestic architecture by asserting their definitions of housing appropriate to the United States. As we find in Chapter Seven on pattern book houses and in the Epilogue that documents extant buildings in a community in the Pacific Northwest, the professionals from what was believed to be the trend-setting Northeast may not have achieved cultural leadership.

This book began almost two decades ago when I documented late-nineteenth-century houses in Los Angeles County, California. Street by street, over four hundred houses were noted and photographed. My interest in the project came from my love of houses and research, but I was also curious about the growing contemporary fascination with the nineteenth century. As I recall, developers in Long Beach and in the San Francisco area were duplicating nineteenth-century houses for their new clients, and the excitement among my peers over these houses brought me to question nostalgia and the desire to reconstruct history through architecture. I could not imagine living in a "Victorian" replica, nor did I want to live in its original. (In my dreams, I live in a Richard Neutra house.) With my current less positivist study, I once again began to think about our relation to the "American" past. The scope of my study developed from my observations of contemporary interpretations of built environments that signify those times in American history when life was "real." Memory, in the form of nostalgia for a less complicated past, is seductive, and many of today's living spaces rework the past in attempts to reconstruct an idealized way of life. Signifying features of selectively remembered notions of home and community—street lights, store fronts, eyebrow dormers, bay windows, family dinners—are overlaid on spaces, and on the activities that enliven them, to make more secure a life characterized by change. These manifestations of a mythologized past helped me to expand my questions about the structured relationships between late-nineteenth-century homes and the development of suburbs, for they entail an intriguing conflation of suburban and small-town life. The most longed-for home of today remains the detached, owner-occupied house surrounded by lawn. However, this ideal home is not placed in the type of suburban development with endless rows of look-alike houses that is associated with Levittown and its subsequent variants. The suburban house is imagined in a community that has a Main Street.[8] It is located in a small town that has a strong sense of permanence and place, where neighbors know one another, the children are safe, and shopkeepers and their customers share the news of the day. When this historical memory is interpreted for actual built spaces, it merges with the current practices to reveal the desirable. Consider, for example, the new towns that are developed as an antidote to both the contemporary suburb and the city. The now-famous Seaport, Florida, was designed as an embodiment of dreams about small-town life. Interestingly, a problem its residents now face is how to function as a community. Do they work together as residents of a conventional suburb or as a small town? Memory does not always cover the daily practical transactions. In other communities, a characteristic feature of twentieth-century suburban life intermingles with the memory of small towns. New shopping malls are designed to resemble Main Street. So that they sustain a lived authenticity, they are not designed as Disneyland Main Street theme malls but with objects and architectural features that evoke the feeling of a small town, albeit surrounded by parking lot. Alternatively, towns with Main Streets attempt to make them economically viable by making them more convenient for shoppers who are accustomed to shopping in malls.

Of course, these observations about contemporary spaces for living cannot bear upon my analyses of the nineteenth century; nor can the present be explained as a linear progression of influences from the nineteenth century, for meanings are selected from the past for re-articulation. But today's nostalgic emphasis on the small town as the physical context for the suburban house is a vision of the "American dream" that prompted me to consider the maneuvering of cultural power in the process of building American identity in the nineteenth century. While the notion of the suburb as an antidote to the ills of city life was given form, small towns encouraged commercial and industrial development to stimulate population growth.

Communities in the growing southern and western states and territories were especially aggressive in their appeal to gain new citizens.
Growth was progress, and growth meant building new homes that
profited both from a belief in modern progress and a need for a retreat from the demands of modern daily life. That the retreat was a
house situated in the healthy fresh air of suburban nature in a community striving for urban attributes shows the urban-rural dichotomy
that was formulated in the nineteenth century, and which has informed much of our thinking about the nineteenth-century home, to
be a much more complex struggle to bring forward certain beliefs
about national, collective, and individual identity in the United States.

From this perspective, then, the following is not a linear history
of late-nineteenth-century houses and their communities. Although I
begin with the Centennial of 1876 and conclude with examples of
houses built in the last decade of the century, my concern is the complex negotiations for cultural authority over meanings and sites of
representation that had to do with producing the nineteenth-century
modern suburban house. The chapters demonstrate intersections of
related discourses which I conceptualized in terms of spatializing
American identity. Thinking about the dimensions of space extricates
us from viewing buildings and communities as objects imbued with
context-free meanings. It also enables us to form more salient connections with the social context that so often serves as historical
background. Looking at buildings, built environments, and texts as
"spatial practices" reconfigures the customary object/context relationship to one that highlights the social relations produced and
reproduced by their users in the territories of identity.

Attention to space challenges the notion of history as a diffu-
sion of ideas as they come from a leadership of cultural elite and it
gives us greater access to considerations of agency. An important
question for studies of middle-class and vernacular architecture, especially, is how people make use of objects and their meanings—and
I include as objects those ideas that have been made concrete through
discourse, such as the concept of a professional owning the cultural
distinction and title of "architect." What happens in the space between
an object and the holder of the power to accept, reject, or transform
it and what it represents? How does a local carpenter in Minnesota

or Pennsylvania, who in the nineteenth century typically called himself an architect, make use of new fashions from the East Coast members of the American Institute of Architects and their moves toward limiting access to the title architect through professionalization? And will prospective homeowners in California be convinced that simple colonial-style houses purveyed as the new fashion can fulfill their dreams? Each question is about social relations that are produced in physical and conceptual space. These and others that are posed in the topics of this study demonstrate the networks of spatialization that strengthened particular attributes of American identity. Definitions of American character located in house and community gained currency in the nineteenth century as an attribute of nationalism. It was a cultural project in which the ideology of Americanism was given national and localized spaces to which it belonged.

NOTES

1 Ernest Crosby, "The Century of Ugliness," *Craftsman* 6, 4(July 1904): 409.

2 Antoinette Rehmann, "The Modern House Beautiful: An Exhortation," *Craftsman* 7, 5(February 1905): 567.

3 The now popular term stems from Morley Baer, Elizabeth Pomada, and Michael Larsen, *Painted Ladies: San Francisco's Resplendent Victorians* (New York: E. P. Dutton, 1978) and later volumes in the series.

4 Robert Shoppell, *Shoppell's Modern Houses* (New York: Co-operative Building Plan Association, c. 1887), p. 64.

5 Linda Smeins, "National Rhetoric, Public Discourse, and Spatialization: Middle Class America and the Pattern Book House," *Nineteenth-Century Contexts* 16(Spring 1992), p. 159. Shoppell quote, 1887, n.p.

6 George L. Hersey, "Godey's Choice," *Journal of the Society of Architectural Historians* 18(October 1959): 104.

7 See also an article by Martha Marsh, "Suburban Men and Masculine Domesticity, 1870–1915," *American Quarterly* 40, 2(1988): 165–86.

8 Richard V. Francavigilia examines the construction of nostalgia for small town centers in *Main Street Revisited: Time, Space, and Image Building in Small-town America* (Iowa City: University of Iowa Press, 1996).

◿ 1 ◺

National Identity and an American Style of Architecture

> Although an Italian villa is more adaptable to our wants than a Greek temple (and our country-houses have often copied both with lamentable results) it does not readily submit to being Americanized (Brunner, 1884).[1]

Having a home of one's own is an unquestioned feature of the American dream. Owning a home on a small plot of land is imbedded in national history as a mark of distinction when comparisons are made between the United States and other countries. Beliefs about entitlement to home ownership override social and economic contradictions to symbolically link together the elements of diverse geography and population into a national abstraction with people having a common goal. As such, domestic architecture is inseparable from the formulations of national identity and nationalism. The concept of nation needs its symbols, for a belief in shared identity distinct from other national identities is an abstract notion that must be built in the imagination to make it concrete. Flags, parades, coinage, holidays, monuments to the fallen in wars and to political dignitaries, all make the otherwise difficult-to-comprehend geographic boundaries of nation more tangible.[2] The individual home for a nuclear family was established firmly as a national attribute in the late nineteenth century. As millions of immigrants entered the United States, with many of them crowding into city tenements, buying a home became more than a personal act. Individually owned, detached homes—in contrast with multiple housing collectively—were a sign of being truly American. In the conception of nationhood, becoming a citizen of the United States required assimilation by shedding one's alien cultural ways to become American. The house, too, must be American.

26

I begin the chapters on building American identity with an introduction to Centennial year celebrations of nationhood. A hundred years as a nation was a remarkable achievement. Not only was the United States a new experiment in the course of history, but the country recently had overcome the divisions of Civil War. The nation now could work competitively to join the prestigious circle of British and European industrial leaders. Here, we find the beginnings of a powerful mandate for Americanism. In response to disruptions brought by the war, various early nineteenth-century themes on nationalism cohered into a more effective conception of the meanings of "America."[3] During the years leading to the Centennial and through the next decades, ideas of national definition and national character fused with a need to have great pride in the nation and to express this as love for the country. However, the need to structure a pride-filled identity to some extent derived from a perceived lack of national achievement. Nineteenth-century writers on the national condition reveal that, in the midst of expressions of pride in a tested but enduring American democracy, there was a sense of insecurity about the standing of the United States among western nations. In actuality, the United States was but a fledgling nation when compared with the histories of European and British development. Although the land was rich with minerals and ores, the United States admittedly had yet to match England's industrial leadership.[4] Believed to be sorely lacking in high culture, the creative arts continued to rely on Britain and the Continent for leadership. Public discourse acknowledged that the United States was an inheritor of western cultural traditions and was a contemporary ally in western cultural and economic domination, but finding means to locate symbolic separation and international leadership was paramount. Gaining force with the Centennial and continuing through the century, the United States' status as a nation depended upon reworking its heritage to demonstrate its uniqueness—its "Americanness." Being perceived as a peer and an inheritor of western cultural and economic dominance was central to American identity, but the nineteenth century was a time of intense nationalism. Frequent struggles for statehood here and dominant power abroad contributed to the fostering of nationalism as a controlling theme in the public arts on both sides of the Atlantic. Each nation struggled to define unique achievements that were attribut-able to the character of its people, and each nation sought emblems of national solidarity. Among the emblems, architecture stood out as crucial to communicating nationhood to the world. Architects and cultural leaders in the United States, too, argued for symbolic nation-hood in buildings, but producing national identity through architecture was difficult in a nation whose people were defined more by dissimilarity than commonality. The task was made more difficult when they considered the reality of foreign precedents for their ar-chitecture as well. As architect Alfred Brunner explained in the quote above, the buildings themselves had to be Americanized.

The Centennial Exhibition, 1876

With relief over the end of the bloody War between the States, a group of politicians and businessmen from the North proposed a national celebration of the reunited country. By 1871, members of Congress had acted on the proposal, and President Grant appointed a commis-sion to plan the Centennial Exhibition of 1876, to be held in Philadelphia's Fairmount Park. The Centennial Exhibition plans were about the United States having overcome political division to achieve a full century of nationhood, and the organizers recognized the need for operative emblems of national unity that would physically bring together the people of the nation. From its inception and through 1876, the Centennial Exhibition was an action to bolster belief in the future of the nation. Reconstruction was working toward economic and social stability in the north and south, but there was much work yet to be done. Former governor of Pennsylvania William Bigler deliv-ered a speech to the organizers, saying that visitors to the fair would see that in America, ". . . the mass of the people whilst engaged in their daily and necessary pursuits, enjoy a larger measure of personal comforts and dignity than those of any other nation."[5] Reports show that the organizers' fears that unity was not fully achieved were not misplaced. The Mobile Daily Register, as one voice from the South, went so far as to call the Exhibition activities "a bold humbug and open fraud in its assumption of patriotic motive."[6]

The coming centenary of nationhood and the Exhibition brought eloquent exercises in national self-examination in various newspapers, popular periodicals, and trade journals. Many questioned whether the nation was actually fulfilling the dreams of its forefathers. As the year 1876 progressed, national order continued to face many challenges.[7] The economy was not fully recovered from the depression brought by the Panic of 1873. President Grant's government was vilified in the press amidst threats of impeachment. Confrontations between troops and Native Americans in the West continued, lynchings in the South escalated, and disabled soldiers panhandling on city street corners remained as graphic reminders of the war. But despite these obstacles to sustaining pride in the nation's achievements, and to override these impediments to perceptions of well-being, the exercises in introspection predominantly were self-congratulatory. The Centennial Exhibition provided a timely environment for a forum on the national condition, but for the most part, the forum became a platform to extoll the country's accomplishments, especially regarding its growth in commerce and industry. At its opening in May, scarcely a newspaper or magazine could be found without some mention of the Centennial and its attending issues of the nation, and the public responded enthusiastically. Through the months, an average of over a quarter of a million people each day came to see the buildings and exhibits put up by the United States and other nations. The displays from other countries, including such distant places as Japan and Egypt, brought the world to the American fair goers. Exotic decorative objects from the eastern lands and the colonial outposts of the represented European countries boosted their enthusiasm for the event, as did the new, but old-looking, half-timber British government buildings and displays of art from Britain and Europe.

But the Centennial was not about the accomplishments of other countries. It was about the United States. As a celebration of one hundred years of national history, it was premised on instilling pride in the present for the purposes of building a future. Robert Rydell emphasizes the patriotic tenor of the Centennial in his study of world fairs, saying, "Patriotism was explicitly linked to the need for continued economic growth as well as political and social stability."[8] The fair goers participated in this grand production. Visitors attending an international exposition sponsored by their own country engaged in forming estimations of themselves as national citizens. Planners arranged the spaces of the Main Exhibition Building to place the United States and its citizens at the center of the world to facilitate measuring the nation's performance. Displays from around the world were organized in a typical textbook-style cartographic manner, with the United States surrounded by the other countries. Latin America was directly across from (below) the United States section, the Asian nations were on its left, and France, England, and Germany were given prominent spots on the right.[9] At the Centennial Exhibition, amidst the array of international demonstrations of pride, the United States-sponsored buildings and displays announced America's anticipations for legitimate standing among nations of the world. Crowds thronged the Machinery Building to see the amazing 2500-horsepower Corliss Engine at work. In the same building, they saw the typewriter, the telephone, and other recent inventions that would transform the world. The exhibitions underscored the message conveyed by the proponents of American nationalism: the United States was prepared for an auspicious future. National unity had been maintained. The triumph of national consolidation now allowed a pursuit of economic and industrial ascendance.

Repeatedly, the public was fortified with the belief that the progressive character of Americans made it possible for the nation to rapidly overcome seemingly insurmountable obstacles and move toward international leadership in manufacturing. As I will explore in the following chapters, the public discourse on nationalism explained Americans as uncommonly enterprising and diligent. In this land of (perceived) unlimited resources, prosperity awaited the industrious, and those who worked hard to attain success contributed not only to their own standing but to the progress of the nation. Thus, it was a citizen's responsibility to contribute to the nation's good by upholding and actively communicating national beliefs. This theme of American character and nation, found in speeches, sermons, and printed materials ranging from McGuffey's Readers and dime novels to household manuals and professional journals, formulated the power of a common articulation of national identity. The nation's many peoples were undifferentiated and reminded of common identity with the many uses of the adjective "American" for products, leisure activities, and notations of progress. The 1876 revised edition of *Hobbs's Architecture,* for example, contained thirty-nine house plans and eight of them were "American" (Figs. 4, 5). At the same time, the unified vision was divisive, for it expressed the interests of the varied middle classes. The belief in social mobility as a distinctive feature of American life mapped out distinctions among its diverse peoples. Through the nineteenth century, newly arrived immigrants who did not pursue the hegemonic dream of success were in need of being "Americanized." Indigenous and African Americans, as well as Chinese immigrants along the Pacific, were largely absent in the proclamations of American character. When present, they often were posed as a contrast with the paradigmatic. Pattern book author George F. Barber in the early 1890s set up a visual distinction of American homes and social mobility by showing a "Negro cabin." From the early years of nationhood, definitions of American character developed on western conceptions of race and on idealized memories of its founding citizens from colonial history. A month after the opening of the Centennial Exhibition, Thomas M. Anderson explained American uniqueness in *Galaxy,* a periodical having an editorial policy permitting the illumination of America's ills but supporting the tenets of nationalism. The title of his article posed a question, "Have We a National Character?" His answer echoed prevailing sentiments when he described a narrowly defined citizenry having a northern European heritage. Americans had the "old Saxon passion for utility, their respect for wealth" and the "Norseman feeling of . . . restless energy."[10]

Architecture and national identity

From our perspective well over a century later, the Centennial seems to have been the time and place to exhibit a distinctive statement on American architecture. We merely need to look at the white classical buildings of the Chicago Columbian Exposition (1893) and Seattle's Space Needle (1962) to recognize the posed relationship between building design and the national identity of the host country of a world fair. The United States government buildings at the

Fig. 4. Leading to the 1876 centennial, pattern book authors participated in the search for symbols of national identity by designating houses as "American." An "American Suburban Residence." (Hobbs, Hobbs's Architecture, 1876)

Fig. 5. "An American Cottage." (Hobbs, Hobbs's Architecture, *1876)*

Centennial Exhibition were representative of building of the time, but they did not present an identifiable American style of architecture. As the centennial brought a commitment to the nation's future and, with it, a concerted effort to identify those things which were singularly American, the United States' buildings on the Exhibition grounds to many were a disappointment. Authors of guide books for the Exhibition grounds and buildings excitedly described the wonders to behold, but the architectural press and architectural critics whose articles were published in periodicals such as *American Architect and Building News, Scribner's,* and *Harper's,* did not share this enthusiasm for the buildings. A reviewer for the *American Architect* described the Horticultural Hall (Fig. 6), designed by H. J. Schwarzmann, the German-born directing architect for the Exhibition, as "quasi Moresque . . . but with an odd tinge of Renaissance and modern German in the detail, with occasionally a gothic touch."[11] The Main Exhibition building (Fig. 7), although covering thirteen acres, enough acreage to be the largest building in the world, had few distinguishing characteristics. It prompted lackluster comments similar to those of the *Atlantic Monthly* reporter who wrote, "It is not handsome nor agreeable, though not positively the reverse . . ."[12] He evidently agreed with the *American Architect* reviewer's impression of the Exhibition shortly after its opening. With some discouragement, he suggested

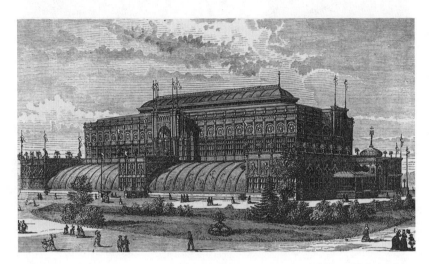

Fig. 6. H. J. Schwarzmann, Horticultural Hall, Centennial Exhibition, Philadelphia, 1876. (McCabe, History of the United States, 1877)

Fig. 7. H. J. Schwarzmann, Main Exhibition Building, Centennial Exhibition, Philadelphia, 1876. (McCabe, History of the United States, 1877)

that a world's fair was not the place where the public should expect to see architecture of lasting artistic or monumental value.[13]

The Centennial Exhibition cannot be claimed as a turning point in American architecture, but it arguably brought focus to the nineteenth-century endeavor of Americanization in which formulations of American character were inseparable from the pursuit of concrete manifestations of American identity. The search for an American style of architecture, which had been ongoing from early in the century, had not reached a satisfactory conclusion. Reports on local architecture attested to a myriad house styles across the land, noting that one would find Greek revival, gothic, Italianate, Swiss and French roof (mansard), and worse, these styles were often freely interpreted, even mixed together in one building. Architectural critics described public buildings in classical and gothic stylistic variations, some of which were judged as highly admirable, but others much less so. A common criticism of small-town main streets in the west was the prevalence of unlearned imitations of architecture. With this actual and perceived condition of the built environment, defining a national style of architecture became one of the major projects of late-century nationalism. In tandem with the production of a more cogent definition of a shared American character, architects, critics, builders, pattern book authors, and social commentators debated ways to organize the processes of building design to achieve shared American features. Whether architects of mansions and office blocks or of suburban cottages, most agreed that the United States surely needed a national style of architecture to communicate American national character. Philadelphia architect Samuel Sloan was one of many who professed the urgency to prospective middle-class homeowners. He applied resonating patriotic language in his 1871 pattern book, *City Homes, Country Houses and Church Architecture*, to claim, "The time must come, sooner or later, (and why not now?) when an original American style must be born of the National genius. This will be our *Naissant* style which would be *of* the country, as well as *for* the country. . . . Let everything be American, in feeling and effect. Such is our idea of what a National style ought to be."[14]

The belief that architecture embodied and exhibited the character of nations or groups of people was well established in Britain and

Europe, and those who shaped architectural theory from across the Atlantic were frequently invoked as authorities in the United States. Late-eighteenth-century proponents of environmental determinism had convincingly argued that geography and climate formed a people's history and a nation's character and that the arts were eminent visual expressions of these attributes. From the eighteenth to the nineteenth centuries, theorists in Britain, France, and Germany claimed that a native style of architecture, the most public art, was a physical manifestation of a nation's character, its moral quality, its present condition, and its history. English author John Ruskin, whose works on art and society were circulated extensively in the United States, encapsulated the substance of the belief when he explained his goals in his first published book on architecture. The final chapter began, "It has been my endeavor to show in the preceding pages how every form of noble architecture is in some sort the embodiment of the Polity, Life, History, and Religious Faith of nations."[15] This message was carried forward for five decades of nineteenth-century readers in the United States. *Seven Lamps of Architecture* was published in 1849 in London, but John Wiley & Sons, New York, published an unauthorized American edition in the same year. The publisher continued regularly to publish *Seven Lamps* into the 1890s. Followers of the French architect-theorist Eugene Emmanuel Viollet-le-Duc found a similar message in his writings, even though Ruskin and Viollet-le-Duc represented a separation between proponents of art (Ruskin) and science (Viollet-le-Duc) in architectural debates. Some thirty years after the introduction of Ruskin's treatise, U.S. government architect John L. Smithmeyer spoke eloquently to the Association of Architects in Washington, D.C. An admirer of Viollet-le-Duc's theoretical works, he claimed architecture to be "one of the clearest exponents of civilization . . . speaking a language from age to age, and from country to country, which is intelligible to all . . ."[16]

Theory based on such environmental and ethnographic determinism did not intend architectural expression as a passive enterprise. The public role for architecture was much more significant than exhibiting national identity, for buildings were seen to strongly affect the social, moral, and intellectual development of a country's people. Given impetus by the moralizing writings of Ruskin and his fellow enthusiasts of the gothic in Britain, architecture as an instrument of uplift was accepted as a certitude in America well before the Civil War. Oliver P. Smith, author of *The Domestic Architect* (1854), earnestly asserted, "Our minds and morals are subject to constant influence and modification, gradual, yet lasting, by the inanimate walls that surround."[17] The moral charge given architecture established a rationale with which later nineteenth-century architects argued the consequence of good or bad design from their profession's hands as well as the importance of educating their clients in matters of good taste. Architects who were engaged in defining professional criteria, by ascribing to the conception of architecture as an active contributor to national moral character, found an opportunity to emphasize their significant role in producing well-designed national architecture. Authors of pattern books directed to prospective home builders and owners, too, took up the message and assigned responsibility. Daniel Atwood, for example, told his readers of *Country and Suburban Houses*, "As social beings, we are required to rebuke and banish that selfishness which could lead us to build only for our own convenience. . . . As moral beings we require that buildings should be expressive, and yet yield definite emotions, indicating their quality and purpose."[18]

Shaping the definition of style

By its physical presence, architecture, more than other arts, was a preeminent public expression of national character. Buildings had immanent potential for contributing to the good of the nation. Yet, a crucial question remained. What would constitute a national architecture? Could there be a unique American style that would differentiate the United States from its British and European heritage? By the 1880s the architectural establishment clearly doubted the possibility of devising a unique style, but the desire for something new and specifically American continued to circulate to such an extent that John Stevens and Albert Cobb from Portland, Maine, admonished those who wanted a new style in their 1889 pattern book, ". . . it is vain to discuss the possibility of inventing 'a new style' in Architecture. To build rationally in an 'original style' is no more possible than to furnish society with a useful code of 'original statues,' in which shall appear no trace of the commands of Moses, or the laws of Greece and Rome."[19] This certainty that a style could not be invented did not stifle aspirations that a new, distinctly American architecture might eventually emerge. The solution to the dilemma for American architects was again one shared with the British and Europeans. British architectural historian James Fergusson suggested in his *History of Architecture in All Countries* (1874) that a new style could develop through the process of change. The practice of delving into history to find styles for the present was not congruous with history or contemporary needs. Instead of copying from the past, architects needed to build on it, for the development of a representative architecture depended on "an aggregation of experiences."[20] Fergusson was not alone in his conclusion, for his suggestion was common to contemporary architectural understanding. Already in 1871, Russell Sturgis, an American architect who favored the gothic and, later, a voice in architectural criticism, had assessed the nation's modern architecture in an article that included specific references to Viollet-le-Duc and used phrasing similar to that of Fergusson and German architect and theorist Gottfried Semper. He concluded, "It is not desirable that people should annoy themselves about the invention of a new style; it will come of itself when we have common sense and simplicity enough to let it come."[21] Slightly over a decade later, critic Montgomery Schuyler grew tired of the public's demands that architects, in the slang of the day, "talk United States." The search for an American style was provincial; it would come of itself.[22] Nonetheless, in the first volume of *Architectural Record* (1891), twenty years after Sturgis's commentary, Barr Ferree bemoaned, "With us, one of the most popular of modern architectural ideas is that there will someday be devised a truly original American style."[23] And, he, too, professed that a style could not be invented.

An American style would develop through time just as national architecture had developed in other countries. However, American architects continued to face a difficult predicament. Was a progressively unfolding American style feasible, even possible, in a country such as the United States? From the architects' perspective as participants in a trans-Atlantic dialogue, and with nineteenth-century blindness to Native Americans, the United States was a country that lacked indigenous forms and traditions upon which to build a nationally characteristic architecture. Because it did not have a lengthy history comparable to that of the British and European nations, and because America's heritage was drawn primarily from across the Atlantic, its architecture must naturally rely on external stylistic sources. Emblemizing a singular American identity and history in architecture was a problematic task that brought a distinct uneasiness about the incompatibility of historical determinism and nationalism even while both were accepted.

Other situations unique to the United States added to the difficulties. In the commonly held tenets of nationalism, a country's history, native people, and geography were inseparable components in the formation of national character. The United States was without a legitimate history and both its population and geography were characterized by diversity more than similarity. The United States was an immigrant nation with a population of mixed ethnic origins. At the same time, its architects shared the beliefs on which nineteenth-century racial classification rested. Fergusson expressed the dominant view with, "When properly studied, it [architecture] consequently affords a means as important as language for discriminating between the different races of mankind . . ."[24] And in the United States, geography, from which a country's native peoples gained their character, was also too diverse. Territorial boundaries encompassed climatic conditions ranging from arid desert to lush grain fields to snow-capped mountains. Although the problem of a diverse population could be solved to some degree by nonconforming members of society becoming American in character, a narrowly circumscribed national architecture could not be aesthetically, or functionally, suitable to different climates.

Charles Howard Walker, a young architect who later became the head of fine arts at M.I.T., addressed the situation in a paper for members of the Architectural League of New York in 1881. After noting the startling and sometimes absurdist list of names for styles being produced across the country, he drew attention to the issue at hand—producing a style that is publicly recognizable, and one that allows for freedom among differences:

> . . . when one and all are urging us to give them a
> new, a distinctly new and American style—it is well
> to see what claims the old styles have to our alle-
> giance, whether a new one is possible, and if it were
> presented to our friends the critics and the public,
> whether they would recognize it as such, and whether
> there is not some common and broad basis to start
> from, which will allow freedom of design in all di-
> rections, without incurring the clash of different
> advocates of this or of that style.[25]

Speaking to architects who were carving out parameters of professionalism, Walker recognized the limitations placed on architectural
creativity within traditional conceptions of architecture as historically
based style. Others, too, recognized that progress in the debates on
national style was stymied if architects persisted in their use of the
word "style" only to mean a prescribed formula of architectural characteristics. Most modern architects already had turned away from the
pursuit of archaeological accuracy when they invoked the past for
new building fashions. An *American Architect* respondent to an article
on English architectural style that had been published in the London
Architect lamented the tendency toward historicism in British architecture. In contrast, however, architects in the United States were free
from the "tyranny of archaeology" and this freedom was a "national
privilege." Americans could master the past but the past would not
master the Americans.[26] With similar words, the eminent Henry Van
Brunt praised the genius of American architects whose "freedom from
the tyranny of historic precedent . . . encouraged them to a far wider
range of experiment in architectural forms."[27] Essentially, progressive
architects who designed for the modern age needed a freedom not
allowed by present formulae, and the nation's lack of history actually worked to their advantage. These architects and critics, however,
refrained from supporting the prospect of unlimited freedom, for the
notion of style as a controlling mechanism was integral to nineteenth-
century architecture. Architect Leopold Eidlitz observed, in his book
The Nature and Function of Art, More Especially of Architecture (1881),
that the complexity of modern society made necessary a new style.
Political, social and religious changes required buildings with a

"new expression." Turning to science and, in doing so, revealing his own position in the debates on art and science, as well as on archaeological versus eclectic architecture, he criticized Ruskin's rigid use of past forms, then argued for a broader conception of style. "Methods of building as determined by prevalent ideas, by materials used, and by the progress of architects in the science of construction in the art of expressing ideas in matter, all go to make up style in architecture."[28]

Later-nineteenth-century writers on the subject acknowledged, too, that the use of the word "style" had long contributed to more than one meaning. After a decade of discussions, American critic and historian A. D. F. Hamlin reviewed for *Architectural Record* readers the course of its meanings, and he invoked the authoritative voice of Viollet-le-Duc's *Discourses*. In this essay specifically addressing American architectural style, he explained the word as having both definitive and qualitative meanings. Employment of the definitive approach to style, implying classification based on historic precedent and its contemporary interpretation, offered more distinct visual results. But a building could exhibit an identifiable style and lack inherent qualities of character, integrity and refinement. If a building had qualitative style, it had "character, unity of effect proceeding from some dominant quality in the design." Architectural elements forced into a stylistic mold without an underlying principle of design resulted in architecture without qualitative style. With this distinction, the critic refuted the custom of using the word "style" simply to mean categorizable fashion. Hamlin used a phrase earlier suggested in an article by Montgomery Schuyler to define style as an "understood way of working." Then adjusting it to a modified ethnographic view that accommodated requirements of the modern age and, not least, one that allowed for an architect to exercise his individual genius, style was "a particular manner of designing peculiar to a race, age or person."[29]

Categories of style and eclecticism

An appeal for principles of design and considerations of the meaning of style such as Hamlin's notwithstanding, there was no clear route for the majority of American architects. The theoretical conclusions drawn by architects and critics were not directly translatable into buildings without mining the past to devise contemporary styles of building. Architects typically adopted one of two historical traditions with which to build their careers—medieval and classical. The many styles in circulation through the nineteenth century were developed from these two categories that were seen as the primary threads of historical development in the western tradition. Through much of the century, participants in the debates over national architecture disputed the merits of each as the most representative of life in the United States. Classicist opposed gothicist and, within each alliance, archaeologist opposed the eclectic who permitted combining forms from the historical uses of each respective category. The choices were difficult because a well-designed building must not only be functional and beautiful but expressive as well. For the architect in the United States, it must be, above all, American.

Interpretations of the classical retained a strong following in the United States from early in the century when buildings of ancient Greece were perceived to better symbolize the nation because they displayed a rational style of simplicity and austerity. From monumental public buildings to plantation homes in the South, and from the War of 1812 to the Civil War, the interpretation of Greek architectural models was apparent. Modest wood frame houses with Greek temple fronts were the most familiar feature of this fashion, perhaps because it was inexpensive and easy to transform a simple gable-roofed farmhouse into a fashionable white residential temple. But such revivalism, using forms from what some conceived as one definable historical era within the classical, was for others too redundant and they adopted a broader architectural vocabulary. From the end of the 1830s many architects who designed buildings allied with civic and economic authority turned to eclectic classical stylizations that encompassed Greece, Rome, the Italian Renaissance, the French Renaissance, and subsequent expressions of the classical. Their popularity was fueled by the fact that from mid-century to the end of the century, increasing numbers of American architects studied at the most prominent school for classicism, *l'Academie des Beaux-Arts* in Paris or with those who had a Beaux-Arts education.

Meanwhile, as interpretations of classicism expanded from the 1830s, the medieval began to win adherents with revivals of gothic architecture. Gothic was extremely fashionable across the Atlantic, most notably in England, and associations made between gothic buildings and botanic growth made the style compatible with America's own version of environmental determinism. Theorists of contemporary gothic pointed out that the structure of gothic architecture emulated organic growth, and towering gothic spires and steeply pitched roofs echoed the uplifting lines of the forest's trees. Further, it was practical because it provided more planning flexibility than symmetrically organized classical buildings which had been popular in the eighteenth century. John Ruskin enthused, it offered "accommodation to every architectural necessity. . . ."[30] Gothic was judged especially suited to churches, libraries, and collegiate buildings, but it caught the imagination of the American public as a style for homes, just as it had in England. Alexander Jackson Davis, a successful architect who had designed many buildings in Greek and Italian styles, was one of the leaders in the new fashion, and he introduced a small book of house architecture, *Rural Residences* (1838), that contained drawn perspectives and floor plans of houses in styles he considered more picturesque than the Greek temple form. The book contained a variety of fashions, but Davis suggested that he preferred the "English collegiate" with its bay windows, oriels, turrets, and chimney shafts.[31] Davis' book did not circulate widely, but other antebellum pattern book authors followed with much the same intent: improving house architecture by educating the public and introducing contemporary styles considered "picturesque." Houses with steeply pitched roofs, board and batten siding, decorative barge boards, ogival windows, dormers, and finials began to be featured in pre-Civil War pattern books, including those by Alexander Jackson Downing, Calvert Vaux and Gervaise Wheeler (Fig. 8). Calvert Vaux, among others, emphasized the need for houses that would inspire a family's well-being as well as a sense of beauty and culture. Literature directed specifically to women, too, promoted the gothic. *Godey's Lady's Book* and Catherine Beecher's household instructional materials introduced house designs and essays on the moral influence that such houses had on the character of the families who lived in them.

As late as 1875, pattern book author Amos Jackson Bicknell predicted gothic as the style of the immediate future because it was the most beautiful, economical, and adaptable for domestic architecture. Modern Italian and French stylizations also were introduced to the public and embraced as high fashion, but local builders sustained the popularity of gothic in one form or another into the last quarter of the century, even while architects and architectural critics had begun to question the propriety of translating a style with pointed arches and vaults intended for churches into a style for houses.

A year after Bicknell's prediction, *Harper's* magazine published an article by British architect John J. Stevenson, who was a leader in the development of the latest English fashion, popularly known as Queen Anne. The thesis of his essay dealt with the limitations inherent to pointed architecture for homes, in contrast with more modern fashions that drew from a different period of English history.[32] Architectural historian Caroline Horton, a strong supporter of modern gothic derivations in general, had already observed in her *Architecture for General Students* (1874) that new sources, most notably the

Fig. 8. A gothic cottage with board-and-batten siding, steeply pitched roof, decorative barge boards lining the gables, and ogival portico openings. A "Cottage Ornee." (*Wheeler,* Homes for the People in Suburb and Country, *1855*)

Elizabethan, were being used by contemporary architects.[33] These new British buildings broke current rules of design by mixing together classical and medieval forms, but the practice was justified by historical precedent. The gothic had served its purpose by providing a link with the nation's architectural past; it had provided a foothold for examining related periods of British history. Contemporary borrowing from Jacobean, Elizabethan, and sixteenth-and seventeenth-century cottage architecture for the new fashion was thus an appropriate expansion of stylistic interpretation because it was legitimized by history.

For many, this expanded eclecticism portended a greater freedom in design. There was little room for an archaeological motive in architecture for the modern world. For architects who believed in contemporary progress, revivalist architecture, superficially, at least, discounted the reality of new materials, new methods of construction and new functions for buildings. At the same time, nineteenth-century architecture was too rooted in the century's historicism to be anything other than consciously eclectic. The architects' alternatives were to select from one of the opposing stylistic classifications, each of which provided a plentiful supply of forms, or to integrate the two, which generated an almost infinite number of variations. But architects from each of the positions, even those who sought the prerogative of mixing stylistic categories, were alarmed because these changes reduced the likelihood of educated control over architectural design. An acceptance of merging styles threatened a form of eclecticism that was not easily managed, especially in light of the current abundance of models available to the architect. Small and full-scale plaster casts of architectural details, photographs of buildings, builder and architectural journals, popular magazines, and exhibitions provided an embarrassment of riches for aspiring designers searching for inspiration, and unsuspecting architects could easily be tempted to employ a random mix of styles.[34] One critic in the *American Architect* suggested that architects were "like children in a toy-shop, dazed with the multitude of . . . opportunities."[35] Another grudgingly admitted that eclecticism must be considered seriously because it was already so prevalent. Although he believed that eclecticism set before American architects "a more difficult task in architecture than has ever been set before a people," conditions in the United States made it inevitable. Therefore, it was all-important to "prepare ourselves for our difficult task by large acquirement and culture. . . ." The central argument for his readers was a pivotal point in the current debates on professionalism—the need to demonstrate that eclecticism required knowledge. "Eclecticism," he claimed, "is much more exacting, requires more deliberate adjustment . . . a stronger mastery and finer skill to force into union parts that have never been adapted to each other."[36] The ways in which designers of buildings used historical styles marked a crucial divergence between architects defining themselves as professional and their competitors in the building trades. While a more systematic approach to architectural design was sought for modern buildings, those who designed homes for the middle classes produced an inventive array of stylistic interpretations. Adhering to an expression known and cherished by their clients, the homes were invariably termed "picturesque."

Style and the aesthetics of architecture: the picturesque

The situation faced by late-nineteenth-century architects was the culmination of a direction that had been long cast. Early in the century, the conception of the picturesque both allowed for freedom from inviolable academic rules and afforded some guidance for assessing building design. The picturesque was an aesthetic judgement given shape by late-eighteenth-century and early-nineteenth-century landscape designers and theorists who compellingly argued that taste, meaning the cultivated appreciation of beauty, was an indicator of social status. The early formulations of the picturesque in architecture primarily were requisites for exterior and visual properties that were drawn from the pictorial convention in painting. A picturesque building had irregular exterior contours and produced a coloristic play of light with its shapes and materials. Although the conception of the picturesque encompassed classic and medieval interpretations, gothic forms were considered most naturally picturesque. As A. F. Oakey's 1881 designs for American bungalows show, by the last quarter of the century the appellation "picturesque" was no longer readily identified with a particular style (Figs. 9, 10). It was associated

Fig. 9. Modern houses were picturesque. A.I.A. architect A. F. Oakey demonstrated the picturesque with his interpretations of a fashion that would not become popular until the twentieth century. A bungalow of "extreme simplicity." (Oakey, Building a Home, *1881)*

Fig. 10. The bungalow made picturesque with multiple gables and applied decoration. (Oakey, Building a Home, *1881)*

frequently with buildings composed of styles blended to produce complex silhouettes. Pattern book authors applied the attributes of the picturesque to their house descriptions, and contributed to its construction as a desirable quality in terms of fashionable beauty as well as recognition of the public's desire for cultural refinement.

Andrew Jackson Downing was the foremost early exponent of the picturesque in the United States and he was, appropriately, a landscape gardener as well as architectural pattern book author. In his *Cottage Residences*, 1842, he borrowed freely from late-eighteenth-century and early-nineteenth-century British publications to criticize Greek Revival architecture and the practice of situating white buildings in the muted but rich colors of nature. Downing defined the major requisites of picturesque as it applied to American architecture for readers from the 1840s and, with later editions of his books, well into the 1880s. Both the text and his many drawings of houses in gentle landscapes framed by trees demonstrated irregular visual qualities and arranged architecture and landscape into a composition in which the building and its site were conjured as indivisible, as if in an idealized, painterly scene viewed from a distance (Fig. 11). Downing stressed the importance of an aesthetic and conceptual association between what a building looked like and the attributes of nature in this configuration. Both color and shape must harmonize with the landscape, for a picturesque building was not a building alone but a part of nature. Its irregular volumes were geometric projections of the corresponding irregularities of nature and the colors were the colors of nature. A crusader for suburban country living, he proposed houses nestled in tree-dappled sunlight, caught in the play of sun and shadow, and quoted eighteenth-century theorist Uvedale Price to persuasively describe the beauty of such houses in contrast with Greek Revival houses, ". . . an object of sober tint, unexpectedly gilded by the sun, is like a serious countenance suddenly lighted up by a smile; a whitened object like the eternal grin of a fool."[37]

The picturesque was an aesthetic consideration with ties to nature. It was about the external appearance of a building, but its advocates also found it a more practical approach to building design than the classical and archaeological. The asymmetrical silhouette of a picturesque building enclosed a floor plan that was correspondingly free from the constraint of classical balance. Sizes of rooms and their placement were regulated by their intended uses rather than by proportional ratios and custom. In the picturesque, they pointed out, function and beauty were naturally united as they were in nature. Downing was one of many who maintained that such a house grew "as a tree expands which is not crowded by neighbors in a forest, but grows in the unrestrained liberty of the open meadow."[38] His words were similar to those of his contemporaries Ralph Waldo Emerson and Horatio Greenough, who were equally impressed by the union of function and beauty in growing things. In effect, this identification of the picturesque with function provided a direction for accommodating a traditional means of aesthetic judgment to contemporary theoretical developments. The associations of landscape with the picturesque were particularly germane to ruminations on American style, nature, and national character. Through the end of the century, many, most notably pattern book authors, effectively manipulated the conception of the picturesque to present both its visual and functional

Fig. 11. A composition of house and landscape in the picturesque manner. A "Bracketed Cottage." (Downing, Architecture of Country Houses, *1850)*

properties as appropriate for the United States. These designers of homes built across the United States merged the language of nature and adaptation, beauty and taste with picturesque design to enlarge the familiar rural image of the picturesque home to become synonymous with the modern suburban home. However, to many architects working toward professionalism in the building trades, profligate applications of these aesthetic guidelines made the picturesque a demonstration of rampant eclecticism. By the time of the nation's Centennial, architects pursuing professional recognition for their occupation no longer deliberated the merits of the picturesque nor recognized a need to promote it, but they continued to apply the word as a relatively benign descriptive term in their discussions about new buildings.

Nature, from metaphor to scientific principles

From early in the century, considerations of the relationship between architecture and nature were offered as potential solutions to unraveling the American problems of national style and eclecticism. Both followers of Ruskin and Viollet-le-Duc discerned principles of design in nature that were eternal and immutable, yet allowed for change and progress. Plant shapes, they observed, expressed their functions and they developed from the needs of the plant. In a metaphorical construct, botanical process explained the principles of architecture. Architecture, too, adapted. It grew and changed as inexorably as nature to meet physical and social conditions. A direct relationship between form and function was established as a relationship that was as necessary to the life of architecture as it was to the life of nature, and an emphasis on the relationship of function and form appealed to those American architects who considered meeting practical necessities of building a fundamental requirement of architecture. By the late nineteenth century, references to nature already were thoroughly incorporated into architectural thought, but the laws of nature were now conceived differently, for the amplification of building as an organic process provided a legitimate course for architects in the United States to develop theories of organic functionalism. Montgomery Schuyler's language in the *American Architect* was typical in this endeavor to define architecture when he explained, "A building is an organism of which the architecture is . . . the expression of its functions and conditions."[39] Architects and critics in the final quarter of the century readily applied biological references, especially that of adaptation, to explanations of architectural principles and judgments of buildings, for scientific considerations of nature had begun to supplant the hieratic. Although architecture was undoubtedly an art, constant, eternal, and unifying scientific principles were needed to balance the vagaries of design which had been permitted by the aesthetics of taste. Henry Van Brunt, in the introduction to his translation of Viollet-le-Duc's *Discourses*, criticized the "tyranny of aesthetics" and literary theory brought by the popularity of John Ruskin's writings. He praised the French author because he was a practical architect who worked from a scientific basis.[40] Montgomery Schuyler continued his exposition on distinctive architecture, "If it has any vitality, it must have a vital principle." The vital principle, he found, was "independent of any particular set of forms, but . . . adequate to meet with new forms, new exigencies of requirements and material." Architecture continued to be defined as an exercise in both art and science, as it had been for centuries, but architectural theorists participated in a larger social process of bringing scientific studies to preeminence as they found in science the source for both principles governing the art of architecture and answers to their practical engineering problems. Contemporary society, they argued, required principles rather than rigid rules, for principles assured unity in building without restricting freedom. Principles accommodated adaptation to current "requirements, the habits, the tastes, the traditions, the materials, the methods of employing them."[41] At the same time, regarding art, principles insured against uncontrolled combinations of architectural forms.

An organic analogy emphasizing adaptation was particularly attractive to architects at a time when the speculations and vocabulary of evolution were being incorporated into painting, literature, theology, and political, social, and economic theories. Histories of architecture and architectural literature, from the *American Architect* and Chicago's *Inland Architect* to builders journals and pattern books, introduced language to parallel architecture with the evolutionary process of nature. Architects, critics, and pattern book authors suggested that following the adaptive processes of nature was the answer to finding an American architecture of merit. Direct and indirect references to Charles Darwin's theory of biological evolution fortified the integration of science and art in architecture and encouraged greater latitude in the definitions of style. Darwin, too, considered beauty a product of the process of nature, for beauty resulted from competition and organisms' adaptation to environmental conditions.[42] The writers on architecture also participated in the production of beliefs about architecture and society by drawing on Herbert Spencer's theory of social evolution. Frequently, the ideology of social evolution was applied as a logical extension to discussions of houses and housing. Architectural critic Mariana Griswold Van Rensselaer used the language of social evolution when she directed her estimations of contemporary housing fashions to the readers of *Century Magazine* in 1886. Her readers were largely of the professional and managerial middle classes and could be anticipated to share the later nineteenth-century belief in social mobility. With censorious commentary on houses which most likely had been inspired by popular pattern books, she deplored the products of miscreant builders and their overly ambitious clients. She then invoked a Spencer phrase that already was becoming a cliché to convince the public to turn away from popular representations of eclectic house design: "And can we say that their species is not still prolific? Now at last it has come into active competition with another and better species. But that the 'fittest' shall survive in this one special struggle for existence, depends almost entirely on you to whom I speak. . . ."[43]

Herbert Spencer's theory of social evolution provided a scientific foundation for the ideology of progress and social mobility in the United States. As such, he entered the mainstream of both social and architectural theory. Admiration of Spencer by the nation's powerful and wealthy was unmistakable in the laudatory speeches at the banquet held in his honor in 1882 at the famous Delmonico's in New York. The subscribers for the festive banquet represented a broad sampling of prominent professionals, scientists, industrial magnates, theologians, publishers, politicians, artists, and architects. Among the latter were Albert Bierstadt, painter of the American western landscape, and the venerable architects Calvert Vaux and Richard Morris Hunt.[44] Herbert Spencer's theories had been well known before the Civil War, and they were more widely circulated in the next decade when *Popular Science Monthly* published *The Study of Sociology*. The language of social evolution soon filtered into newspapers in small towns and cities alike. Institutions and individuals contributing to the construction of national identity found Spencer's vitalistic theory to be particularly relevant to the complex make-up of American society and its products, including architecture. It articulated a sense of order for change and multiplicity and provided a rationale for economic competition. By the 1880s, many elements of Spencer's social theories had become thoroughly integrated into the entrepreneurial attitudes that Mark Twain dubbed the "gilded age." In brief, Spencer argued that society actively improved when the strongest members asserted their superiority. The ability to compete and adapt constituted the fitness of a social organism and formed its vitality. The change inherent to life was regulated by a universal principle, or vital force, and the social organism evolved progressively if the process occurred without interference. Without the obstacles of legislation, the vital force behind evolution caused organisms to change from the unstable homogenous to the complexity of the heterogeneous, and finally, to perfection.[45] The United States could be easily construed as a model for Spencer's heterogeneous stage of societal development in which diversity was unified by the underlying vital principle of nature. His emphasis on non-interference was particularly attractive, too, for it scientifically supported a nation's *laissez-faire* doctrine. And while the theory described a people working together for the benefit of the society, it also allowed for, even mandated, individual action and personal initiative. With a belief that competition in economic action fostered vitality in the people and contributed to the development in personal character, further justification could be found for the unimpeded accumulation of wealth. In Spencer's theory and American hegemonic thought, such change was natural, thus favorable and moral.[46]

References to Herbert Spencer by name occurred infrequently in popular literature, but the tenets of his theories were naturalized. As we find in the following chapters, architecture and social evolution joined in a narrative of American families living in self-owned houses having picturesque settings of lawn and trees. The detached house, separated from neighboring homes by its plot of tamed nature, became imbedded in national identity, even while professional architects such as Samuel Sloan and John Smithmeyer suggested that American architects should develop a national architecture through public buildings. The trans-Atlantic dialogue on national architecture emphasized government buildings, museums, and monuments as direct manifestations of national image and commercial buildings as representations of the economic interests of a nation. In this context, architects in the United States who grappled with the complications unique to their search for a national style recognized the prestige in gaining commissions for civic and commercial buildings, but a number of factors brought forward the house as the emblematic form for the United States. From a pragmatic perspective, there was a developing market for houses—summer homes for the affluent, speculative housing for developers, homes for the nation's growing population and ever-mobile middle classes. There was as well a strengthened alliance of beliefs in the rights of home ownership and social mobility as identifying features of American character. A conviction that the United States was a land of opportunity was an underlying ingredient for allying nationalism with domestic architecture, and in the architectural literature, it was articulated as an evolutionary process of adaptation from the historical underpinnings of the nation's founding. In the formulation of a history for American architecture, the architects described the character of the nation's early buildings as having developed from colonists making accommodations to new climate and new geography. In these authors' formulation of national architecture and environmental determinism, the American house, more profoundly than any other type of building, was a unique product of adaptation. Modern houses, if designed properly, continued to adapt to conditions of the fast-changing world. Responses to advanced technology, new social needs, and the spread of populations to diverse climates demonstrated a coordination of house design with the evolutionary process of nature. National character and national architecture were ascribed to the house, and the popular press sent the message to the middle classes.

Harper's New Monthly Magazine published a series of articles by New York architect Henry Hudson Holly in 1876, and Holly's underlying message was a proposal to codify a vernacular domestic architecture to represent American character, to be American.[47] A decade later, Palliser, Palliser, and Company, one of the more successful entrepreneurial pattern book companies, assessed recently built houses and informed their readers, "there is springing up a National style which is becoming more distinctive in character and unlike that of any other nation. . . ."[48] It is not surprising that their most "national" design was a complexly silhouetted house titled, "Modern American Renaissance," and was most appropriate for "those who are looking for permanent homes" (Fig. 12).[49]

Fig. 12. Architects and pattern book authors continued to develop the notion of a uniquely American style of house. It was a single, detached dwelling with a picturesque complex silhouette. A modern "American Renaissance" house. (Palliser, New Cottage Homes, *1887)*

NOTES

[1] A. W. Brunner, *Cottages, or Hints on Economical Home Building* (New York: William T. Comstock, 1884), p. 28.

[2] Benedict Anderson, *Imagined Communities: Reflections on the Origin and Spread of Nationalism* (New York: Verso, 1983), is a fundamental source for contemporary studies of nationalism. See also Joanne P. Sharp, "Gendering Nationhood" in Nancy Duncan, ed., *Bodyspace: Destabilizing Geographies of Gender and Sexuality* (London and New York: Routledge, 1996) for a review of other authors on the subject.

[3] See Eric Foner, *Reconstruction: America's Unfinished Revolution 1863–1877* (New York: Harper & Row Publishers, 1988).

[4] England was the world's industrial leader in 1876, but by 1894 U.S. manufacturing production nearly equaled that of Great Britain, France, and Germany together. Herbert Gutman, *Work, Culture and Society in Industrializing America* (New York: Alfred A. Knopf, 1976), p. 33.

[5] Quoted in Robert W. Rydell, *All the World's a Fair* (Chicago: University of Chicago Press, 1984), p. 19.

[6] "Centennial Morbidity," *The Mobile Daily Register*, 19 January 1876, p. 2.

[7] See Foner and the introductory chapter in Robert H. Wiebe, *The Search for Order 1877–1920* (New York: Hill and Wang, 1967).

[8] Rydell, p. 18.

[9] Ibid., p. 21.

[10] Thomas M. Anderson, "Have We a National Character?," *Galaxy* 21(June 1876): 737.

[11] "Centennial Architecture. II," *American Architect and Building News* 1(June 10, 1876): 186.

[12] "Characteristics of the International Fair. II," *Atlantic Monthly* 38(August 1876): 233.

[13] "Centennial Architecture," *American Architect* 1(June 3, 1876): 178.

[14] Samuel Sloan, *City Homes, Country Houses and Church Architecture, or the American Builders' Journal* (Philadelphia: Claxton, Remsen & Hafflinger, 1871), p. 612.

[15] John Ruskin, *The Seven Lamps of Architecture* (New York: John Wiley, 1849; reprint ed., New York: Noonday Press, 1961), p. 188.

[16] John L. Smithmeyer, *Our Architecture, and its Defects* (Washington, D.C.: C. W. Brown, Printer, 1880), p. 2. Delivered to the Association of Architects on 22 December 1879.

[17] Oliver P. Smith, *The Domestic Architect* (Buffalo: Phinney & Co., 1854), iv.

[18] Daniel T. Atwood, *Atwood's Country and Suburban Houses* (New York: Orange Judd, 1871), p. 141.

[19] John Calvin Stevens and Albert Winslow Cobb, *Examples of American Domestic Architecture* (New York: William T. Comstock, 1889), p. 19.

[20] James Fergusson, *A History of Architecture in All Countries from the Earliest Times to the Present Day* (London: John Murray, 1874), pp. 44–47.

[21] Russell Sturgis, Jr., "Modern Architecture," *North American Review* 112(January 1871): 165.

[22] Montgomery Schuyler, "Recent Building in New York," *Harper's New Monthly Magazine* 67(September 1883): 561–62.

[23] Barre Ferree, "An 'American Style' of Architecture," *Architectural Record* 1(July 1891): 39.

[24] Fergusson, p. 2.

[25] Charles Howard Walker, "The Use of Architectural Styles," *American Architect* 9(April 16, 1881): 184.

[26] *American Architect* 4(August 10, 1878): 47.

[27] Henry Van Brunt, "On the Present Condition and Prospects of Architecture," *Atlantic Monthly* 57(March 1886): 380.

[28] Leopold Eidlitz, *The Nature and Function of Art, More Especially of Architecture* (New York: A.C. Armstrong, 1881): p. 30.

[29] A. D. F. Hamlin, "The Battle of Styles," *Architectural Record* 1(January-March 1892): 272. Hamlin adapted Viollet-le-Duc's *Discourses on Architecture*, lecture 6, for this discussion.

[30] Ruskin, *Seven Lamps*, p. 153.

[31] Alexander Jackson Davis, *Rural Residences* (New York: By the author, 1838), advertisement. The Metropolitan Museum of Art exhibition catalogue, *Alexander Jackson Davis: American Architect 1803–1891* (New York: Rizzoli, 1992) shows the scope of Davis's work. Jane B. Davies, "Introduction," and Susanne Brendel-Pandich, "From Cottages to Castles: The Country House Designs of Alexander Jackson Davis," address Davis's admiration for English architecture.

[32] John James Stevenson, "Gothic Architecture," *Harper's New Monthly Magazine* 52(January 1876): 239–40.

[33] Caroline W. Horton, *Architecture for General Students* (New York: Hurd and Houghton, 1874), p. 261.

[34] "Art," *Atlantic Monthly* 33(January 1874): 122.

[35] "American Architecture-Present," *American Architect* 1(August 5, 1876): 251.

[36] "Eclecticism in Architecture," *American Architect* 1(January 1876): 18–19.

[37] Alexander Jackson Downing, *Cottage Residences*, new ed. (New York and London: Wiley & Putnam, 1873; reprint ed., New York: Dover Publications, 1980), p. 15.

[38] Alexander Jackson Downing, *The Architecture of Country Houses* (New York: D. Appleton & Co., 1850; reprinted., New York: Dover Publications, 1969),pp. 22–23.

[39] Montgomery Schuyler, "Concerning Queen Anne," *American Architect* 1(December 16, 1876): 404. He paraphrased Viollet-le-Duc for this discussion.

[40] Henry Van Brunt, Intro., *Discourses on Architecture* (Boston: James R. Osgood, 1875), in William A. Coles, ed., *Architecture and Society. Selected Essays of Henry Van Brunt* (Cambridge: Belknap Press of Harvard University Press, 1969), pp. 101–02.

[41] Schuyler, p. 404.

[42] Charles Darwin, *On the Origin of Species* (1859; reprint ed., New York: Heritage Press, 1963), pp. 163–64; 430.

43 Mariana Griswold Van Rensselaer, "American Country Dwellings. I," *Century Magazine* 32(May 1886): 14.

44 Edward L. Youmans, comp., *Herbert Spencer on the Americans and the Americans on Herbert Spencer* (New York: Appleton and Company, 1883; reprint ed., New York: Arno Press, 1976), pp. 22–24.

45 See Stanislav Andreski, *Herbert Spencer: Structure, Function and Evolution* (London: Michael Joseph, 1971) and David Wiltshire, *The Social and Political Thought of Herbert Spencer* (London: Oxford University Press, 1978).

46 See Richard Hofstadter, rev. ed., *Social Darwinism in American Thought* (New York: George Braziller, 1959), pp. 31–50.

47 Henry Hudson Holly, "Modern Dwellings: Their Construction, Decoration and Furniture," *Harper's* 53(May 1876): 855–67; (June 1876): 49–64; (July 1876): 217–26; (August 1876): 354–63.Published in book form by Harper & Bros., 1878.

48 Palliser, Palliser and Co., *New Cottage Homes and Their Details* (New York: By the Authors, 1887): Intro.

49 Palliser, *New Cottage Homes*, Plate 6.

⚜ 2 ⚜

A House in Civilized Nature

> The ideal and real home will always be found in the
> country. Satisfactory and desirable homes abound in
> villages where space is allowed for disconnected and
> independent properties and dwellings. . . . A
> moment's intelligent reflection will suggest that the
> sum required to purchase an ordinary city residence
> would provide an elegant suburban home [where] the
> owner's personal identity would be recognized in the
> community, and thoroughly established and realized
> through his presence, example and general interest.
> (Reed, 1885)[1]

When pattern book author Samuel Reed shared these sentiments in
his book of suburban houses, he located the ideal family home on a
lot of its own in a rural village within commuting distance from the
city (Fig. 13). As a producer of designs for middle class homes, Reed
wrote for a clientele who lived in cities of many sizes, fringe suburbs,
satellite suburbs, towns, and villages; yet, the drawn illustrations of
the houses shared common features that were attributed to suburban
living. They were far enough from the city center to have vistas of
the countryside and large lots for plantings of lawn, trees, and shrubs.
Reed's book joined newspapers, professional and popular periodicals,
household manuals, school textbooks, fiction, scientific reports, religious tracts, and speakers across the political spectrum that
contributed to a narrative of American life which placed husband,
wife, and children in a picturesque detached house in civilized
nature—not in the urban fabric of a city. The authoritative voice of
the Wharton School of Finance offered evolutionary and historical
validation with a history of housing that culminated in the develop-

FRONT ELEVATION.

Fig. 13. The narrative of true American life situated the home in a small community within commuting distance of a city. Entrepreneurial pattern book author Samuel Reed acknowledged his prospective clientele with houses named after suburban communities near New York. "Passaic," New Jersey. (Reed, Dwellings for Village and Country, *1885)*

ment of the detached house, for "it gave scope for the large and free development of the life of the true or natural family—that great so-cial unit which lies at the foundation of all sound social growth."[2] By moving out of the urban fabric of a city to become suburban, the nation's citizens could achieve a moral, healthy, and prosperous fam-ily life. Although many families of the middle classes chose to live in cities and many recent immigrants living in city tenements struggled in their poverty to uphold family values similar to those attributed to the model classes, extended families living in row houses and tenement buildings were posited as examples of unsuitable family life in the city. Cities were places for crowded, unsanitary tenements, loose morals, crime, family disintegration, fomenting socialism, even the ostentatious display of greed. Apprehensions about the contradictions of modern society, which in actuality were not specifically rooted in the city, were assigned to a known geographic space to keep them manageable and keep neurasthenia-inducing apprehensions at bay.[3]

Containment of the nation's problems in the urban sphere worked in tandem with another ordering spatial element: the suburban. Residential sites in nature represented family domesticity, quiet, uplifting solitude for the harried businessman, a haven from disease and crime, and, not least, an opportunity to participate fully in morally appropriate upward mobility. Here, too, the traits of national character could be exercised, for in the suburb more than the city, enterprising Americans had the opportunity to become distinguished participants in community building. Pattern book author Elisha Hussey described city dwellers as "thousands of men and women, of the various callings of life, crowded and pinched together . . . waiting, watching and anxious" and offered these unfortunate people an alternative. They could live in city suburbs, villages, or towns that were independent of the city. His book described over two hundred fifty small cities, suburbs, towns, and hamlets as future homes for his clients. With assessments of each community's climate, moral bearing, and economic stability, he distinguished non-urban communities as places where the citizenry who lived among "enterprising, highminded, sober, industrious, refined Christian people" in houses that were "the retreat and shelter for all the family. . . ." More, in these communities, Americans found "health, education, culture, and a generous reward for the expenditure of talent, time and money. . . ."[4] The conception of a house as a cozy family retreat in the healthy, safe environment of the countryside joined desires for community, and the city did not serve as a locus for community in the normative story of an American life. A true American lived in a suburban home in a community having the cultural and economic advantages of a city and the neighborhood familiarity of a village.

In the late-nineteenth-century conception of home, the word "suburb" indicated geographic space in the form of residential developments and towns within daily commuting distance from a city, while the omnipresent adjective "suburban" was articulated for national space as a shared vision of community ideals. This vision, however, encompassed communities and housing in the United States that were by no means uniform. Suburbs were clusters of houses and communities forming a patchwork of residential areas near cities, including some that were pleasantly developed and some that were similar to "a limbo or ragged edge" between the country and town where "no piece of real estate is quite sure whether it is still part of an old field or has become a building lot."[5] New developments and existing villages and towns were scattered only one, two, or three miles apart along the railroad, providing the city with employees. These communities served as suburbs, but many functioned with their own civic structures and business districts. Rural, autonomous towns continued to dot rail lines and the junctions of roads where trains did not yet travel. Some were settled communities that endured the late-century boom-and-bust economy, while others grew overnight and died as their residents moved to seek opportunities elsewhere. Old colonial villages, dreary industrial towns, harsh mining settlements, quiet or bustling rural farming centers, and rugged cattle towns added to an assortment of communities and types of houses that no European nation could match. In the city, belying the descriptions of squalid tenements, housing included individual houses, row houses, small multiple-residence units, and large tenements, as well as makeshift shelters built by the homeless. Non-urban housing was even more diverse. Isolated prairie homes, sod houses, log cabins, hastily built mining town shanties, shotgun houses developed by African American carpenters in the South, adobe houses in the Southwest, and many others with origins in various cultures and immediate needs joined the model suburban home.[6] With this extreme heterogeneity in housing and community, a broad network of contributing factors was necessary to produce so firmly the suburban home as an American ideal.

The conceptualized suburban home organized the diversity of domestic sites across the nation, and the logic of owning a detached house in a community of like-minded, semi-rural people was mapped over the lived actuality of the nation's residents. In practice it was played out with multiple interpretations. Through the past several decades of this century, scholars have examined the shifting meanings of the word "suburb" and its formulation as a social antidote to urban problems. Following Sam Bass Warner's ground-breaking study of Boston in *Streetcar Suburbs* (1962), Kenneth Jackson's *Crabgrass Frontier* (1985) and John Stilgoe's *Borderlands* (1988) add to our understanding of the development, structure, and meanings of suburbs in the late nineteenth century. Their work emphasizes suburban expansion in the cities on the east coast, while others examine suburbs of cities farther west. Regional and national studies highlight such pertinent issues as class and ethnic diversity in suburbs, variations on suburban residential patterns, and differences between those suburbs on the fringes of the city and the suburbs separated from the city by undeveloped land. However, their work largely is limited to the suburb in its definitive form, as a residential community from which income-earners commuted daily to the workplace. Nineteenth-century authors writing from an urban perspective often made the same distinction. An editorialist in *Scribner's* (1891) further clarified the distinction by explaining the difference between suburban residences and country homes. He cautioned readers that suburban life should not be confused with country life. Country houses were second homes for the wealthy whose permanent addresses were in the city, or they were homes for those who earned their living from the soil. The latter, the author found, was not a desirable alternative for city dwellers who wished to embrace the romance of rural life. Early morning cow milking and insects that destroyed garden vegetables were not necessarily the stuff of pastoral dreams and financial security.[7]

When authors writing from a less urban-centered perspective spoke of American residential leanings, the words suburb and suburban were applied with less precision. The words of suburban life were used in conjunction with words and phrases connoting village, town, country, and community. The symbolic American home was structured on a dichotomy between city and suburb that implied the suburb as a cohesive notion, but when the contrasting element of non-conforming city dwellers was made absent from writings and visual portrayals of home, meanings of the suburban home became more complex. Situating the suburb in opposition to the city did not erase the city from the discourse on suburbs nor did it prohibit communities from striving to achieve physical, governmental, and cultural attributes that were associated with cities. While American identity and architecture were secured in the ideal of a picturesque detached house as a homey retreat from the city, they were at the same time rooted in the belief in progress, which was often represented by urban growth. The city, too, was instrumental in the formation of national identity, for the city was the vital center of commerce and industry. Cities signaled to the world the nation's competitive standing, and civic leaders in the United States, as across the Atlantic, introduced expansive building programs that celebrated their cultural achievements with new opera houses, museums, and libraries. The city was the vitalizing and civilizing force of a nation. For the United States, especially, its cities were symbols of the exhilarating force of progress. For commuter suburban dwellers, the city's business district remained their commercial and cultural center. It was their place of employment, and shopping and proximity to its cultural offerings was important to their suburban identity.[8] Communities that were not in commuting distance of the city centers aspired to city-like success. They competed to lure new residents, businesses, and industry; some western towns conducted vigorous advertising campaigns to attract investors and new citizens from the eastern United States, Britain, and Europe. Community growth was believed a natural product of social evolution, thus moral and desirable. It ensured individual prosperity, and with the citizens' work, a community could become as culturally "civilized" as a city.[9]

Building suburbs

Developments in transportation, real estate development, and building technology facilitated accommodations to the construct of the American home. In 1869, the final spike was struck in Utah to connect east and west by rail; soon parallel lines were laid in the north and south, adding to the web of greater and lesser railway transport

routes. Where once roads and trails crossed the endless miles of prairie and rugged mountains, a network of more easily traveled railway
was laid for the emigres from more settled regions, business speculators, and tourists. Railroad track was laid at a phenomenal rate in
the 1870s—5,690 miles in 1870; 7,670 in 1871; 6,167 miles in 1872; and
4,105 in 1873. The Panic of 1873 slowed the rate of expansion only
momentarily, and by 1877, approximately five billion dollars had been
invested in railroads.[10] Although the economics of railroad building
included graft in enormous sums and precipitated the great depression of 1873, romance with the railroad remained high through the
decades. The railroad was a means to bring the nation together, to re-
unite North and South and to unite the disparate geography and the
peoples. In the same month that General George Custer died in the
Battle of the Little Big Horn, *Galaxy* magazine published his version
of confrontations with the Sioux, which included the generally shared
claim that railroad building across Native American land was a peace-
engendering process.[11] The *Omaha Daily Republican* (1883) editorialized
with the language of Americanization, "In a quarter of a century,
[railroads] have made the people of the country homogenous, break-
ing through the peculiarities and provincialisms which marked
separate and unmingling sections."[12] Expanded communication
through railroad travel was posed as a solution to many problems,
including the spread of cultured knowledge to ameliorate the common citizens' lamentable ignorance about literature and art.[13]

Railroads were necessary for the economic viability of small
towns and emerging cities. Competition was fierce to gain the bless-
ing of a major line, and local entrepreneurs built feeder lines when
their towns were by-passed. When the transcontinental Union Pacific
was routed through Cheyenne, Wyoming, city investors in Denver
countered this potentially devastating situation by building the Denver Pacific line to connect with it.[14] To become a terminus for a major
line was a most sought-after boost to the local economy. In the far
Northwest, Seattle and Tacoma fought vigorously by promoting themselves in newspapers, entertaining dignitaries, and constructing new
buildings when the Northern Pacific Railway announced its plans for
the coastal network. When Seattle lost the competition in 1873,
the city looked to another market and attempted to establish a

connecting line with growing communities on the eastern side of the mountains. Tacoma's reputation as a city prime for civic and financial investment brought within a decade an opulent hotel built from plans by McKim, Mead and White, a nationally respected architectural firm from the New York and Boston circles of the American Institute of Architects.[15] Seattle's boom was yet to come.

The nation was developing rapidly and many cities and towns underwent extraordinary growth in the last decades of the nineteenth century. San Francisco grew to over two hundred thousand people by 1880, and the population of many smaller western and Pacific coast communities increased a dramatic 100 to 300 percent from 1880 to 1890.[16] Chicago, fast becoming the hub of the nation, increased in land size fivefold with its annexation of suburban development. Villages grew into towns, towns became cities, and cities expanded into the countryside with suburban residential development.[17] From mid-century, as inner cities grew with numbers of immigrant and rural poor laborers, the middle and laboring classes moved to the developing suburbs and commuted to the workplace. A network of horse car tracks from the city center to residential areas served as the predominant form of urban transportation from the 1860s to 1880s. The horse car was a major factor in the transformation of the early-nineteenth-century pedestrian city, having mixed-use neighborhoods with housing, employment, and shopping, into sprawling cities having housing segregated from commerce and industry. In the 1880s cable cars were introduced to a number of cities, but they were soon replaced by the more efficient electric street cars. By 1900 most cities had electric street car systems for city transport and trolleys to reach nearby communities that were geographically separated from the residential developments of the urban fringe areas.[18]

Residential development already was moving outward from the city center, but city and private investment in transit systems facilitated an effective shift of population. Earlier, laborers moved to the outer urban areas to be near industries that had moved to cheaper land. In Chicago, they were the first to leave the city center.[19] This migration portended opportunity for those whose interests it served. Building rapid transit systems brought financial gain and was seen to contribute to city and national order by diffusing urban density. A report on city transit in *Scribner's* enthused, "It is fast abolishing the horrors of the crowded tenement. It is shortening the hours of labor. It makes the poor man a land-holder. It is doing more to put down socialism . . . than all other things combined." But the author saw a down side, too. Although city growth was "a necessary part of the evolution of our social structure [thus] for the benefit of the country," transportation made the outlying areas more accessible and, he implied, crowded, too. Suburban land now was accessible to both city dwellers and rural people who looked for city employment. His solution further established the borderland communities for the middle classes: Build tall multi-story residences for the masses in these fringe areas and rapid transit to communities outside of them for others.[20]

Sam Bass Warner's study of the Boston suburbs of Roxbury, West Roxbury, and Dorchester shows that it was the lower middle class, which included both skilled laborers and a growing number of office and sales employees, who lived in the outer regions of the walking city. These fringe residential areas rapidly became crowded with multiple-residences and small houses on narrow lots to make them affordable. They little resembled houses in nature. The type of suburban experience that manual laborers and white collar employees attained was modified by their employment more than the cost of suburban lots. Exploitation of the demand for houses actually made land values higher there than in borderland suburbs, but many of their jobs required moving from shop to shop or working overtime during busy seasons or on Sundays. A home in a location that depended on one transportation route did not permit this flexibility. Warner finds the "central middle class," whose types of employment insured a stable workplace, among those who commuted from suburbs connected to the city by rail.[21] Nonetheless, wage earners with unsteady incomes and salaried workers alike found it difficult to purchase homes with more substantial lots. In many city suburbs, the daily commute was too expensive for home ownership in an outlying suburb. The countryside became more invisible for these city-edge suburban dwellers as apartment houses joined the detached houses that developers had built on narrow lots, and the movement of population pressed outward to serve dreams of suburban life. Trolley rails reached several miles from the city center and railroad lines took commuters to somewhat more distant villages and towns. With trolley and train, increasing numbers of towns were connected as satellite cities. A promotional book published for Passaic, New Jersey, and reported in *Scientific American, Architects and Builders Edition* (1886), celebrated the ease of an eleven-mile commute to New York City that took less than forty minutes. Its illustrations demonstrated the signifying features of suburb—homes on verdant lots, a new high school, an eighteenth-century home and rural countryside.[22] Suburban life became synonymous with commuting into the city and, more largely, a separation of work and home.

Patterns of employment, building houses, developing land, and speaking and writing about city and suburban life were practices that contributed to defining suburbs as spatial enclaves of the more well-off middle class. A subscription periodical from 1870 ardently presented the social distinctions that were taking form:

> How I wish some good angel would guide my pen, while I portray the dark side and wonderful disadvantages of city life! How many thousands can tell the tale of doleful poverty! How many, a step higher on the scale, can utter bitter complaints of hard work and scant pay! Higher yet, there comes a class of shop-keepers, faithful toilers, whose daily gains barely pay the expenses of a livelihood; and to whom the oft-recurring face of the landlord is like an apparition of terror. But between these and the rich classes, who sit down to costly suppers and dress in purple and fine linen, there are found thousands of families of the energetic business or professional men of the city, who, apparently in comfortable circumstances . . . sigh for a home in the country.[23]

Frank J. Scott in the same year pleaded for country living in villages and new suburbs at the perimeter of the cities with his treatise, *The Art of Beautifying Suburban Home Grounds.* Writing twenty-two years before the author quoted above who had seen the growth of suburban density, Scott proposed lots from one-half to four or five acres. Both authors, though, defined suburban dwellers as a particular class of people. They were businessmen, and "men of

congenial tastes and friendly families." They did not live in isolation
from the city or from others. They lived where they could "cluster
their improvements so as to obtain all the benefits of rural pleasures,
and many of the beauties of park scenery, without relinquishing the
luxuries of town life." Scott concluded with pointed social distinction, "The *Suburban* home, therefore, meets the wants of refined and
cultivated people more than any other."[24]

In the same vein in the midwest, Nelson & Bolles, Land Agents
and Brokers, published a book promoting development along the
Marietta Railroad and directed it specifically to the "more enterprising business men" in Cincinnati, Ohio. With the grandiloquence of
nineteenth-century suburban promotion, the developers claimed that
all would find there, "influences are favorable to pure morality, a
higher manhood and their own prosperity." The booklet also planted
a doubled enticement for the astute businessman. He could move to
the suburbs himself and he could invest in property waiting for development there to encourage others to move from the city as he had
done. The imperative of suburban living joined with the heady se-
duction of late-nineteenth-century capitalism as the reader was asked
to think of himself as a capitalist and a philanthropist who contributed to the well-being of the city by reducing its population density.[25]

Social and aesthetic implications of exclusivity were put into
place as suburban life was inscribed with meanings of national endeavor, distinctive community membership, and social status. Frank
Scott, for example, attempted to insure elevated taste and social culture by suggesting that potential suburban dwellers monitor the
appearance of their neighborhoods by joining together to buy land.
Two decades earlier, Llewellyn Park, New Jersey, had been planned
as an ideal retreat to nature by manufacturer Llewellyn Haskell.
Houses designed by Alexander Jackson Davis on streets that con-
formed to nature's geography rather than a city grid system comprised
the fashionable epitome of rural living for the well-to-do.[26] Suburban
planning for the affluent remained a profitable venture for later century developers. Kenilworth, Illinois, was developed as an exclusive
suburban community in the early 1890s. The developer Joseph Sears
advertised the suburban requisites "pure air, quiet green grass, forest
shade, and all the comforts and delights of rural life" and "water, gas,

paved streets, sidewalks, sewage. . . ." Sears established higher lot values for these amenities and promoted them by inviting affluent businessmen and professionals to a picnic on the site. His selection of potential clients on one hand targeted those with sufficient means to buy his lots, but he defined them more precisely as the visibly recognizable "Americans" who enjoyed the current social entitlements to professional status and cultural leadership. Covenants at Kenilworth excluded any but "caucasians." Adding to his strategies for achieving suburban homogeneity, the developer interviewed prospective residents. As one applicant recalled, "I had to give an account of myself, my family, occupations and in the language of the Constitution, my 'age, race, color and previous conditions of servitude.'"[27]

Salvatore Lagumina's study of Italian immigrants who settled on Long Island also notes such flagrant strategies to prohibit selected groups from suburban living. One Long Island developer advertised property with the words, "Italians Excluded," and enough residents commuting on the Long Island Railroad campaigned against having to share coaches with Italian workers to cause the company to relegate Italians to the smoker cars. The 1880s and, more notably, the 1890s were decades of massive Italian immigration and it was this ethnic group's unfortunate turn for immigrant marginalization. Lagumina, however, focuses more on the conditions that contributed to today's large Italian population on suburban Long Island and how immigrant groups established subcultures within the suburban communities while they were assimilating. He demonstrates that amid the exclusionary efforts, other developers encouraged immigrants by advertising their lots in Italian-American newspapers. The desire to live in a smaller community with vestiges of the rural was strong among Italian immigrants. Although most who arrived at Ellis Island in the 1890s settled first in "Little Italies" in New York City, city living was a stark contrast with the small towns and villages of their origins. Many sought employment that entailed living in the suburbs. Early immigrants to Long Island provided manual labor for Long Island railroad expansion and for local industry. With suburban development, they were employed as gardeners and provided other forms of service labor for suburban residents, but they did not commute from the city. They, too, lived in the suburbs, and some of these nineteenth-century immigrants themselves started small businesses that required and supplied manual labor.[28] Late-nineteenth-century commuter suburbs contradicted the image sought by such developers as Sears, for the model successful businessmen comprised only from thirty to fifty percent of the heads of household in such communities.[29]

Some residential developments were marketed to laborers who were lower-middle or working classes. Developers platted new communities along railroads to encourage manufacturers to locate, and subsequently, residents to provide labor. Near Indianapolis, for example, developers encouraged the Bee Line Railroad to build its repair shops in Brightwood, with hopes that it would become a thriving manufacturing center.[30] These communities were situated close enough to major cities to expedite the import and export of raw materials and finished goods, and they became satellite suburbs as well as autonomous industrial communities. Other developers focused on residential lots for working-class commuters whose employment was sufficiently stable to buy homes and pay for transit. Oakwood, Tennessee, a late-century suburb of Knoxville, was largely a community of these "laboring elite" who were able to pursue the symbol American material and social stability.[31] In cities with high immigrant populations in the midwest, immigrants joined together as developers. Chicago's Humboldt Park district was subdivided by a German building and loan association in 1880 for laborers.[32] This type of development introduced pockets of ethnic identity within the larger context of the so-conceived middle-class suburbs, and it was repeated in other communities and commuter suburbs. The desire to live among one's own achieved similar ethnic groupings in the larger scheme of development. Italians settled where their neighbors were Italian, Germans moved into German neighborhoods and Irish into Irish neighborhoods.[33] Suburbs were more diverse in structure and population than the persuasive explanations of their homogeneity suggested. Land value, cost of housing, location of employment, transportation patterns, and desires for community contributed to many variations. Suburbs were home to people of the middle classes and working classes who by their employment, belief in upward mobility, and consumption were drawn into middle-class status.

More on the developer

Kenneth Jackson states, "At the heart of all suburban growth is land development—the conversion of rural or vacant land to some sort of residential use. The process involves property owners, speculators, banks, private lenders, builders and buyers."[34] Real estate developers typically arrived before the new residents of these towns and suburbs. Selling land was profitable for rural landowners, and potentially more profitable for the developers who subdivided their small or large purchases into residential lots. Railroads played a major role as developers in establishing new communities and in transforming villages into suburbs, whether they were the investors or their presence inspired speculators. They extensively advertised their new communities in publications having potential suburban dwellers as their readers. In Robert Shoppell's pattern book, *Artistic Modern Homes*, the Harlem Railroad advertised "Fine Suburban Country" close to New York City where one could find inexpensive lots and houses for a "permanent country home"; the Long Island Railroad advertised its connection to "thriving villages," and the Erie Railway advertised "suburban residences." Real estate development companies who saw potential for growth in an area bought undeveloped land, divided it into building lots, and, at times, built homes. The Real Estate Associates in San Francisco bought land and built more than one thousand houses in the 1870s.[35] From 1880 to 1882 an ambitious developer in Chicago laid out sixteen towns, one hundred fifty subdivisions and a total of 40,000 lots, and he sold over 7,000 houses.[36] These two examples, however, were exceptions. Small speculators who bought land and built one, two, or more houses for sale or developers who sold lots but not homes were more typical.

Speculative land investment for subdivision was not limited to suburbs or commuter towns. Communities located far from cities were also developed by speculators who gambled on a site's future when a boom was expected. Grand Junction was an expanse of "sagebrush and tumbleweeds" when investors arrived to await the removal of Colorado lands from the Ute nation in 1881. Shareholders of the town development company laid out the streets, named them, and divided the blocks of land into lots to sell for businesses and homes. Within two decades, the town site claimed for Grand Junction was lined with tree-shaded streets, businesses and houses.[37] Expectations for a rush of incoming population sometimes were fulfilled and at other times were sorely disappointed. More often, land speculation success fell in between. Newspaper and magazine reports told excitedly about the numbers of people who moved into new communities, and real estate investors were lured by descriptions of towns with insufficient housing. Companies selling tents for temporary shelter were prosperous ventures across the West. But not all of these tent dwellers could afford to buy residential lots or homes even if they were available. Large numbers of the population were transient, soon to move elsewhere to pursue wealth. Often, overly ambitious investors owned more lots than there were people moving into the community who could afford to buy land for a home. Subdivided areas of the city consequently were unevenly built up, with many empty lots separating houses.[38] Today, as we look at local nineteenth-century promotional maps that were drawn in with scatterings of existing buildings, we can recognize that development may have been as large a contributor to the physical distance between houses as a desire for building a home isolated from neighbors.

Building houses quickly and inexpensively

Mass produced building materials paved the way for building the homes, whether for developers, small speculators, or individuals. Rapid growth was incompatible with the traditional building techniques so admired by architects who were attempting to separate themselves from the non-professional builders. Member of the American Institute of Architects Henry Van Brunt characterized the brisk pace of building in western towns as "too impatient to wait for a natural growth in art" in contrast with the "slowly growing indigenous styles" found in Europe and England.[39] Van Brunt was among those who proposed colonial carpentry for building the nation's homes because colonial timber-frame buildings were models of architectural integrity when compared with flimsily built modern homes. Their mental picture of the domestic landscape, however, neglected to consider the practical matter of increased building costs from materials and labor time. Home builders in suburbs and towns took full advantage of more recent construction technology. Machine-made nails, standardization of building materials, and developments in lighter framing techniques had transformed American building between the 1830s and the Civil War. These changes affected masonry and wood domestic architecture. Brick houses were more prevalent in regions of the country where clay soil made manufacturing bricks a profitable enterprise. Denver, for example, was built on clay soil and it was over fifty miles from forests with trees usable for milling timber lengths. It became a "brick city" with fashionable houses for the middle classes in warm fired tones of its native material.[40] The *Inland Architect*, published in Chicago where fire-resistant properties were a priority, introduced brick and masonry homes to their architect readers much more frequently than the *American Architect* on the East Coast or the *California Architect and Building News*, published from a major lumber producing region. Local availability of clay and wood factored into building material preferences, but wood was plentiful and inexpensive. Building materials from raw lumber to finely finished woodwork were shipped on the efficient railroad network from the Pacific west, north and southeast to local suppliers and individuals. Pattern book authors had good reason for marketing plans for wood houses more than masonry houses.

Most homes were wood frame and, of these, most were efficiently built balloon-frame construction. Balloon framing was developed in the 1830s and within thirty years had begun to replace braced framing, which used nails and lighter weight timber than traditional timber framing with its squared timbers and mortise-and-tenon joinery (Figs. 14, 15). In the service of rapid and inexpensive construction, balloon framing improved upon both. Balloon construction introduced a more straightforward approach to building, in which upright wood studs, extending from foundation sill to the roof or second-story supports, were nailed directly to the sill and joists. Angled timber braces were unnecessary. With the use of readily available, mass-produced standardized materials, it could be built by one or two carpenters and with fewer tools. The balloon frame revolutionized national house building. Yet, it was not embraced uniformly. Pattern book authors who included essays on construction explained

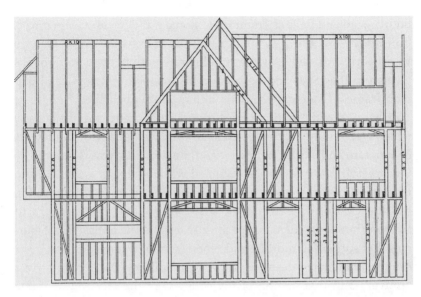

Fig. 14. Braced-frame construction was more expedient than labor intensive mortise-and-tenon timber-frame construction. (Comstock, Modern Architectural Designs and Details, *1881)*

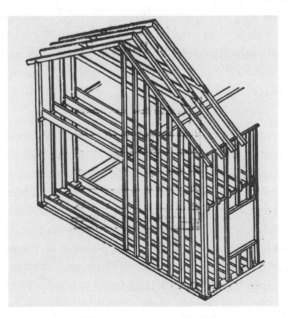

Fig. 15. Although many established architects argued that balloon-frame construction was too flimsy, local builders and carpenters made it the norm. Isometric projection of balloon framing. (Woodward, Woodward's Country Homes, *1865)*

both braced and balloon framing for home builders who were uncertain about the stability of the new lighter framework. George Woodward included drawings to illustrate both in his pattern books written in the 1860s and persuaded his readers to make use of balloon frames. Later pattern book authors described their houses as "substantial" and "solid" to assure their future clients that the houses, which were implied as balloon frame, would indeed withstand years of sun, rain and storm. Professional trade literature was divided. The *California Architect* was largely aligned with the *American Architect* on the subject of the need for professionalization in the building trades, but the California editor took a different stance with regard to balloon-frame construction. Specifically responding to East Coast journals that supported mortice-and-tenon framing as stronger and more durable, they stated the reality of western building. Balloon frame was "universal in this section of the country, in the erection of frame buildings, which constitute ninety-five per cent of buildings erected west of the Rocky Mountains," and contrary to the suggestion that such buildings had a life span of less than ten years, many buildings in the region were thirty years old and in good condition.[41]

Factory-produced exterior and interior woodwork was readily available to embellish the basic balloon-frame structure. An 1875 advertisement for the C. P. Fobes Manufacturing Company of Crown Point, New York, highlighted a long list of wood products they could produce:

> Architectural work of every description executed from the Drawings of Architects, in any wood desired. Vestibules, front doors, porches, verandas, cornices, bay windows, balconies, canopies, blinds, inside and out. Sash, plain and ornamental. Library fittings, Book-cases, Window cornices, mantles and wainscoting, etc. All from the plainest to the most extravagantly rich and beautiful designs. Winding or straight staircases, with rails, fitted to put up. Elegant and original newels made a specialty. Work securely packed and shipped to any part of the United States and Canada.[42]

Companies sold marble fireplace mantels, glass, tile, and decorative iron work. Numerous companies, especially in the midwestern states, circulated nationally their catalogues of mass-produced woodwork. M. A. Disbrow in Lyons, Iowa, was a typical manufacturer of wood-work for homes. Established in 1856, incorporated in 1884, and opening branches in Omaha, Nebraska, and Cheyenne, Wyoming, in the 1890s, the company advertised a full spectrum of exterior and interior woodwork and glass. Elaborate spindle work to span wide doorways, bulls-eye corner blocks for door frames, turned veranda posts, bay windows, gable decorations that were adjustable to the pitch of the gabled porches and other familiar features of late-nine-teenth-century houses were designed to appear hand-produced.[43] Today, these wood embellishments continue to elicit awe over craft-ing skill that belonged to a machine, albeit governed by a skilled hand. By 1887, the use of pre-fabricated parts was so prevalent that the *American Builder* staff was prompted to comment, "Modern houses are put up pretty much as Solomon's temple was, the parts are brought together all prepared and fitted, and it is short and easy work to put them together."[44] Manufacturers shipped their pre-fabricated materi-als to city suburbs and rural towns. Although their customers chose from a wide array of items, their selections were limited by the com-panies' offerings and by their own budget. As with the house plans sold in architectural pattern books (see chapters six and seven), the end result was variety within a genre of design. Many suburban streets were lined with houses bearing similarity to the "modern house" in Robert Shoppell's history of domestic architecture but with embel-lishment (Fig. 16). Less expensive versions were simpler one-or two-story cottages with decorative gables; others employed the full panoply of decoration.

Suburbs and towns and the city

Suburbs, despite their having been framed as living environments in nature, were built with houses made possible by the machine. The streets on which the houses were built, too, opposed notions of the natural, for they registered gridded communities with parallel lines of intersecting streets that glossed over the contours of nature. The

Fig. 16. Factories produced bay windows, doors, and all forms of exterior and interior decoration, making the new fashion attainable and affordable throughout the United States. Home in Bellingham, Wash., 1890s. (Photograph by Barbara Plaskett)

United States early had adopted the efficiency of the grid for city schemes and in 1785 organized the land from the Ohio River to the Pacific coast into thirty-six-square-mile parcels. The towns and cities that followed reproduced this reticulation in smaller scale.[45] Grid systems were efficient. They were easier to survey and expedited town platting. Straight streets were less costly to build and maintain and they facilitated the flow of traffic into and out of the town. Once implemented from east to west and north to south, grid plans presented newcomers with a familiar layout. Following the organization of city centers, land speculators platted new towns with Main streets, Front streets, and Center streets to denote each community's commercial and civic heart. Main Street typically ran perpendicular to the railroad and provided access from the countryside to the train station, grain elevators and other storage facilities as well as to local businesses. The main street was often designated by a town square patterned after a village green, from which streets spread out neatly. With few exceptions, a national identity that merged urban progress with rural nature gave dominance to the physical urban pattern in city, suburban and rural communities alike.[46]

Functional relations to the city within this conventional urban grid were less straightforward. For suburban residents, the city was appropriate for employment and shopping, but it did not serve the daily needs of the family. For fresh produce, many took advantage of their location to grow vegetables and fruit. Groceries, drugstores, and small hardware stores were built on corner lots among the rows of houses to supply them with other necessities. To serve commuters who traveled longer distances, businesses cropped up along trolley lines, and at the most convenient locations, businesses soon abutted one another, giving both convenience and variety of shopping.[47] Access to consumable goods was solved, but a more formidable problem was introduced by the numbers of families living in unincorporated communities. A civic infrastructure was needed to build and maintain public utilities, including water, sewer, gas, and, later, electricity. Suburban children required schools for their education.

One solution was annexation of a suburb into the larger metropolitan area to which it was physically connected. The phenomenal rate of urban geographic expansion in the late nineteenth century was accomplished by cities annexing suburban lands. Bigger was indeed better in the rhetoric of nineteenth-century city growth. Statistics were compiled as never before to compare populations, their composition, and their movement, and competition was high among the cities to be ranked the largest in the region or recognized for closing the gap between them and the nation's largest cities. For promoters of city growth, annexation brought the prestige of size, and it brought urban professional expertise, which resulted in a larger and more efficient civic organization.[48]

Not all suburban residents saw integration into a larger civic entity as a beneficial course of action, but *whether* to annex was not always a decision available to suburban communities. Forcible annexation of unincorporated developments and towns was the rule until late in the century, and it served the inexorable sprawl of city limits outward. Formerly autonomous communities were subsumed, and these maneuvers proposed a shifting of community identity from the local to the metropolitan. Some commuter towns resisted becoming appendages to the city by incorporating before annexation could take place. Others resisted by sustaining community identity within the larger metropolitan area. In both situations, community boosters took advantage of their nearness to city employment and high culture, as well as their community's affinity with nature, to proclaim superiority of suburban living. Their community identity, however, remained local as suburban residents of each community defined themselves as having distinct civic character from neighboring suburbs, even when they were only a mile or two apart. Friendly town rivalries in sports were a common exercise in building town identity.[49]

Towns, too, were signs of the advance of civilization on the landscape of the nation. Boosterism to promote town growth was raised to an art form, or perhaps I should suggest a vaudevillian art form, in the prairies and West. Town leaders exercised their entrepreneurial imaginations to make their towns appear prosperous and civilized so as to draw industry, commerce, and future residents, to become more city-like. They gave special attention to visiting politicians, reporters, authors, and artists who would broadcast the community's fine attributes to the nation, and they sponsored cultural activities that brought to town famous entertainers and orators. Their quests for good press for the community joined with wishes for culture and pleasure that consequently supported a vast national railroad entertainment circuit. American, European, and British troupes gathered crowds in theaters from small cities to remote mountain mining camps, and with the famous came a stamp of civilization.[50] Promotional literature produced by town leaders unabashedly claimed their towns to be flawless. They were prosperous, cultured, and to suggest the upstanding character of their citizens, they were claimed as moral. Helena, Montana, with customary town bombast advertised "a society in its moral structure as pure as in any community on the face of the earth."[51]

The boom-and-bust mentality of these towns increased the intensity with which city promoters sought success. The hegemonic belief that American land was there to conquer intersected with beliefs in progress as city-building and as entitlement to individual prosperity, but fierce competition among towns and the sometime actuality of economic recession and depleted natural resources made triumph uncertain.[52] Rural midwest and mid-Atlantic states already faced the reality of young people leaving to work in cities or to find their fortunes elsewhere, and their populations were dwindling. Industrial towns were suffering under the weight of their bleakness, and sought means to revive economically and socially.[53] Towns were the testing grounds for a survival-of-the-fittest philosophy, and the activities that demonstrated the initiative of social adaptation defined towns as places with identity in the expansive land of the United States. Boosterism was more about the future than the present haphazard condition of many towns. Although towns were platted in grids, their development did not produce visually cohesive communities. In smaller towns, the business centers contained a mix of retail and industry around which were shacks, small buildings functioning as living quarters, and empty lots. Reports from East Coast visitors told too frequently how high expectations for a town precipitated grave disappointment. Town boosters also were aware of effects of transience and of the circulating stereotypes of wild western towns.

Civic leaders realized that a town's public image could not be conveyed by word alone. The physical appearance of the town was as important as printed communication about the town's prosperity and culture. A newspaper editor in Wichita argued for physical improvements because they "give an air of stability and appearance that the people who cultivated it are not mere birds of passage, but have come to stay."[54] Main Street was a town's first public statement of achievement for the visitor. If a community was to appear civilized, it must be accomplished in the emblematic business center. Although boosters claimed unique identities for their towns, local and regional characteristics in building were less important than conforming to urban precedents.[55] They, as did A.I.A. architect Henry Van Brunt in his article on western architecture, assumed that a lack of influence from the East Coast was detrimental to western town development. In smaller towns, false front buildings with classical cornices and dentils predominated to mask the humble, gable-roofed structures behind. In larger towns, they stood next to new masonry buildings in the latest Renaissance, Queen Anne, and Romanesque fashions for commercial buildings. Mass-produced materials were used by some communities and their business owners to inexpensively achieve the look of enduring stability. Sheet iron stamped with columns, cornices, moldings, and all forms of classical detail was manufactured in several midwestern towns. St. Louis had eleven such factories in the 1880s. The Mesker Company was one of the more successful, shipping approximately 70 building fronts to small towns in Montana.[56] One visitor to Helena, Montana, who evidently recognized the prevalence of wood frame, false-front buildings, cast iron facades, and uneven residential development in western towns, observed, "Queen Anne in front and Crazy Jane behind."[57]

Imaged community

Perhaps there has been no time in history without its contradictions. The late-nineteenth-century desire to live in suburban nature while relying on community growth for prestige and economic security has been a national condition for over a century, and it has been dealt with by each generation. The nineteenth-century home and its relationship to site and community was framed as a cultured home whose inhabitants engaged in the endeavors of economic and social mobility, but the rawness of rapidly growing suburbs and towns did not always coordinate with the image of a civilized suburban refuge. Through late century, tensions in the struggle between progress and domestic sanctuary in residential spaces of home and community were tempered with nostalgic memory that evoked images of towns with clean, tree-lined streets, flower-filled yards, village greens with smooth, grass lawns, and spirited, cohesive community relations. What many community residents actually faced were de-forested lots, unplanted or untended yards, muddy, treeless greens, and a community with a population entirely composed of recently arrived residents or so many incoming residents that the existing social order was overturned. The imaged town was a conflation of evolutionary progress, moving toward an ideal, and constructed memories of an idealized past. Communities of people for whom wilderness remained a part of national memory planted thousands of trees before and after Arbor Day was instituted by the governor of Nebraska in 1872. From the East Coast, idealized New England villages that had been carved out of the wilderness by colonists were posed as models for modern communities. During the same decades that were marked by national expansion, nostalgia for the late eighteenth and early nineteenth centuries had become a cultural industry, with tourism to real and reconstructed colonial sites, interest in historic preservation and colonial crafts, and histories and fictional tales about life among the colonists in popular periodicals and books.[58] The uncertainties of modern life were softened by—and we may note, kept alive by— myth. The colonial period was believed to be a bygone life when people had dignity, honesty, and respect for neighbors, and they lived in a friendly community, a village.

Living these selective yearnings for life from a century past, authors and visual artists from states with colonial and early federal origins often juxtaposed old and new to overlay visions of colonial home and wholesome village on the suburban community. Architect and architectural critic Bruce Price began his article on suburban houses with an assumption of commuter suburbs, but he immediately turned to the beauty of much older houses found in many towns and villages. With unequivocal language he pitted recently developed "suburban villa cities" filled with "hideous structures of wood" against an ideal that had been inspired by the British buildings at the

Centennial Exhibition. The timber-frame buildings had reminded American architects of the merits of their own colonial and early republic houses. This historical example of architecture and community set a precedent for present-day domestic beauty and, as a result, contemporary counterparts of colonial houses were found nationally, in communities such as Morristown, New Jersey, Kenwood, Illinois, and Tacoma, Washington.[59]

Admittedly, constructing a history of colonial heritage was an East Coast project that had little immediate historical relevance to the larger population who were without colonial and early republic lineage. Nonetheless, this period in history was fundamental to framing American national identity, and it was represented well in magazine articles, books, and prints read by the larger population. Reading materials for children, too, educated them early and subtly into this nostalgic historical scheme. Between the Centennial Exhibition and the 1893 Columbian Exposition in Chicago, the children's magazine *St. Nicholas* interspersed drawings of children in old-fashioned dress and poems about the eighteenth-century making of the nation among African jungles adventures, essays on Japanese and Chinese customs, stories with European characters, and instruction on sports. Curiously, the participants in the newest leisure-time mania of bicycling toured villages with winding streets of ivy-and moss-bedecked half-timber cottages. The villages were English and European rather than American, but the houses were the style and age so often used to show the colonial ancestry of American housing (Fig. 17).[60]

Residents of new towns in the East and West did not reproduce colonial life; they were profound believers in moving forward. Longings for a specific past in American history cannot be argued as a national condition, but nostalgia for life in the remembered New England village combined with aspirations for stable community. The United States was a restless nation of people on the move. Newly arrived immigrants and native-born and foreign-born residents alike moved to new neighborhoods, nearby towns, and across the country. The unemployed, the adventurous seeking new opportunity, and the frail searching for healthy climates migrated to new communities. Some moved thousands of miles; others moved shorter distances. Still others moved but a few miles away to new residential developments

Fig. 17. A children's magazine illustrated the new sport of cycling in British villages with picturesque sixteenth- to eighteenth-century houses at a time when modern desires for a simpler, less harried life turned to nostalgia for the nation's colonial past. (Pennell, St. Nicholas, *1890)*

on the edges of cities or to established and new suburban towns connected to the city center with more rapid transportation. Establishing a home in a new community, however, did not mean permanence. Many families moved several times. For example, only a small minority of families in Omaha remained over a decade in the same home. Changes of address were much more frequent than in the late twentieth century.[61] People in Philadelphia and Boston, too, were highly mobile, and the story was much the same in towns farther west. The average length of residence for families living in Grand Junction, Colorado, in 1885 was less than five-and-one-half years.[62]

Americans continually severed their geographic ties, and many attempted to find community identity in their new homes by forming civic and social organizations. Late-nineteenth-century town dwellers were active community participants, joining social clubs, drill teams, whist clubs, baseball teams, and philanthropic organizations. Residents of rural and frontier towns formed organizations, such as music, art and literary groups, to bring "civilized" culture to the community.[63] Some midwestern and western reading groups ordered periodicals such as *Scribner's, Harper's, Atlantic Monthly,* and *St. Nicholas* then circulated them for others to read. Reading these magazines was a sign of status. Produced on the urban East Coast, they were considered to have a higher standard of culture and intelligence than the pulp fiction and popular magazines for the masses, and not incidentally, the magazines took an active role in the formulation of an idealized colonial history.[64] Professional and fraternal associations enabled members to enhance their business as well as social prospects. As residents of suburbs, small cities, and towns thrived on activities that were modeled by modern city vitality, they smoothed the raw edges of rapid change by building community.

Progress, memory, and town improvement

Life in an ideal American community proposed detached houses with well-tended lawns, closely knit nuclear families, belonging to a community of like-minded individuals, social status associated with middle-class hegemony, and civic pride based on economic and geographic growth. Among all of the active organizations joined by nineteenth-century community members, none so cogently united these suppositions as village improvement associations. Organized village improvement began in a few New England towns before the Civil War, but the impetus came during the years leading to the Centennial.[65] By the mid-1890s town citizens organized in New Jersey, Connecticut, Massachusetts, Pennsylvania, Ohio, Illinois, Nebraska, Minnesota, Colorado, California, and South Carolina. Massachusetts alone had more than sixty village improvement societies.[66] Birdsey Grant Northrup, a secretary of the Connecticut State Board of Education, was one of the most ardent supporters of the movement. From his 1869 tract "How to Beautify and Build Up Our Country Towns" until 1880 he helped organize approximately one hundred societies in New England and the Middle Atlantic states. A decade later, the *New York Tribune* spread the word of beautification by republishing his tract "Rural Improvement Associations." The newspaper sold it for the small sum of three dollars per one hundred, which made it possible for communities to spread his goals to improve civic, domestic and individual lives. The tract encouraged residents

> to cultivate public spirit, and foster town pride, quicken intellectual life, promote good fellowship, public health, improvement of roads, roadsides, and sidewalks, street lights, public parks, improvement of home and home life, ornamental and economic tree-planting, improvement of railroad-stations, rustic roadside seats for pedestrians, betterment of factory surroundings.[67]

The name "village improvement association" was circulated from the East Coast in national publications in the 1890s when the word "village" was taking on meanings of ideal rural life, but communities already had put the program into practice in the form of village improvement associations, town improvement societies, and other civic-minded organizations with a variety of names. No matter the name, the late-century tensions between beliefs in city progress and wholesome nature generated the projects. Above all, participants in village and town improvement saw themselves as progressive, having as one of their challenges to confront "local conservatism."[68] They campaigned for sorely needed public utilities, sewer systems, good soil drainage, maintained streets, and pedestrian walkways. Some ambitious groups worked to bring public libraries into their communities. These improvements had a practical basis, but they signified city-like amenities. Caroline Robbins, recounting the history of village improvement in 1897, explicitly credited city visitors to small towns for the movement's inspiration. City dwellers were accustomed to urban conveniences, and they did not want to deal with "old-time make shifts" when they holidayed in these rural retreats. The requirements of tourism demonstrated the shortcomings of an unprogressive community, and the organizations accomplished bringing the "higher civilization" of the city to rural life.[69] B. G. Northrup went so far as to consider improvement associations the "rural counterparts of the urban boards of trade."[70]

Northrup contributed to its popularization, but women lead village and town improvement. Completion of the work depended on philanthropic support from the community, and women plied their social networks to solicit membership, participation and impressive amounts of money. At times, women stepped out of the supportive role as club organizers and took more instrumental roles in civic leadership. In Oskaloosa, Kansas, in 1888, several took full advantage of their new right to vote in city elections. They had become impatient with muddy and dusty streets without sidewalks and decided to run for mayoral and city council office. Their success remains a remarkable achievement in the history of city governance, for Oskaloosa gained an all-woman government, which was a catalyst for civilizing this prairie town.[71]

Improving city streets and draining muddy public spaces were practical; plus, they added to the visual appeal of a community. Village improvement was a beautification program that promoted an image of a community where the entire population planted flower beds, shrubs, and trees, mowed their lawns, and, generally, kept their residences and towns neat and tidy. With visions of tree-lined streets, the activists planted trees in the thousands. Wyoming, Ohio, with a small population of 700 people, planted over 700 trees from 1880 to 1882. Organizations in some communities offered prizes for the most trees a group or individual planted and awarded prizes for their selection and tending of the trees. Most chose shade trees with stately height and breadth, as was exemplified by the American elm. Without this social imperative for tree-shaded streets and parks, many communities would have been quite barren. The imperative became a civic mandate as some towns appointed tree wardens to monitor the health of the trees and administer fines to those who harmed them. Elsewhere, a soft-gloved form of social control was put into place. Children were given the responsibility of protecting town flower beds from those who would deface civic beauty. More actively, they planted trees and gathered litter into large, but decorative, community waste receptacles. Improvement societies were a means to order the physical character of villages and towns into a middle-class ideal. Lawns were to be neatly mowed, gardens tended, and houses freshly painted. For, as George and Charles Palliser stated in their firm's architectural pattern book, "A true appreciation of a country or suburban home will not tolerate slovenly, ill-kept grounds. . . ."[72] Leading citizens of both genders situated themselves as progressive cultural leaders, and they worked to bring other believers into the fold. Not only conservative citizens needed to be convinced, but laboring classes, too. From the perspective of the town's upright middle-class citizens, workers' houses and yards contributed to the town's overall appearance of prosperity and communal spirit, and gaining their conformity to the norm required concerted effort.

Progress defined through nostalgia framed meanings for these middle-class activities in cultural leadership, and towns and villages were produced as places of memory. The Park Association and the Old Settlers Association in Nebraska City, Nebraska, established a city park, planted trees, and built a reproduction of a pioneer log cabin for the park. They beautified their town with a population of 12,000 people in a way that fulfilled the mythical image of the United States as wooded nation and posited the pioneer experience as a home in a picturesque, bucolic scene. Leadership by long-standing citizens was not unusual. Early settlers formed pioneer associations in prairie and frontier towns to distinguish themselves from transient populations and to establish historical legitimacy for their communities. In New England, old family citizens joined with relative newcomers to produce nostalgic re-presentations of colonial villages.[73] Residents of North Andover, Massachusetts, as in many small communities in New England, responded to the physical and social ramifications of industry introduced to the village and the subsequent migration of workers by adding a visual symbol of friendly social relations—a village green. The community of their collective memory had been dismantled, and to bring it to life, they reached to the American myth of the colonial that defined an imagined time when people lived real, meaningful, and stable lives shaped by commitment to family and community, and their village green was their place for socialization, leisure, and symbolic participation in community. The North Andover Village Improvement Association convinced civic leaders to remove a bandstand and a fire station from the town common and transformed it with lawn and trees.[74] Both Stockbridge, Massachusetts, and New Milford, Connecticut, drained and graded their bare commons, then planted grass to manufacture quintessentially pristine colonial greens.[75] Many of these New England towns converted rutted, largely dirt commons into lush rectangles of shaded lawn, often surrounded by buildings remodeled or newly built to appear colonial. Today's picturesque image of a quiet expanse of lawn with shade trees, around which are two-hundred-year-old white buildings, is a legacy of this movement. Translations of this conception of a village center in towns without colonial history emerged as cleaned-up town squares with benches, bandstands, grass, and trees. These squares, which were the product of earlier-century midwestern and western interpretations of New England town planning, were made into civic spaces by adjacent courthouses, libraries, or other public buildings. For smaller towns without city squares, tree-lined church yards served the community. Suburban towns sought spaces of communal identity, too, but

Fig. 18. Train stations were symbols of suburban progress and the focus of many community beautification programs. Cover. (Smith, Suburban Homes at Wollaston Park, 1890)

this often was subsumed into beautifying prized symbols of progress. Residents in some suburban communities gathered to paint their train stations, surround them with flowerbeds, and appoint them with tasteful exterior furnishings. The emblematic character of these links to urban employment and culture was underscored by architect Frank L. Smith. On the cover of his book of house designs for Wollaston Park, Massachusetts, a drawing of a spacious modern house shared attention with a train station (Fig. 18).[76]

In this conception of the ideal community, residences were located at the peripheries of the civic and commercial center, but they were not symbolically peripheral. That beautiful houses were important to town image is demonstrated on maps and in promotional publications. Bird's-eye view drawings featured houses in the topography of the communities. Often larger drawings of houses surrounded the map to highlight the cultured sensibilities and prosperity of a town's residents. Invariably, the residences typified the suburban ideal of home—the individually owned house in a community where one could distinguish oneself and belong to a group with common values. Pattern books that circulated house designs and their plans turned out to be an excellent place to carry forward this image.

NOTES

[1] Samuel Burrage Reed, *Dwellings for Village and Country* (New York: Orange Judd Company, 1885), p. 121.

[2] Robert Ellis Thompson, *The Development of the House. Annals of the Wharton School* (Philadelphia: Wharton School of Finance, University of Pennsylvania, 1885), p. 15.

[3] David Hamer, *New Towns in the New World: Images and Perceptions of the Nineteenth-Century Urban Frontier* (New York: Columbia University Press, 1990).

[4] Elisha Hussey, *Home Building* (New York: By the Author, 1876), pp. iii and Plate No. 9.

[5] Henry A. Beers, *A Suburban Pastoral* (New York: Henry Holt and Company, 1894), p. 5.

[6] See Dell Upton, ed., *America's Architectural Roots: Ethnic Groups that Built America* (Washington, D.C.: The Preservation Press, 1986).

[7] "The Point of View," *Scribner's Magazine* 9(Jan-June 1891): 392–94.

[8] William J. Lloyd, "Understanding Late Nineteenth-Century Cities," *Geographical Review* 71, 4(1981): 468.

[9] Robert C. Haywood documents the civilizing thrust of community activities and the frequent use of words such as "civilized" to distinguish

cultural difference in *Victorian West: Class and Culture in Kansas Cattle Towns* (Lawrence: University Press of Kansas, 1991).

10 Albert C. Bolles, *Industrial History of the United States*, 3rd. Ed. (1881; reprint ed. New York: Augustus M. Kelley, 1966), pp. 635–46, and Philip S. Foner, *The Great Labor Uprising of 1877* (New York: Monad Press, 1977), pp. 13–14.

11 George A. Custer, "Battling with the Sioux on the Yellowstone," *Galaxy* 22(July 1876): 91.

12 Quoted in Thomas Schlereth, *Victorian America: Transformations in Everyday Life* (New York: HarperCollins Publishers, 1991), p. 22.

13 "Point of View," p. 392.

14 Thomas J. Noel, *Buildings of Colorado* (New York/Oxford: Oxford University Press, 1997), p. 25.

15 Leland Roth, *McKim, Mead & White, Architects* (New York: Harper & Row, Publishers, 1983), p. 92. Thos. Emerson Ripley notes that the furnishings were from Wanamaker's large store in Philadelphia; the waiters, too, came from Philadelphia, in *Green Timber: On the Flood Tide to Fortune in the Great Northwest* (Palo Alto: American West Publishing Company, 1968), n.p. Murray Morgan attributes the design to Stanford White in *Puget's Sound: A Narrative of Early Tacoma and the Southern Sound* (Seattle: University of Washington Press, 1979), p. 253.

16 Kenneth T. Jackson, *Crabgrass Frontier: The Suburbanization of the United States* (New York/London: Oxford University Press, 1985), p. 140; Lawrence H. Larsen, *The Urban West at the End of the Frontier* (Lawrence: Regents Press of Kansas, 1978), p. 115.

17 The differences between villages, towns and cities are indistinct. Late-century architect Henry Van Brunt considered towns as having populations between 30,000 and 50,000. As cities grew, statistical categorization changed in nineteenth-century United States census reports, in U.S. Bureau of the Census, *Historical Census of the United States: Colonial times to 1970, Bicentennial Edition* (Washington, D.C., 1975). I am concerned with cities and small cities (typically a population of 50,000 or more) having suburbs, towns, and the conceptual image of villages. Villages were generally perceived as more rural communities, but town and village designations often were used inter-changeably in the late nineteenth century.

18 Communities separated from the city by expanses of green space are called "Borderlands" by John R. Stilgoe, who considers them more accurate representations of the suburb than the fringe residential developments. In *Borderland: The Origins of the American Suburb, 1820–1939* (New Haven and London: Yale University Press, 1988).

19 Michael H. Ebner, *Creating Chicago's North Shore: A Suburban History* (University of Chicago Press, 1988).

20 Thomas Curtis Clarke, "Rapid Transit in Cities. I.-The Problem,." *Scribner's* 11 (January-June 1892): 567–70.

21 Sam Bass Warner, *Streetcar Suburbs: The Process of Growth in Boston (1870–1900)* (Cambridge and London: Harvard University Press, 1978 [1962]) pp. 55–56.

22 "Passaic, New Jersey," *Scientific American, Architects and Builders Edition* (June 1886), republished in Eugene Mitchell, *American Victorian* (New York: Van Nostrand Reinhold Company, 1979), pp. 40–44.

23 Sereno Edwards Todd, *Todd's Country Homes and How to Save Money* (Hartford: Hartford Publishing Company, 1870), p. 48.

24 Frank J. Scott, *The Art of Beautifying Suburban Home Grounds* (New York: D. Appleton & Co., 1870), pp. 29 and 31.

25 Richard Nelson, *Suburban Homes for Businessmen, on the Line of the Marietta Railroad* (Cincinnati: Nelson & Bolles, n.d.), pp. 6 and 9.

26 Brendel-Pandich, p. 78.

27 Ebner, pp. 65–68. His quotations are from Colleen Browne Kilner, *Joseph Sears and His Kenilworth: The Dreamer and the Dream* (Kenilworth, 1969).

28 Salvatore J. Lagumina, *From Steerage to Suburbs* (New York: Center for Migration Studies, 1988).

29 Jackson, p. 99. Successive ethnic groups were excluded from such suburbs. As noted above, Native Americans, African Americans, and Chinese were too marginalized to be feared as potential residents. Jewish families were ascribed most frequently to the city in the discourse.

30 Ebner, p. xxv.

31 Kevin David Kane and Thomas L. Bell, Suburbs for the Labor Elite," *Geographical Review* 75, 3(1985): 333.

32 Jon C. Teaford, *Cities of the Heartland: The Rise and Fall of the Industrial Midwest* (Bloomington: Indiana University Press, 1993), pp. 79–81. Teaford cites Barbara Posadas, "A Home in the Country: Suburbanization in Jefferson Township, 1870–1889," *Chicago History* 7(Fall 1978).

33 Anne Bloomfield, "The Real Estate Associates: A Land Developer in the 1870s in San Francisco," in Thomas Carter, ed., *Images of an American Land* (Albuquerque: University of New Mexico Press, 1997), p. 29, and Warner, *Streetcar Suburbs*, p. 67.

34 Jackson, p. 133.

35 Bloomfield, p. 16.

36 Jackson, p. 135.

37 Kathleen Underwood, *Town Building on the Colorado Frontier* (Albuquerque: University of New Mexico Press, 1987). Underwood cites similar development in Jacksonville, Illinois, Grass Valley, California, and Seattle, Washington, p. 107.

38 Barbara Ruth Bailey, *Main Street Northeastern Oregon: The Founding and Development of Small Towns* (Portland: Oregon Historical Society, 1982), p. 72.

39 Henry Van Brunt, "Architecture in the West," *Atlantic Monthly* 64(December 1889): 772 and 774.

40 Noel, p. 41.

41 "'Balloon-built Buildings': How False Statements Gather Strength," *California Architect and Building News* 2 (February 1881): 16.

42 Advertisement in Gilbert Bostwick Croff, *Progressive American Architecture* (New York: Orange Judd Company, 1875).

43 Arthur A. Hart, "M. S. Disbrow & Company: Catalogue Architecture," *Palimpsest* 56, 4(1975): 98–119.

44 *American Builder* 23(September 1887): 223.

45 David P. Handlin, *The American Home: Architecture and Society, 1815–1915* (Boston and Toronto: Little, Brown and Company, 1979), pp. 97–98.

46 Noel, p. 23, and Stilgoe, pp. 152–53.

47 Peter G. Rowe, *Making a Middle Landscape* (Cambridge: MIT Press, 1991), p. 110.

48 Consolidation of suburbs was another strategy to achieve a stronger economic base. Jackson, pp. 138–48.

49 Ebner, in his introduction, discusses the competition among suburbs to distinguish themselves from nearby suburbs and explores this factor of community identity in the subsequent chapters.

50 Marion M. Huseas finds that even remote mining camps were entertained by famous actors in "Entertainment on the Western Frontier," *Gateway Heritage* 3, 1(1982): 22-33.

51 *Helena Illustrated: Capital of the State of Montana* (Minneapolis, 1890), p. 24. Quoted in Hamer, p. 62.

52 Julie Wilson demonstrates the ideological intersections of grid-system planning and themes stemming from beliefs in manifest destiny which were articulated in community and state boosterism in, "'Kansas Uber Alles!': The Geography and Ideology of Conquest, 1870–1900," *Western Historical Quarterly* 27, 2(Summer 1996): 171–89.

53 Henry J. Fletcher, "The Doom of the Small Town," *Forum* 19(April 1895): 214–23.

54 Quoted in Haywood, p. 86.

55 Hamer, p. 87.

56 Arthur A. Hart, "Sheet Iron Elegance: Mail Order Architecture in Montana," *Montana Historical Society* 4, no. 4(1990): 26–31.

57 Almon Gunnison, *Rambles Overland: A Trip across the Continent* (Boston, 1884), pp. 86–87. Quoted in Hamer, p. 188.

58 Dona Brown, *Inventing New England: Regional Tourism in the Nineteenth Century* (Washington and London: Smithsonian Institution Press, 1995). Brown also examines the contradictions between commercial development and desires to get away from it.

59 Bruce Price, "The Suburban House," *Scribner's Magazine* 8(July 1890): 3–19.

60 Elizabeth Robins Pennell, "Cycling," *St. Nicholas* 17(July 1890): 733–39.

61 Howard P. Chudacoff, *Mobile Americans: Residential and Social Mobility in Omaha 1880–1920* (New York: Oxford University Press, 1972). He also found that there was little difference between individual and family mobility.

62 Underwood, p. 79.

63 Documentation of organizations and membership in Kansas is found in Carol Leonard, Isidor Walliman and Wayne Rohrer, "Group and Social Organization in Frontier Cattle Towns in Kansas," *Kansas Quarterly* 12, 2(1980): 59–63.

64 *American Builder* condensed articles from the adult periodicals for their readers.

65 Credit for the first organized society is given to Mary Goodrich nee Hopkins. Warren H. Manning, "The History of Village Improvement in the United States," *Craftsman* 5(February 1904): 423–32 and Birdsey Grant Northrup, "The Work of Village-Improvement Societies," *Forum* 19(March 1895): 95.

66 Northrup, and Mary Caroline Robbins, "Village Improvement Societies," *Atlantic Monthly* 79(1897): 212–22.

67 Manning, p. 427.

68 Northrup, p. 103, and Robbins.

69 Robbins, pp. 213–14.

70 Northrup, p. 104.

71 Interview with Nancy Hamilton, April 30, 1998, Bellingham, Washington, the great granddaughter of Oskaloosa city councilwoman, Mittie Ernel Golden. Women in Kansas gained the right to vote in city elections in 1887. Joanna L. Stratton, *Pioneer Women: Voices from the Kansas Frontier* (New York: Touchstone, Simon and Schuster, 1981), p. 265.

72 Palliser, Palliser and Co., *Palliser's Model Homes* (Bridgeport, Conn.: Palliser, Palliser and Co., 1878), p. 34.

73 New England towns were successively developed as interpretations and re-interpretations of the past. See Joseph Wood, "The New England Village as an American Vernacular Form," in Camille Wells, ed., *Perspectives in American Vernacular Architecture, II.* (Columbia: University of Missouri Press, 1986), and J. S. Wood and M. Steinitz, "A World We Have Gained: House, Common and Village in New England," *Journal of Historical Geography* 18, 1(1992): 105–20.

74 Thomas W. Leavitt, "Creating the Past: The Record of the Stevens Family of North Andover," *Essex Institute Historical Collections* 106, 2(1970), p. 66–67.

75 Northrup, p. 96.

76 Frank L. Smith, *Suburban Homes; or, Examples of Moderate Cost Houses for Wollaston Park* (Boston: Wood, Harmon, & Co., 1890).

≥ 3 ≤

Building America with Pattern Book Houses

Local builders and carpenters were the people who built late-nine-teenth-century homes in towns and suburbs from coast to coast. Their ideas, and those of their clients, came for the most part from houses already built in the community, houses seen in other communities, popular periodicals, and building trade publications. From the 1840s, house designs were widely circulated through the sale of architectural pattern books having perspective drawings and floor plans for house types ranging from cottages to villas, presented in the current styles. The practical function of the pattern book was to provide the home-owner with designs from which to choose so that he or she could provide the local builder with a visual model. A local carpenter would then interpret and modify the house design according to his abilities and his client's wishes. The intent of the early pattern book author, however, went beyond the practical, for the bulk of the pattern book text was written as an educational tool to improve the readers' archi-tectural knowledge and taste. The educational function of the pattern book served both the builder and the homeowner at a time when institutional architectural training in the United States was in its in-fancy. Those who claimed the title "architect" usually received practical rather than theoretical and artistic instruction, and most middle-class homes were built by artisans whose education was hands-on training. Many antebellum pattern book authors responded to this situation with a conclusion that most local builders could not be trusted to integrate appropriately the two crucial elements of ar-chitecture—beauty and function. Nor could their unenlightened clients readily appreciate a well-conceived building. As an antidote, the authors established precedents for professionalism and presented themselves as cultural authorities to a public considered to be sorely lacking in aesthetic knowledge.[1] This was no small matter, as Calvert

Vaux concluded in his book *Villas and Cottages* (1857): "The lack of taste perceptible all over the country in small buildings, is a decided bar to healthy, social enjoyments; it is a weakness that affects the whole bone and muscle of the body politic. . . ."[2]

Pattern books, such as Vaux's and Andrew Jackson Downing's popular *Cottage Residences* (1842), became sources for defining architecture in the United States. The authors advanced architectural theory with a concentration on standards of aesthetic judgment. At the same time, they provided visual and verbal incentives to build in a utilitarian, as well as tasteful, manner, and usually included information on the function of the floor plan, the coordination of site and architectural style, the historical foundation of the principles of architecture, aesthetics, and the critical relevance of scientifically sound plumbing and ventilation to the family's health. There can be little doubt that these books fulfilled a need for such information. Four editions of Downing's book were printed during his lifetime, and frequent republication continued until 1887. The second edition of Vaux's *Villas and Cottages* (1864) was re-issued in 1867, 1869, 1872, and 1874. These are but two of the many pre-Civil War architect-authors who established a precedent for comparable publications of the last quarter of the century. Pattern books containing drawings of houses as well as essays on style, taste, beauty, and proper building techniques continued to attract an audience despite growing diversity in building practice.

By the mid-1860s more innovative pattern book authors began to explore means by which they could take advantage of the potential for increased sales of books and services in an expanding market for house-building literature. This resulted in significant changes to the traditional pattern book format in the last quarter of the century. As participants in the nation's competitive entrepreneurial activity that was encouraged by nineteenth-century theories of social evolution, authors and publishers vied with one another to introduce more services to their public and make the services seem necessary. By the end of the century, architects and related companies provided architectural plans, specifications, loans, consulting services, even building materials, all of which could be mail-ordered from pattern books.

Instrumental changes to this customary means of circulating house designs were made at a time of a fluctuating and highly competitive market in the building trades. Charles Lakey, editor of the *American Builder*, monitored the effect of the economy on local builders each month from the centennial year of 1876 through the remainder of the decade. Despite intermittent predictions of improvement, he deplored the staggering numbers of unemployed skilled carpenters, and he marveled that so many pattern books were being published.[3] At the same time, he explained the depressed prices of building materials and labor as an opportunity for the building professions to return to work as well as for the public to take advantage of the lower cost of home building. This speculation was echoed by pattern book publisher Amos Jackson Bicknell, who in 1878 encouraged prospective homeowners and builders by claiming that many of the designs in the fifth edition of his *Village Builder* could be constructed now at a cost of thirty to forty percent less than the given estimates.[4] From the West Coast, San Francisco's *Quarterly Architectural Review* (soon named the *California Architect and Building News*), too, found high carpenter unemployment in the midst of opportunities for building.[5] In brief, pattern book authors, builders, architects, and their clients faced the incongruity of an unstable, often depressed, economy and a strengthened belief that investment in home ownership was a mark of national character and entrance to middle-class status. An owned home was also security, for there was no family or social network to provide shelter for people who were on the move to new communities.

Indeed, a demand for new houses existed. In a nation with an expanding and mobile population, communities grew. Although the general building market was depressed and carpenters outnumbered available jobs, there was sufficient vigor in the construction trades to provide an opportunity for a thriving commerce in architectural literature, or at least provide an arena for competition for clients. The *American Builder* frequently published letters whose authors boasted of buildings under construction or recently completed in their communities. The town of Arlington, New Jersey, for example, was reported to have grown from the unremarkable size of only two or three houses to at least two hundred buildings of note within three years.[6] Other communities across the United States and territories grew rapidly, even doubling and tripling in size. Such growth required expedient methods for producing architectural designs to complement the time-saving methods of building made possible by new tools, balloon-frame construction, and manufactured housing parts. However, growth statistics cannot allow us to assume an unlimited and universal clientele for pattern books. Pattern book authors, while offering occasional houses for mechanics, farmers, and the wealthy, more specifically targeted individual, middle-class, prospective homeowners as their primary audience. As noted above, the boundaries of middle-class definition were expanding from changes in employment while the ideal of home ownership as a sign of middle-class status was being stimulated more forcibly. Despite a higher rate of home ownership among the blue-collar working classes, pattern book authors directed most of their business to those who would aspire to the American dream of achieving not only home ownership but ownership of a house which was of a particular status-communicating type. That the pattern book authors directed their verbal content to individuals more than to the more profitable investor market was also an astute marketing device at this time of suburban expansion. Small speculators who owned one or more rental units, as well as real estate developers and investors, were building rental units to appeal to the middle classes. Their houses were more rentable and saleable if they met the physical and social requirements which fulfilled the hegemonic image of home ownership promulgated in popular and architectural literature.

Modifications were introduced to traditional pattern book formats in order to meet changing market demands. But for the most part, entrepreneurial pattern book authors were not simply reacting. They were defining their market and they also found it necessary to convey a need for their services. To achieve this they began to offer architect-related services, sell products, and employ language that was persuasive because it was aligned with the articulations of American character. Some changes to traditional-format pattern books had already been effected by mid-century, and they offered more services to the prospective homeowner. But in the 1870s, increased competition among pattern book authors and companies having regional and national clientele dramatically changed the pattern book.

A tradition of pattern books

Traditional-format pattern books based on the Andrew Jackson Downing and Calvert Vaux models yielded profits for the authors and publishers by sales of the books, in spite of their cost. For example, Samuel Sloan's two-volume work *The Model Architect* sold for twelve dollars in 1855. Sloan's volumes, first published in 1852, were among the popular pre-Civil War pattern books, and in 1860 they were produced in a new edition that maintained sales into the 1870s. *The Model Architect* was instructive in the manner of popular mid-century pattern books by Downing and his contemporaries. Subjects from the theoretical, such as architectural style, to the more practical, such as ventilation and the preservation of timber, were explained. However, Sloan's books differed from the earlier models because his contained proportionately more architectural drawings than text. Delicately drawn lithographic perspectives of the houses in their appropriately landscaped settings were accompanied by floor plans and drawings of those architectural details that made a house distinctive—doors, windows, decorative carving and sawn work, posts and balusters. Plans and details were drawn to scale in order to facilitate their copying by local builders. Sloan also helped the builders approach their tasks in a much more professional manner. Estimates of unit material costs which could serve as examples for the builder when he projected the cost of a home accompanied some of the plans. Descriptive specifications for excavation, construction, and materials for several homes provided a reference for the builder to follow when he contracted with his clients. In addition, the author submitted legal aid with a sample contract drawn up by a Philadelphia lawyer stipulating contractor's or builder's fees and dates of completion.[7] Samuel Sloan's contributions to the education of the builder were evidently pertinent, for they were subsequently included in numerous popular pattern books, including those of the last quarter of the century.

Architectural detail drawings were another significant selling point for pattern books. Without such drawings, the builder needed considerable carpentry and mathematical skill in order to duplicate houses selected from the pattern book. Considering the quality and small size of some perspective drawings of pattern book houses, he also needed a fertile imagination. In fact, detail drawings were so useful that pattern books exclusively illustrating these also gained a market, being usable for remodeling older homes as well as for completing the design of new houses (Fig. 19). Their continued popularity and the custom of piecing together architectural elements at whim may have been the source for one critic's article on "Crazy-Quilt

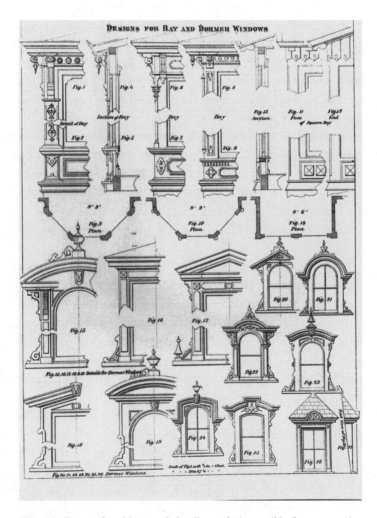

Fig. 19. Pages of architectural details made it possible for prospective home builders to design their own homes with fashionable architectural features. "Designs for Bay and Dormer Windows." (Bicknell, Detail, Cottage and Constructive Architecture, *1873)*

Architecture."[8] Shortly after the Civil War, more pattern book authors began to accompany house designs with detail drawings. In this way, the decorative details would more assuredly match the character of the house. Two architects, Marcus F. Cummings of New York and Charles C. Miller of Ohio, co-authored *Architecture: Designs for Street Fronts, Suburban Houses, and Cottages*, in which they declared that elevations and details were more substantive building aids than perspective drawings. They considered their book singular because it contained front facade elevations and decorative details drawn in "so large a scale that anyone familiar with the construction of work cannot fail to comprehend their forms and their construction."[9] Although the book sold, their clients were not completely satisfied because the architects had not included floor plans. Cummings and Miller had determined that floor plans which were prepared to coordinate with the exterior elevations were not practical. The requirements of each family dictated an arrangement of rooms which would be specific to their activities, and they must plan the home. Customers objected to this notion and wrote to suggest that the architectural team's expertise was also needed for designing the appropriate arrangement of rooms.

Pattern book authors continued to modify their publications for the market during the short period of economic stabilization between the War and the Panic of 1873. Bicknell recognized the demand for a straightforward book with successive pages of elevations, plans, and details. He, too, included descriptive specifications, cost estimates, and contract examples, but he did not introduce the reader to architectural history, tenets of taste and principles of beauty, nor to educational essays on construction. A sales agent for architectural books, including Cummings and Miller's *Architecture*, he had then turned to architectural publishing. From this experience he evidently became aware of a national market for a type of pattern book which was largely a visual inventory of houses. His *Village Builder* (1870), followed by the *Supplement to Bicknell's Village Builder* (1872), consisted of designs by a number of architects rather than by one or two. The selection of "fifteen leading architects, representing the New England, Middle, Western and South-Western states" provided house designs suitable for "North, South, East and West."[10] In this way, the designs and, no less importantly, the cost estimates for specified locations appealed more directly to the purchaser of the books, who, at a cost of ten dollars for the two volumes, could turn the pages and readily select a house design and gauge a geographically relative price. Bicknell changed his format little from 1872 to his publication that was reviewed in the *American Architect* in 1878.

The early pattern book author had little personal contact with his clients. The sale of the book both initiated and completed the communication between the two parties. Some architect-authors, however, began to use the pattern book as an advertising medium to expand their architectural business by encouraging their readers to write for further information, details and specifications and to hire them as professional architects. Answers to the new clients' queries were provided for a modest fee; complete architectural services were offered at a percentage of the resultant building's cost. Cummings and Miller advertised their willingness to furnish detail drawings for their buildings, as well as to "superintend the erection of buildings."[11] Gilbert Croff, who worked in New York and in 1875 published *Progressive American Architecture*, placed greater emphasis on selling his architectural services and products by mail. He invited the public to purchase plans and drawings, elevations and full-size details, specifications, and bills of material for the homes in his pattern book. As a bonus, the client would also receive a free pencil sketch of the house as soon as he/she provided the architect with a description of the location and the order for plans. Everything was shipped Express C.O.D.[12]

This expansion of entrepreneurial activity continued into the last quarter of the century as more architects produced pattern books and as those entering the market competed to offer more services and products than their competitors. Some, especially those allied with those seeking professional status, such as New York architect and member of the American Institute of Architects Henry Hudson Holly, continued to follow antebellum precedents, having the content as much a literary effort as a book of styles for the local builders to interpret. His book, *Modern Dwellings* (1878), was a lengthy essay on the new fashion from Britain and its potential for adaptation to an American architectural vernacular. It previously had been published as a series of articles titled "Modern Dwellings: Their Construction, Decoration and Furniture" in *Harper's New Monthly Magazine*. He was among several who included educational essays on interior planning and decoration. Alfred C. Clark's *The Architect, Decorator and Furnisher* (1884) consisted of house designs and essays by authors other than himself, several of whom were women addressing issues considered important to the housewife.[13] Others, for example, Bicknell and his partner and successor in the architectural publishing business, William T. Comstock, eliminated most of the commentary to produce books of architectural patterns—perspective drawings, elevations, and details. Still others produced books of perspective drawings of houses, most of which had already been completed for clients, as a form of advertisement. The prospective clients were informed that the drawn examples within the book were samples of the firm's mastery of architectural skills and not representations for carpenters' interpretations. A dramatic shift occurred when author-architects began to produce pattern books which were much like mail-order catalogues. Robert Shoppell of New York and George F. Barber of Tennessee, among others, sold working drawings and specifications needed for building a home but they did not give prominence to individualized architectural services. Some, like Croff and Palliser, Palliser and Company, sold mail-order plans and working drawings but pointed out that the illustrated designs in their books could not be adapted to individual needs without their personal architectural assistance. The pattern books with mail-order services typically contained a balance of text and image.

Entrepreneurial expansion in pattern book publication

Changes in the aim and format of pattern books were not introduced to the public in an easily distinguished chronological order. For the most part, pattern book authors recast existing ideas, while the more entrepreneurial devised new marketing techniques in order to reach a broader audience. In the centennial year of 1876, the diversity of approaches was already evident in the new publications by Daniel Atwood, Elisha Hussey, George Palliser, and William Woollett.

William Woollett recognized the diverse needs of his audience and offered his *Villas and Cottages* as "a collection of dwellings suited to various individual wants and adapted to different locations."[14] But he was an established East Coast architect who did not explore new methods for selling his buildings. *Villas and Cottages* was produced in a traditional educational format. His house designs, however, showed some influence from the latest British fashions.

Atwood had earlier produced *Atwood's Rules of Proportion* (1867) and *Atwoods' Country and Suburban* Homes (1871), a volume that was republished in 1883 and 1885. The earlier book was instructional in intent, directed to the builder; the second was essentially a pattern book, but it offered constructional and theoretical instruction. His 1876 book, *Atwood's Modern American Homesteads*, was different. Lacking educational essays, it was designed to reach the pattern book audience in several different ways. A relatively small volume with forty-six plates of perspective drawings, elevations, and floor plans for a wide selection of house styles, and one-page descriptions accompanying the designs, it selectively informed the reader of stylistic characteristics, constructional details, and cost estimates for locations where the houses had been previously built, a type of assurance to prospective home builders introduced by many pattern book authors to confirm that their plans were indeed buildable. For several designs, an enlarged set of plans and elevations including details drawn in one-fourth full size, complete specifications, and a bill of required materials could be ordered from him. The complete set of drawings for his "Swiss Gothic Cottage" cost ten dollars (Fig. 20). Finally, he insisted on contact with the home builder stating that all work was subject to his approval, a position that led an 1879 reviewer of his book to comment on just how busy he would have been if all his clientele responded to his ambitious request![15]

Atwood made available pattern book house models, ready-made plans, professional assistance, and even a survey of "Modern American" stylistic choices. As the nation celebrated its centennial and a national style was sought in literature, the arts, and architecture, many pattern book authors sought to enhance their sales by designating houses as "American." Isaac H. Hobbs and his son enlarged their 1873 *Hobbs's Architecture* in 1876 to contain more designs, including more

Fig. 20. A "Swiss-Gothic cottage" with stick work and decorative details associated with traditional Swiss architecture applied to a house with steeply pitched gothic roofs. (Atwood, Modern American Homesteads, *1876)*

"American" cottages, villas, and residences.[16] Atwood and Hobbs of course offered "modern" houses but they were "Tuscan," "mansard roof" (Fig. 21), "Italian" (Fig. 22), "Renaissance," "English Gothic Rural," as well as "Semi Swiss Ornee" and others. Their offerings of stylistic choices to suit individual preferences were typical of pattern books of this time that used titles to draw attention to unique house designs, for creative stylizations required descriptive titles, such as

Fig. 21. Mansard roof houses were shown in pattern books in the 1870s but many considered them old-fashioned. (Atwood, Modern American Homesteads, *1876)*

the difficult-to-visualize "Swedo Gothic." Others, however, avoided such designation and would discard naming or use more general descriptive terms, such as "modern" and "suburban."

A more entrepreneurial New York pattern book author, Elisha C. Hussey, invited the builder and future homeowner to consult him for his architectural expertise. Or, on request, Hussey shipped working plans and specifications for any of forty-five original designs found in his book *Home Building*.[17] Mail-order sales of plans would soon become the primary method for the dissemination of architectural designs, but Hussey did not capitalize on this opportunity. Instead, he added to the sales appeal of his moderately priced three-dollar book by including information which was directed more specifically to a nationwide market of readers than Bicknell's selection of house designs from regional communities. The largest proportion of pages in Hussey's *Home Building* fulfilled the promise of the book's subtitle, "A reliable book of facts, relating to building, living materials, costs at about 400 places from New York to San Francisco."

Hussey had conducted a study of communities across the nation in order to compare land and building costs, healthfulness of climate, industries, churches, community organizations and other data pertinent to relocation, and then presented the information to the house-building public. With this section of the book, he acknowledged the fact that Americans were highly migratory. From Hussey's book, these migrants could learn about future places of residence, the cost of constructing a home, even someone in the community to contact for more information. Of course, the comparative costs of the homes were based on designs in *Home Building*, which returned the

Fig. 22. A house in the Italian fashion. (Atwood, Modern American Homesteads, *1876)*

reader to the subject of Hussey as the architect. Following the survey, the builder (to distinguish between the home owner and the one who constructed the home) was given construction and materials specification information. Hussey now captured a broader geographic and consumer market for the sale of his volume. His earlier pattern book had been directed specifically to the builder whom he exhorted, "Do all that is necessary to provide all materials, labor, and cartage to fully complete, in a workmanlike manner, according to the plans, specifications, and details, to the full intent and meaning thereof as expressed or implied in either or all of them, satisfactory to the owner."[18]

Hussey's search for profits did not end with sales of his book, plans, and specifications. He was a masterful late-nineteenth-century businessman who also introduced the reader of *Home Building* to his American Home Company, a "center of inquiry" and a central supply house for products needed for the completion of the home's exterior, interior, and accessories. The home products were available by mail order, similar to sales in the new mail order journals, which were subscription magazines that sold products by mail. Although only two products were featured, the Patent Home Lock and the Patent Brush Washboard, the author implied thousands. Hussey's contribution was his expertise in coordinating everything from the landscape to interior decoration. As he explained to his clients:

> The author has undertaken the duties of adviser on all subjects pertaining to building, decorating, or furnishing a house, laying out or planting its grounds, and shall enter upon his labors with great pleasure. All charges for advice, instruction, or any drawings or specifications required, will be one of the most moderate rates, and in proportion to the time required only.[19]

If the head of the household questioned whether such an expenditure was necessary, he was persuaded by an article titled "Furniture and Decoration," excerpted from the May 1875 issue of *Scribner's Monthly*. Here, the pattern book reader learned of a new kind of expert and emerging professional, the interior decorator, who helped the client realize a tastefully coordinated home. This shrewdness in

the business of pattern book marketing resulted in sales which justified a second printing of *Home Building* the next year.

Hussey did not foresee, however, the extent of the market for
mail-order house plans, unlike Connecticut architect George Palliser,
who was to become the most successful of the 1876 pattern book
authors. Palliser's *Model Homes for the People* was only a small pamphlet of twenty-three pages plus advertisements, but most of the five
thousand copies printed were "sent into every State and Territory in
the Union, and many to the provinces."[20] The appeal of Palliser's
pattern book was simple. At twenty-five cents per copy, it was more
affordable than its competitors. Further, the simply drawn elevations
and floor plans were more inducements to the reader to order professional working drawings at a low cost than models for local
interpretation. Front, side, and rear elevations and floor and roof plans
were offered for the first two designs in the book, a "Centennial Villa"
and a "Model Gothic Cottage," at the amazingly low price of fifty
cents. If more detailed specifications were needed for these or other
houses in the book, they could be ordered at the cost of approximately
two percent of the total building cost. Although the plans and specifications were readily available, Palliser did not consider them mass
produced. He was aware of the general concerns about mass production in the building trades and how this was applied as an important
distinction made by the American Institute of Architects. Professional
architects did not sell plans without having had consultation with their
clients. To mediate this requirement, Palliser asked clients who ordered detailed plans to provide him with precise information relative
to the desired cost of the home, its size and materials, the site, and
local weather conditions. It would seem that little persuasion would
be necessary to sell these inexpensive plans, but this was a relatively
new practice. Palliser, together with Hussey, verbally persuaded his
public of the need for his architectural services and, echoing Andrew
Jackson Downing, warned them against the all-too-prevalent buildings which were

> discordant in appearance, pernicious to the eye of the
> cultivated, and out of all keeping and harmony with
> their surroundings, a great many of them being the

square house, painted white, with green blinds, which
would not be countenanced for a moment by any one
who prides himself on good taste.[21]

George Palliser's success was founded not on book sales but on
the sales of plans and specifications that could be ordered by the
consumer. He was not the first to introduce this idea to the American
consumer as he has been credited, but he was the first to develop an
uncomplicated marketing of the concept. The first complete page of
Model Homes for the People announced his purpose, whereas earlier
pattern book authors and his contemporaries had informed their
public less directly. Others made their offers of plans for sale difficult
to find. Hussey had inserted the information in his firm's advertisement at the rear of the book, while D. T. Atwood had noted the service
only with selected house designs. Palliser's concentration marked a
division between pattern books that earned income primarily by
royalties from sales of the books and those whose authors profited
by the sales of plans and associated services from the books.[22]

Nonetheless, it is too facile to attribute Palliser's success to the
mere repositioning of his statement of business intent; his success was
based more on the scope of his intent. He combined the concept of
mass marketing with traditional individualized architectural services
by encouraging dialogue between the architect and his client for the
purpose of adapting the chosen house design to each client. The
Palliser client, who could not afford to hire a professional architect,
was able to contract with a pattern book architect for a very low fee.
Although the newly individualized house plans were simple modifications of a prototypical plan, they were not in precise terminology
mass-produced and could be argued to hold the prestige of an architect-designed home. After George Palliser and his brother Charles
formed Palliser, Palliser and Company in 1877, they continued to sell
plans but did not prominently advertise the availability of their ready-
made plans. Ironically, they castigated mass-produced plans when
competitors began to market them, even while their business depended on this service. There is no doubt that the Pallisers were aware
of the American Institute of Architects' low estimation of architects
who sold house plans, for they extensively plagiarized essays by

A. F. Oakey, a young New York architect and contributor to the *American Architect*, and one of the members most critical of this practice.[23]

The Pallisers demonstrated other astute judgments about their audience. The houses represented in their books were in the modern style as defined by pattern book descriptions of the late nineteenth century (Fig. 23). After the 1876 pamphlet, the by-then less-fashionable French mansard roofs were no longer included, and the new style houses were examples of those already successfully built for Palliser clients rather than unrealized products of the architect's imagination. Furthermore, commencing in 1877, they promoted their work to the building trades by submitting designs for publication in the *American Builder*. The trade journal then served as an advertising medium which reached not only local builders who contracted for single projects but also speculative builders. The advantage of promoting residential designs to attract real estate speculators as clients

Fig. 23. An early pattern book example of the new fashion based on so-called Queen Anne houses in England. A house "well in advance of old styles." (Palliser, Model Homes, *1878)*

probably stemmed from Palliser's early career when he had designed blocks of investment housing in Bridgeport, Connecticut, for P.T. Barnum.[24] Such a clientele was an important potential source of revenue as land was increasingly bought for suburban development. The client designation, "capitalist," or someone who earned income above and beyond wages, became a recurrent and favorable term applied to investors in late-nineteenth-century pattern books. At the same time, however, builders and carpenters were fundamental to the popularization of a pattern book for both investors and home owners frequently went first to their local artisans when they considered building. To help local builders form a business relationship with the clients, the Pallisers included sample specification sheets and contract forms for their use, and additional forms were available at a cost of only pennies each.

Varied psychological and practical client needs were also addressed when the firm diversified their pattern book publication. While they offered plans for sale in all of their publications, several formats were used. The content of their next book, *Palliser's American Cottages* (1877), with its brief preface followed by drawings of houses and floor plans, was similar to *Model Homes*. The presentation, however, was much different. The binding of the book was similar to their competitors' traditional (professional) pattern books, as was the five-dollar price. *American Cottages*, produced in quarto size, bound in dark green cloth and dark red Morocco leather, and titled in gold letters, was a handsome edition appropriate for the desk of any professional architect or prosperous (cultured) homeowner. The following year, 1878, a new version of *Model Homes* was published in the same inexpensive pamphlet format of the earlier *Model Homes for the People* but was enlarged by sixty pages. In contrast to the richly bound *American Cottages*, it was paper-bound and fully one-fourth of the pages consisted of practical and educational material: site selection for proper drainage, definition of architecture, comments from the history of architecture, adaptation of building to site and owner, character and training of the architect, reference to the picturesque and organic function, taste and the scientific basis of beauty, necessity of hiring an architect, responsibilities of the client, and at greatest length, the responsibilities of the architect. Thereby, the Pallisers made the educative content of the traditional pattern books available in an inexpensive volume.

The brothers evidently knew their market well. Also published in 1878 was a seventy-five-cent book of printed specification forms ready to be cut out and used by the local builder. Three years later, Palliser, Palliser & Company published its first book of architectural details, simply titled *Palliser's Useful Details*, and with this type of volume they covered the entire pattern book market for house-building. *Model Homes* sold over fifteen thousand copies; *Useful Details* was claimed to have sold 50,000 copies by 1887.[25] *American Cottages* was reissued in 1878. Ten years later, it was combined with *Model Homes* and published as a new and larger volume, *American Architecture*, which was reissued in 1889. In a quarter of a century, the Palliser brothers published over twenty books.

Selling plans without apology

Perhaps inspired by the financial success of the Pallisers, New York-based Robert W. Shoppell entered the mail-order service pattern book market in the early 1880s and remained a Palliser competitor through the 1890s. In the manner of Amos Bicknell a decade earlier and his successor in 1881, William T. Comstock, Shoppell provided house plans drawn by different architects. But these architects comprised his own staff whose names and reputations were not attached to the house designs. Shoppell gathered around him some twenty architects to furnish designs for his new company, the Co-operative Building Plan Association. The publications reached a large audience with his low prices ranging from ten cents to one dollar, and near the end of the decade, Shoppell declared his company the largest architectural firm in the United States, stating that in the year 1887 it had provided designs for nearly five thousand homes in the United States and Canada.[26] If Shoppell's claim was accurate, this number of sales may well have outdistanced the sales of Palliser, Palliser & Co., who in the same year claimed that they had corresponded with "upwards of two thousand" satisfied customers living as far away as 3,000 miles.[27] However, a comparison is difficult because the Pallisers did not define the nature of their "correspondence" and hyperbole was common to nineteenth-century advertising.

There were several reasons why Shoppell may have achieved such success at a time of ambitious pattern book publication. Shoppell emphatically stated that his company sold mass-produced house plans and working drawings. Expediency was more important than face-to-face client contact, although his staff would make alterations to the plans if the client so desired. His method of business could be characterized by an appeal from a client in 1883: "Enclosed find $20, for which send me specifications and full working plans of No. 17. Quick! Our house was destroyed by a tornado last night" (Fig. 24). Shoppell responded that plans were shipped out of the office within three hours.[28] Meanwhile, many of the pattern book authors of the 1880s, among them Samuel Burrage Reed, William Burnet Tuthill, David W. King, and Henry Kirby, continued to publish books in the traditional format which did not offer mail-order plans.

Fig. 24. "No. 17. Gothic Cottage" chosen from a pattern book by a client whose home had been destroyed by a tornado. The plans were sent within three hours of receipt of order. (Shoppell, How to Build, Furnish, and Decorate, *1883)*

Shoppell's mass-market operation was more closely attuned with the growing popularity of subscription mail-order magazines and catalogue sales and it was emulated by subsequent companies, including the New York Building Plan Company and the National Architects Union in Philadelphia. In *How to Build, Furnish and Decorate* (1883), *Modern Low Cost Houses* (1884), and *Modern Houses, Beautiful Homes* (1887), Shoppell also explained more explicitly than his rivals the procedure for using the services of the company. The client was clearly informed of what constituted a complete set of plans: working plans, detail drawings, specifications, bill of quantities, color sheet, supplemental sheet with sanitation information, supplemental sheet with designs for fences, and blank contracts. Paper three-dimensional models were also available at no cost to help clients visualize their future homes. Costs for the sets of plans, ranging from ten dollars for small cottages to six hundred for a mansion with alterations, were listed with each perspective drawing and its accompanying floor plan (Fig. 25). In the 1883 and 1884 volumes, a base price was given for the materials as well as the price for the materials if the client requested Shoppell's recommended alterations. After each plan in *Modern Houses, Beautiful Homes*, specific modifications, such as elimination of the cellar, an enlargement of the kitchen, or raising the height of a tower, were listed. These modified plans were available for a slightly higher fee. A reversed plan of each home was available at no extra charge. In contrast, Palliser, Palliser & Co. avoided the distasteful subject of money and did not list prices for their plans, the practice having been discontinued after George Palliser's first publication. A price list would have communicated too readily an image of mass production for the Palliser brothers. Shoppell also estimated building costs for the homes, with one estimate for locations having high material and labor costs and a second for less expensive locations. And for a modest fee, Shoppell guaranteed the estimate. This practical and exacting method of doing business may well have been more assuring to prospective home builders than the Palliser brothers' later re-use of 1878 house construction cost estimates in their 1888 publication, *American Architecture*.

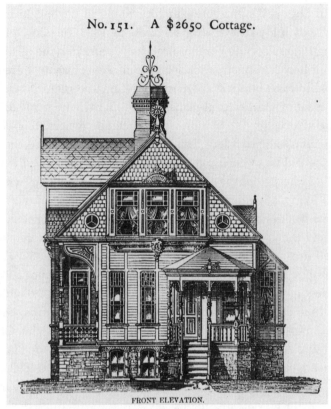

Fig. 25a. Exterior. A set of plans for this elaborate "Renaissance
Cottage" cost $30.00. (Shoppell, Modern Low-Cost Houses, 1884)

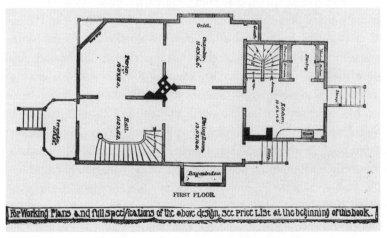

Fig. 25b. Plan. (Shoppell, Modern Low-Cost Houses, 1884)

But Shoppell's entrepreneurship extended beyond improving already existing pattern book services. In 1883, his Co-Operative Building Plan Association announced its venture into the business of financing homes. Construction loans from the company were made available to local builders (perhaps targeting speculators) who purchased a set of architectural plans. For builders living some distance from New York, the Association would facilitate the granting of loans by contacting other lenders. This new service actually was the product of the public's confusion over the company's name. Evidently, many had interpreted the name to be that of a new cooperative building and loan association of the type being formed to provide loans for home builders, and the response elicited by this confusion had impressed the company. Shortly before loans were offered by the Shoppell firm, an essay in *How to Build a House*, entitled "What is the Co-operative Building Plan Association?," began, "It is not a loaning institution, as its name suggests to some. . . ." The extent to which his clients took advantage of this opportunity is not known, but this project was seldom imitated by other pattern book authors. One exception was Alfred F. Leicht, who published a small book of twenty pages to advertise his professional architectural services in 1892. Leicht introduced his book with a section on "Buildings on Monthly Installments. Satisfactory arrangements can be made with those desiring to build on the installment plan."[29] To advertise all the services and the house designs, Shoppell's Association introduced an architectural quarterly titled *Shoppell's Modern Houses* in 1886. While the Pallisers had advertised by contributing designs to the *American Builder*, Shoppell published his own architectural periodical filled with Association designs.[30] Once again, broadening the scope of his clientele, he offered the periodicals as cloth-bound books. Shoppell also broadened his offerings by occasionally including a time-tested design drawn from other pattern books. His picturesquely quaint "ornamental cottage" in *How to Build, Furnish and Decorate*, although not attributed, had been earlier published in A. J. Bicknell's *Cottage & Villa Architecture* and *Specimen Book of One Hundred Architectural Designs* (1878) and Almon C. Varney's *Our Homes and Their Adornments* (1882) (Fig. 26).

Fig. 26. A design "suitable for a gardener's cottage or a seaside vacation cottage" featured without alteration in several pattern books. (Bicknell, Specimen Book of One Hundred Architectural Designs, *1878)*

Pattern book authors offered education, architectural plans, details and specifications, interior decoration, and loans, tending toward selling fully pre-fabricated homes. But instead of turning to the business of home-building kits, such as would appear at the end of the century, these architects sold advertising space in their books to manufacturers of building components. Availability of mill work allowed the homeowner to make individual changes to plans purchased from pattern book authors, but it did not ostensibly lessen the need for their services. Pattern book authors to the end of the century purveyed themselves as architects who were needed to formulate a house plan appropriate to its site and the owner's needs, designed in accordance with contemporary architectural theory, and imbued with meaning.

Pattern book authors as architects

One subject on which pattern book authors were most persuasive was the need for architects in designing the homes of America. Entrepreneurial expansion in pattern books developed concurrently with efforts by the American Institute of Architects and other architects' associations to define architectural practice as a profession. Both groups sought cultural ownership of the title "architect" as well as its suggested economic and social privilege, at a time when the word "architect" was a broadly used term that did not hold today's distinctions. As Oakey bemoaned, anyone occupied in building fabrication could, and often did, take on the title.[31] Distinctions between professional architects and those builders judged to be less qualified by these architects but seeking professional status were not generally known to the public at large. Nor were the differences necessarily recognized within the building trades, for local carpenters and contractors, too, advertised themselves as architects. Although the entrepreneurial pattern book authors typically did not have academic architectural training, they verbally distanced themselves from builders and carpenters and presented themselves specifically as architects. To a large extent, their success in marketing their plans, specifications, and other materials depended on the public's realization of this essential point, and the substantial amount of material dedicated to the subject indicates that they found it necessary to establish a need for their architectural services over the carpenter's. George Palliser, for example, was among the more eloquent on the subject of the architect. He had a very successful architectural practice; one of his designs was published in the *American Architect*. He was recognized as an architect, but he was not among the self-defined professionals who advocated university educational programs and licensing examinations as requirements for the title. He was from an apprenticeship tradition. From his perspective, architecture should be learned by practicing it. An education that did not emphasize the practical taught students to plan buildings that could not be built. Nonetheless, entrepreneurial pattern book authors shared the language of professionalism also being forwarded by the nation's established architects and carried forth arguments of professionalization similar to those published in the *American Archi-tect*. In pattern book textual portions, many authors persuaded readers that an architect was necessary to building a home, and, of course, they were competent architects whose drawings, plans, and services could be trusted. Some, in their petition for a nation of pattern book architect-designed homes, aligned themselves with their architect-competitors and criticized the deplorable condition of earlier residential architecture. They, too, placed the blame on people who hired local builders to design their homes, reasoning that these carpenters and builders, not having appropriate training, produced their house designs by copying and miscopying other houses in the community. This practice of hiring untrained carpenters and builders was denounced on both practical and artistic bases. The National Building Plan Association of Detroit stated the need for an architect quite succinctly:

> So, if we want a beautiful and artistic home, conveniently arranged, with the best known methods for light, heat, ventilation, etc., and constructed economically and substantially, we should depend for all this upon our architect, and employ the builder to carry into effect what our architect designs for us.[32]

In the developing thrust for the authority of professionalism, their middle-class public may have had pretensions for architect-designed homes as they began to carry greater cultural capital, but at the same time, the author-architects who sold plans were acting against custom. Entrepreneurial pattern book authors were usurping a position held by the local craftsman. Most middle-class homes had been constructed by local carpenters. When these craftsmen followed the artistically drawn perspective drawings or simple line drawings found in the traditional pattern books, they had the opportunity to exercise a great deal of liberal interpretation because few views of the home were provided. Completion of such a home required discussions between the builder and the homeowner in which the latter established the family's needs and artistic preferences while the former contributed his planning, artistic, and constructional skills. The local builder was an artisan who had considerable authority in determining the outcome of the house. For the most part, pattern books were to be used by local carpenters, builders, and prospective home owners to gain ideas, not necessarily to copy.

In order to validate their claims that they as architects were indispensable in the process of building homes, pattern book authors continued to appropriate much of the message of professionalism and took it as their task to articulate for the public distinctions between the function of the builder and the architect. The architect was the generator of the plans for a house, the builder a mechanic who instituted the architect's ideas. But while the distinction between architect and mechanic was becoming established among the *American Architect* members, selling this division of labor was a more difficult proposition for the entrepreneurial pattern book authors. The makeup of their audience was different. Carpenters and builders purchased their publications, and in this schema, they needed to accept a revised and less instrumental function in their local communities. To counter this problem, the Pallisers, again, ever ambitious, advertised a self-help booklet, saying, "Ambitious young Carpenters and Builders, who are desirous of taking a lead in their respective villages and towns, should send a full account of their experience, capabilities, etc., etc." and the Pallisers would send them information on "how to get this and succeed in their line."[33]

Often, traditional and entrepreneurial pattern book authors alike strongly criticized the builders and posed a vivid contrast between the two. The Palliser company, George F. Barber, who sold plans from Knoxville, Tennessee, in the 1890s, and Alexander Oakey, for example, claimed that too many builders were dishonest and too many carpenters were careless. Local carpenters were old fogeys who insisted on following outmoded methods; builders were not familiar with correct sanitation and ventilation.[34] Hussey was more politic when he recommended that prospective homeowners seek out honest builders. Aware of building custom in towns and villages, he acknowledged that the local carpenter most likely served as contractor for the job, too. Therefore, it benefited the homeowner to ". . . employ the best, most honest and straightforward carpenters, or other mechanics. . . ."[35] Others praised the builders who worked within their own province, or, as D. S. Hopkins viewed it, with an architect, ". . .

the builder knows what his part is on the program."[36] Some of the more entrepreneurial authors, on the other hand, assigned this subsidiary role with more respect to the carpenter. The National Building Plan Association of Detroit explained the difference between the architect and builder by adapting the common medical analogy to call them "two professions equally responsible and honorable," enjoying relations similar to those between a physician and an apothecary.[37]

The entrepreneurial authors also found it necessary to delicately negotiate the question of their own status, one which was becoming highly questionable in the ongoing formulation of professional criteria among the members of the American Institute of Architects. The Palliser company proposed a distinction between the pattern book architects and academically trained architects which would have addressed the American distrust of the impractical and superfluous. Although the Pallisers argued that they did not sell mass-produced plans as a means to align themselves with acceptable professional practice, they argued that many architects, "under the shallow pretext of preserving high art," were trained to design only on paper. Academically trained architects could prepare beautifully drawn and rendered designs for prospective clients, but they were too infrequently practicing architects.[38] Countering this presumed inadequacy, entrepreneurial pattern book authors who entered into the debate claimed practical knowledge and skills, which then associated them more closely with the builders' function and appealed to a public wanting practical results. The Pallisers evidently felt the difficulty of negotiating the positions. Portions of their pattern book essay directly plagiarized the same essay in the *American Architect* that criticized the practice of selling architectural plans. This point, not surprisingly, was omitted by the Pallisers.

The other segment of the pattern book audience, the homeowners, needed to be persuaded that professional services were needed and were not merely an unnecessary added expense. It was important that the homeowners not be marginalized in this organization. Homeowners read the books, too, and selected plans from them. Entrepreneurial authors did not as readily criticize their clients who, in contrast with the home-building clients of the *American Architect* readership, directly read the pattern book architects' words.

Whereas the "professional" architects were conducting an internal dialogue among themselves and were intent upon increasing numbers among their own body of authorities, the entrepreneurial pattern book authors were speaking to the home-building public. Samuel B. Reed, in his 1885 book of modern suburban homes, explained that in architecture, more than in any other profession, it was necessary to study the clients. Through careful study, the architect could ascertain his clients' "previous history, general character, financial ability, personal habits, and tastes, and family."[39] Of course, there was a practical purpose. They, as architects, then were able to assess American family activities and arrange floor plans accordingly.

Recognizing that pragmatic considerations were perhaps the most immediate for prospective homeowners, authors stressed efficiency, sanitation safety, constructional stability, and, of course, economy. To make this message more salient, they shared language that was resonant in the popular, dominant culture. Words used to describe their work and the houses enforced the discourse on American character defining a people who were industrious, efficient, hard working, and frugal. Houses by these architects did not introduce wasteful space; they were "roomy" yet "compact." Robert Shoppell formed verbal analogies with the efficient space planning found in boat design (Fig. 27). He provided homes with enough storage space to keep the rooms "as clean and clear of obstructions as the decks of a ship." Other authors did not introduce sea-faring comparisons but suggested that compact homes were not only less expensive and thus more attainable for a broader group of prospective owners, they were more "convenient" as well. Such homes required less labor to maintain, a message set in motion by household books written ten to twenty years earlier by such authors as Catherine Beecher, including her *American Woman's Home* (1876), co-authored by Harriet Beecher Stowe.[40] Shoppell was concerned with large and inconvenient houses because only incompetent servants would accept positions in such houses and their supervision would be injurious to the women of the household to the extent of shortening their lives.[41] Although many house plans provided rooms for servants, the women addressed did not run their homes with the aid of large staffs. More typically the woman of the house conducted her duties with the assistance of one

Fig. 27a. Exterior. Interior planning for efficient use of space was emphasized. This Queen Anne house was described as a "compact plan" where "not an inch of space is wasted."

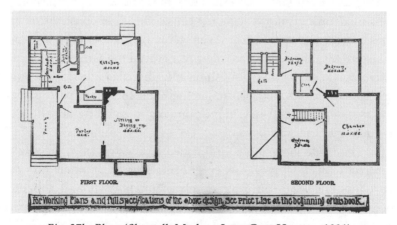

Fig. 27b. Plan. (Shoppell, Modern Low-Cost Houses, 1884)

day-help servant or did without. "Compact" and "convenient" also implied both the saving of time and money for the householder during the decades when Frederick Winslow Taylor was conducting his time and motion studies in the work place and when a home was to be as efficiently run as the factory. The Pallisers proposed a public display of this consciousness "of the flight of time" with the inscription "Tempus Fugit" on the chimney exterior of one of their country homes.[42]

The well-planned house, much like its owner, was also "substantial" and "solid." It was built with the soundest construction methods and materials for the cost of the home. The fact that most of these homes were to be built with balloon-frame construction was seldom noted. Arguments about this method's reliability persisted in the *American Architect*, and the critical conservative A. F. Oakey directly opposed balloon-frame construction in his own traditional format pattern book, *Building a Home* (1881). When entrepreneurial pattern book authors mentioned balloon framing, they usually attempted to convince the public of its viability. The more common treatment of this subject was a simple reference to framing and an examination of other issues related to structural solidity. The Pallisers, for example, claimed that the uneducated builder could not estimate the cost of a building as accurately as could a professional architect. The builder's errors would cause unanticipated expenses and force unfortunate substitutions in material and construction, resulting in a far less structurally and visually substantial building.[43] Perhaps the pattern book authors were criticizing those builders and carpenters who were unscrupulous with just cause. Stories of construction failures causing injury and death were common features in newspapers and journals. The *American Builder* recognized the same problem and attempted to rectify it by publishing educational articles for the builders, on such topics as construction methods, the use of tools such as the steel square, and new developments in building and housing technology.[44]

The trade journal also published articles on bookkeeping. In contrast with the typical carpenter or builder, an architect was purveyed as one who could accurately estimate costs and anticipate necessary material construction changes in order to build properly and within a specified budget. Pattern book authors followed the professional architects' description of the architect as both an artist and a practical businessman whose duty it was "to get the most of the best for the money . . . as much in economy of construction as in preventing impositions of all sorts."[45] Frank L. Smith, in *A Cosy Home* (1887), emphasized the architect's skills in a lengthy reconstructed dialogue with a typical client and explained how he, as the architect, could reduce the cost of the client's home by using less expensive, yet durable and beautiful, materials in its construction.[46] Further, the appearance of the home would not suffer. The architect could make a cheap house appear to be of better quality than many expensive houses.[47] In these matters, the entrepreneurial pattern book authors again allied themselves with the established architects who defined themselves as professionals. In 1887, the Pallisers, again plagiarizing, copied Henry Hudson Holly verbatim when they referred to the decreased value of houses after the Panic of 1873 and claimed that their value would have been sustained if their plans and coordinating exteriors had been well studied.[48]

Sanitation was emphatically argued as an important consideration when determining the need to hire an architect-pattern book author. It was the duty of the householder to provide his family with a healthy home; and the architect, not the plumber, was the reliable authority.[49] Pattern book authors may have been justified in their mistrust of plumbers, too, since none were (professionally) trained and plumbing a house was becoming a difficult prospect. Water closets, or toilets, had become much more common, and venting the wastes and gasses required skill and knowledge of the latest scientific developments. Most followed the theories of George E. Waring, Jr., who opposed the germ theory of disease and proposed that sewer gas was the main cause of disease. The public was cautioned that breathing poisons from dampness, decayed vegetable matter, and animal and human wastes was to be avoided at all costs, and horror stories were circulated telling of sudden deaths in improperly vented hotels and houses.[50] The Pallisers' passage on the subject began with an alarming note: "'Died of bad air.' How often these words might, with truth, be inscribed on the headstones of both old and young." Their warning about poor soil drainage and sewer systems was graphic and clear regarding the role of the knowledgeable architect:

"When the people who build homes have had the experience the writer of this has, and had to fight scarlet fever and diphtheria and grim death himself through the want of a proper system of sewerage . . ."[51]

The modern house

In addition to forwarding concerns about construction and safety, the pattern book authors both followed and shaped public taste with descriptions of houses that indicated their designs' symbolic cultural value. The most prevalent designs in the pattern books were the types of houses which could be termed "modern" and "novel." As William R. Leach has explained in his study of the rise of consumer culture in turn-of-the-century United States, "Newness and change themselves had become traditional in America."[52] Acquisition of the "modern," the "novel," and the "new," even if the "new" embodied sentiments of nostalgia for the past, was a signifier of one's social acumen and was argued to serve as inspiration for others to become "American-ized" into the prevailing work ethic. Most frequently, the modern houses appeared with "picturesque" silhouettes. Through the 1880s the genre of design that was characterized by a broad eclecticism, an abundance of wood decoration, complex massing and asymmetrical exterior silhouette rapidly replaced more staid outlines (Fig. 28). These modern houses also were contended to represent socio-economic and cultural status through the display of cultured taste, progressive character, and the cozy home life of the owner. Prospective residents of such homes were induced to compare themselves with paradigmatic owners who were "intelligent," "cultured," "dignified," and "genteel" Americans. Pattern book houses described as picturesque were considered to communicate the artistic taste of the owners, to fulfill both practical and cultural requirements, and, not least, add value to the property. Pattern book authors took pride in offering the modern styles to the public and they gained a larger audience for their books by being up-to-date.

Pattern book authors used the increasingly popular new genre of design to assert a further need for pattern book services. The modern styles more than those of the past required expert guidance

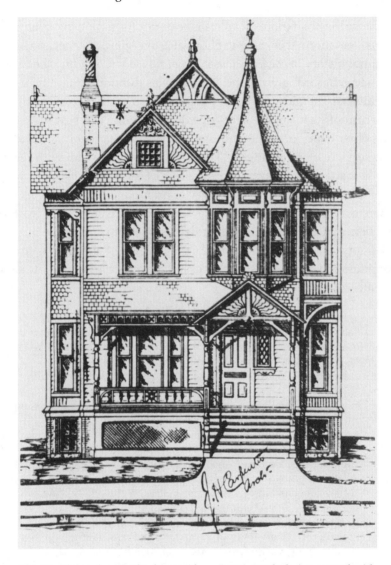

Fig. 28. The modern "suburban residence" was popularly interpreted with complex massing, an asymmetrical exterior silhouette, and colorful decoration to display the cultured taste, progressive character and cozy home life of its owners. (Carpenter, Complete Housebuilder, *1890)*

because they had more complicated exterior forms and, usually, more ornamentation. According to Shoppell's overview of American architectural history in *Modern Houses, Beautiful Homes*, building the earlier classic, mansard, gothic, and Italian styles did not require the use of architects. The older styles of houses were merely "boxes" with different roof forms and easily copied decoration. The new styles, on the other hand, produced houses of "bewildering detail," requiring the services of an architect.[53] This is an interesting point with regard to the pattern book authors' promotion of their services. They were, in effect, creating a demand by way of promoting complex styles. The more complex the style, the more need for an architect, or at least for a book of details or working drawings. Not only were the authors claiming a need for their services, they provided an impetus for the proliferation of the highly eclectic and ornate styles of the late nineteenth century.

NOTES

[1] See Dell Upton, "Pattern Books and Professionalism: Aspects of the Transformation of Domestic Architecture in America, 1800–1860," *Winterthur Portfolio* 19(Summer/Autumn 1984): 107–50.

[2] Calvert Vaux, *Villas and Cottages*, 2d. ed. (New York: Harper & Brothers, 1864), p. 48.

[3] In a review of Palliser's *American Cottage Homes* in "New Publications," *American Builder* 14(February 1878): 44–45.

[4] Amos Jackson Bicknell, *Supplement to Bicknell's Village Builder*, 5th ed. (New York: A. J. Bicknell & Co., 1878).

[5] "Better Times Coming" and "Unoccupied Houses in San Francisco," *Quarterly Architectural Review* 1, 1(January 1879): 20.

[6] "Miscellaneous Notes," *American Builder* 15 (July 1879): 169.

[7] Samuel Sloan, *The Model Architect* (Philadelphia: E. G. Jones & co., 1852). See also, Harold N. Cooledge, Jr., *Samuel Sloan, Architect of Philadelphia, 1815–1884* (Philadelphia: University of Pennsylvania Press, 1986).

[8] "Crazy Quilt Architecture," *American Architect* 18(July 11, 1885): 20.

[9] Marcus F. Cummings and Charles Miller, *Architecture: Designs for Street Fronts, Suburban Houses, and Cottages* (Troy, New York: Young and Benson, 1865), intro. The title continued, "comprising in all 382 designs and 714 illustrations."

[10] Amos J. Bicknell, *Village Builder* (Troy, N. Y. and Springfield, Illinois: By the Author, 1870), title page and introduction.

[11] Cummings and Miller, *Architecture*, n.p.

[12] Croff, advertisement.

[13] Alfred C. Clark, *The Architect, Decorator and Furnisher* (Chicago: Cowdrey, Clark & Co.), 1884.

14 William M. Woollett, *Villas and Cottages, or Homes for All* (New York: A. J. Bicknell & Co., 1876), title page.

15 *Atwood's Rules of Proportion* (New York: By the Author, 1867) and *Country and Suburban Homes*, 1873.

16 Isaac H. Hobbs and Son, *Hobbs's Architecture*, 2d ed., rev. and enl. (Philadelphia: J. B. Lippincott & Co., 1876).

17 Elisha Charles Hussey, *Home Building* (New York: By the Author, 1876).

18 Elisha Charles Hussey, *National Cottage Architecture* (New York: George E. Woodward, 1874), p. 22.

19 Hussey, *Home Building*, p. 203.

20 Palliser, Palliser and Co., *Palliser's Model Homes* (Bridgeport, Conn.: Palliser, Palliser & Co., 1878), Preface.

21 George Palliser, *Palliser's Model Homes for the People* (Bridgeport, Conn.: By the Author, 1876; reprint ed., Watkins Glen: American Life Foundation, 1978), pp. 4–6. See also Michael A. Tomlan's introduction to the reprint edition.

22 James L. Garvin has suggested a distinction between traditional format books and those selling plans by terming the latter type of publication "plan books." In "Mail-Order House Plans and American Victorian Architecture," *Winterthur Portfolio* 16 (Winter 1981): 309–34. For my study, however, the various approaches to selling plans and services make it this bipartite separation limiting for analysis.

23 For example, A. F. Oakey, "Architect and Client," *American Architect* 1(August 26, 1876): 275–77.

24 Palliser's work for Barnum is noted by Michael A. Tomlan in his introduction to the reprint edition of Palliser, 1876. Palliser's design joined those by Woollett and other established architects who were also published in the *American Builder*. The brothers George and Charles Palliser published jointly over twenty pattern books that served as vehicles for selling their plans, specifications, details, and consulting services.

25 Palliser, Palliser and Co., *New Cottage Homes and Details* (New York: Palliser, Palliser & Co., 1887), Prefatory.

26 Robert W. Shoppell, *Artistic Modern Houses at Low Cost* (New York: The Co-operative Building Plan Association, ca. 1887), p. 2. The date of *Artistic Modern Houses* has been suggested as 1881 in both the *National Union Catalogue* and Henry-Russell Hitchcock's *American Architectural Books* (New York: Da Capo Press, 1976). National Building Plan Association advertisements would dispute this date. The book was a compilation of designs from earlier Shoppell books and contained designs from *Shoppell's Modern Houses* which began publication in 1886. In the same volume, reference is made to business success in the year 1887.

27 Palliser, *New Cottage Homes*, advertisement.

28 Robert W. Shoppell, *How to Build a House* (New York: Co-operative Building Plan Association, ca. 1883), n.p.

29 Alfred F. Leicht, *A few Sketches of Picturesque Suburban Homes* (New York: By the author, 1892), n.p. Leicht did not sell plans; his small book, with lettering in script and houses drawn in an artistic, sketchy style, was published as an advertisement for his professional practice.

30 Volumes one through four were published as *Modern Houses, Beautiful Homes* in 1887; volumes five through nine were later published as *Shoppell's Modern Houses*. Both were cloth bound and cost respectively five and two dollars, placing them closer to the more expensive category of traditional format or established architect publications.

31 A. F. Oakey, "Architect and Client," *American Architect* 1(August 26, 1876): 278.

32 National Building Plan Association, *Artistic Homes* (Detroit: National Building Plan Assoc., 1888), n.p.

33 Palliser, Palliser and Company, *Miscellaneous Architectural Designs and Details* (New York: J. S. Ogilvie), p. 1891, p. 66.

34 George F. Barber, *Cottage Souvenir Number Two* (Knoxville, Tenn.: S. B. Newman & Co., 1891), p. 6; Palliser, *Model Homes*, 1878, pp. 14–24; Alexander F. Oakey, *Building a Home* (New York: D. Appleton and Company, 1881), p. 105.

35 Hussey, *Home Building*, Plate 9.

36 David S. Hopkins, *Houses and Cottages*, No. 4 (Grand Rapids, Mich.: By the author, 1891), p. 5.

37 National Building Plan Association, n.p.

38 Palliser, *Model Homes for the People*, pp. 1–2 and *Model Homes*, pp. 7–8.

39 Reed, *Dwellings*, pp. 48-49.

40 Catherine E. Beecher and Harriet Beecher Stowe, *American Woman's Home, or, Principles of Domestic Science* (New York: J. B. Ford & Co., 1876), p. 227. See also Catherine Beecher, "A Woman's Profession Dishonored," *Harper's New Monthly Magazine* 29 (November 1864): 76.

41 Shoppell, *Modern Houses*, Des. 229.

42 Palliser, *New Cottage Homes*, Plate 5, Des. 14.

43 Palliser, *Model Homes*, p. 62.

44 "Builders' Book Keeping," *American Builder* 14(November 1878): 251–52.

45 Oakey, *Building a Home*, p. 105.

46 Frank L. Smith, *A Cosy Home* (Boston: Press of T. O. Metcalf & Co., 1887), passim.

47 For example, Barber, *Cottage Souvenir*, p. 3 and David S. Hopkins, *Houses and Cottages* (Grand Rapids, Mich.: By the Author, 1889), p. 5.

48 Holly, *Modern Dwellings in Town and Country Adapted to American Wants and Climate with a Treatise on Furniture Decoration* (New York: Harper & Brothers, Publishers, 1878, p. 45. Palliser, *New Cottage Homes*, Prefatory.

49 Palliser, *Model Homes*, p. 22.

50 May N. Stone, "The Plumbing Paradox: American Attitudes toward Late Nineteenth-Century Domestic Sanitary Arrangements," *Winterthur Portfolio* 14(Autumn 1979): 283–309 and Gavin Townsend, "Airborne Toxins and the American House, 1865–1895," 24(Spring 1989): 29–42.

51 Palliser, *Model Homes*, Preface.

52 William R. Leach, *Land of Desire: Merchants, Power, and the Rise of a New American Culture* (New York: Pantheon Books, 1993), p. 4.

53 Robert Shoppell, *Building Plans for Modern Low-Cost Houses* (New York: Co-operative Building Plan Association, 1884), Des. 154.

4

True Americans Own Homes

Producers of pattern books were consummate businessmen who participated in the prevailing ethos of success through competition, and they solicited their carefully targeted audience with potent sales techniques. Among the most persuasive was their use of language in the written material accompanying the drawings of their houses. This language resonated with an already present set of dreams and convictions while at the same time making them stronger and more concretely articulated. Pattern books verbally integrated the rhetoric of nationalism, the search for a national architecture, and the definition of American character in a consumer society and put them into visual form. Their authors resorted occasionally to an expected cautionary allusion to the poor, but concentrated on reinforcing the prevailing conception of American progress in which hard work and success were moral imperatives. Both became manifest in home ownership, for the virtue of the American people was founded in the home and held strong by the homeowner. In his 1876 *Home Building*, Elisha C. Hussey encapsulated the commonly held assumptions regarding the paradigmatic middle-class American when he described a suburban community populated by "enterprising, high-minded, sober, industrious, refined Christian people" for whom there was "generous reward for the expenditure of talent, time and money. . . ."[1]

This pairing of architecture and national identity operated in a larger public discourse that served to strengthen the values and practices of a broadly defined middle class who encountered contradictions to the belief in social mobility thought to be inherent in a democratic market society. This middle class was confronted with the practices of late-century industrialists commanding inordinate shares of the nation's wealth as well as by the social disruption represented

by the activities of growing numbers of immigrants, striking workers, and political radicals. From this position they participated in an
internal dialogue that served to legitimize their own activity and its
meaning. Scientific studies, public speeches, and popular literature
written by and primarily addressed to members of the middle classes
persuasively emphasized the contrast between the individually owned
middle-class home in the village or suburban setting and urban housing, especially the tenement. Within the prevailing belief in social
mobility that urged trust in the notion of equality for all Americans
through common opportunities for self-improvement, owning a home
was defined as a democratic right for all Americans. It was also a duty,
for home ownership contributed to national progress and was an
emblem of good character.

However, the United States was in the midst of decades of economic recession, and building a home was not always a simple
prospect. Thus the belief in success through work and thrift required
negotiation with a family's economic reality. Pattern books, by establishment architects as well as by the aggressively entrepreneurial, were
one site for this negotiation. In effect, the authors and their audience
vitalized their cultural dominance as they reaffirmed for themselves
the legitimacy of their beliefs, values, practices and customs. Self-
defined as high-principled Americans who progressed economically
through work and thrift, they functioned as self-conceived standard
bearers of a democratic society and sustainers of "American" standards. In the pattern books, essays, captions, and titles accompanying
the drawings of houses encompassed themes of home ownership,
nationalism, American character, and social mobility. From house plan
to realized suburban community, the empowerment of the middle
class during a time of crisis was given physical definition.

Barriers to national expression

The vigor with which home ownership was promoted grew from
concerns about economic and social security. The peaceful late-nineteenth-century life that is enshrined in today's memories was in reality
a life that brought uneasiness over rapid social and technological
transformation in the midst of enthusiasm for new opportunities.

Among the many cultural histories of the late nineteenth century, Robert Wiebe characterizes the period as a search for order amidst change, and T. J. Jackson Lears points out the prevalence of stress and depression, which was known as neurasthenia, stemming from unremitting personal confrontations with the new and unknown.[2] During and following the centennial year some editorialists countered the claims for American unity and excellence put forward within the rhetoric of nationalism. Before the opening of the Philadelphia Exhibition a reviewer in *Galaxy* recognized that America may not have fulfilled the promise of democracy envisioned a century earlier. Visual evidence of the upcoming celebration were indeed abundant. There were so many items designated as "centennial" that the public could expect to see "centennial pumpkin pies" at any moment. Yet the author could find little genuine enthusiasm for the event. He explained, "We are not quite sure that we are not, as a people, a very great failure," then concluded with an appraisal holding only a rather dubious point of promise: "The liveliest feeling the great centennial fair awakens is the vague hope that it may help to brighten one of the gloomiest business years the country has seen within a century."[3]

The rhetoric of the Centennial Exhibition optimists belied the fact that the late nineteenth century was a time of economic, political, and social instability. Centennial-year Americans, described in the *Atlantic Monthly* as "anxious" in an otherwise laudatory assessment of the United States and the Exhibition, were struggling through an economic depression that had begun with the financial panic of 1873.[4] Economic stagnation lasted until 1878, recurred with an economic slowdown from 1884 to 1885, and culminated in another financial panic and depression in 1893. Unemployment accompanied the persistent economic downturns and was an endemic problem for all levels of wage earners and small business owners up to the close of the nineteenth century. Laborers, especially, were affected when manufacturers and industrial leaders attempted to meliorate the industrial slowdown by means of wage reductions. Many rose in protest. The extent of worker unrest was most clearly exemplified for the public during the Great Strike of 1877 against the railroads. Although the strike was not nationally organized, massive demonstrations spread along the rail lines from community to community and across state lines. This and the many other strikes of the time clearly subverted assumptions that American capitalistic enterprise and democratic government provided equal opportunity for all citizens. Apprehension grew among the middle and upper classes as union organization proliferated, labor organizations were formed, and participation in socialist movements escalated. For many Americans, the official termination of Reconstruction was overshadowed by the violence surrounding them. Those who encouraged and engaged in such dissension seemed to be putting the stability of the nation itself at risk.[5] In 1888, for example, one commentator on the Chicago Haymarket Riots of 1886 expressed the ever-present fear of opposition to capitalism when he offered, "The tragedy of the Haymarket had brought to the knowledge of our citizens the depressing consciousness of the extent and danger of the communistic element in our midst. . . ."[6] Contrasts between the doctrine of moral progress and the nationwide disruption of social order became increasingly apparent. From political corruption of Grant's government to General Custer's death at Little Big Horn and disputes over Chinese contract laborers in California, no geographical area was free from unrest, and the news of regionalized disorder quickly spread to become a national concern. The emblems of unity produced for the Centennial were, for many, hollow.

Social distinctions in American values

In 1884, Rev. Josiah Strong voiced the reactive fears which had developed from the 1870s in *Our Country: Its Possible Future and its Present Crisis*. The popular volume sold over half a million copies. In eight chapters entitled "Perils," Strong explained the dangers of immigration, Romanism, Mormonism, religion and the public schools, intemperance, socialism, wealth, and the city. He warned his "American" readers against optimism, for they must be prepared to contend with "the perils which threaten our Christian and American civilization," and he identified the enemy: the poor, southern and eastern European immigrants, inebriates, socialists, Roman Catholics, Mormons and the wealthy.[7] Strong's tract was, of course, only one among many in the same vein. Newspapers, magazines, and educational literature consistently identified nonconforming groups—strikers, unemployed workers, native Americans, blacks, new immigrants— and marked them as antagonists who functioned outside an ordered society and who lacked the rational intelligence of the civilized. In some, the language became insistent and vituperative. The *Chicago Tribune* claimed, for example, that striking immigrant bricklayers were not "reasoning creatures," and the Chicago *Post-Mail* called Bohemian immigrants "depraved beasts, harpies decayed physically and spiritually, mentally and morally, thievish and licentious."[8] School textbooks joined in with similar estimations. William G. Swinton, in his 1875 textbook, *Elementary Course in Geography*, concluded that the Chinese were not civilized because they were not progressive.[9] A later standard school text in 1887 found the existence of the Chinese laborers "socially undesirable and injurious" to "civilized communities."[10] The dominant culture represented by Strong appeared to be in constant danger.

In short, belief in the unity of American enterprise encountered the reality of social inequality and dissent through the last quarter of the century. Riots and strikes were forcibly quelled, but the response to the danger they represented was not manifest in authoritative action alone. Rather, pronounced differences between acculturated Americans and the dissenters were textually expressed so as to define more firmly the ideological domain of the middle classes. Those who did not show a desire to adhere to the normalized and normalizing "American" values were perceived as opponents of the solidarity, thus progress, of America. It is important to recognize that this discourse of conforming, right-thinking nationalism was not directed solely to the dissenters. Most articles were published in periodicals read by the middle classes, for the most part a public who already supported the tenets of progress and social mobility. A key operation of the portrayal of the relationship between self and nation was to establish more clearly the differences between groups as a means to build a collective confidence and internal strengthening of the middle classes and securing these values in national space.

Dwelling on the immigrant poor

It is not surprising that in this organization of differences the living conditions of the immigrant poor should become a major object of attention. The number of immigrants entering the United States during the last decades of the century was unprecedented. In 1880 more than seventy percent of the population of San Francisco, St. Louis, Cleveland, Detroit, Milwaukee, and Chicago were immigrants or the children of immigrants.[11] The number of immigrants, however, was not the crucial issue, for the perceived problem of this massive influx was their native origins. Primarily of southern and eastern European extraction, they became readily identifiable as "foreign." Throughout the United States, ethnic and racial diversity became an increasingly divisive rhetorical tool as foreign beliefs and cultural traditions seemed to threaten American societal practices. In the estimation of the *Democratic Chicago Times*, late-nineteenth-century America had become the "cesspool of Europe."[12]

Fears that massive immigration and a high birth rate among the immigrants may "foreignize" Americans aroused arguments to "Americanize" them.[13] Again the discriminatory mark of otherness was used to further establish the meaning of "American." By their poverty, the immigrants, the unemployed, and the working poor were perceived as groups devoid of those qualities that ultimately supported national interests. Studies of the causes of poverty—conducted by government agencies, professional social scientists, even charity organizers and activists for social reform—upheld a conviction that poverty was the fault of the poor because they lacked the ambition to work and the discipline to save their earnings when they did work. Because workers evidenced participation in the American ethos by their employment, sympathy for their plight in time of economic hardship was indeed expressed. There were also philanthropic reformers who pursued solutions to the dilemmas of housing the poor. Yet, the impoverished were at the same time criticized for the lack of proper conduct that contributed to their own condition.[14] In New York, the secretary of the State Board of Charities, Charles S. Hoyt, studied the causes of poverty among the inmates of the state poorhouses and concluded, "By far the greatest number of paupers have reached that condition by idleness, improvidence, drunkedness, or some form of vicious indulgence. . . ." Considering the "weaknesses" frequently hereditary, he concluded that few were "reduced to poverty by causes outside of their own acts."[15]

Inevitably the comparison was made between the living conditions of the well-off and those of the poor, and the disparity between the two groups became starkly evident (Figs. 29, 30).[16] Although immigrants indeed moved to small communities eventually, or, as in

Fig. 29. *Ownership of a suburban home was formulated as a trait of American character by posing harsh contrast between those "American-ized" and city dwelling immigrants. "An Old Rear Tenement." (Riis,* Scribner's Magazine, *1889)*

the case of northern European farmers, began their American experience there, many by necessity settled in the noisy city centers and crowded into tenements notorious for lack of privacy, sufficient ventilation, and sanitary facilities. Characteristically, southern and eastern European immigrants landed in such circumstances. As the number of newcomers added to the already large populations of apartment-dwelling workers, investors built multiple rental units in cities along the northeastern seacoast and in other metropolitan areas across the nation. In Cincinnati, for example, the proportion of residents living in dwellings housing three or more families rose to approximately 70 percent between 1877 and 1882.[17] The increasing physical presence of

Fig. 30. "The Dark Side" of tenement family life. (Elsing, Scribner's Magazine, 1892)

the tenements provided a visual symbol to underpin fears of social disruption. Inhabited by immigrants, working-class families, and the poor, tenements were identified as centers of social power for those groups responsible for the unremitting signs of resistance to American mores. Conservatives and liberal reformers alike saw tenements as settings for propagating radicalism. The *Chicago Tribune* reported in 1877, "We too have crowded tenement houses, and our entire streets and neighborhoods occupied by paupers and thieves. We now have communists on our soil."[18] Active reformer and philanthropist Helen Campbell concluded in her study of *The Problem of the Poor* (1882), ". . . it is in the tenement houses that we find the causes which, combined, are making of the generation now coming up a terror in the present and a promise of future evil beyond man's power to reckon." The statement was reiterated in a three-part study of New York city life in which she reported slum dwellers as "human beasts" who had no desire to improve their lot, after which, she wrote, "with a little added intelligence they become Socialists, doing their heartiest to ruin the institutions by which they live."[19] One of the more influential liberal clergymen (and a proponent of Herbert Spencer's theories of social evolution) Lyman Abbot, found in the tenements characteristics that endangered "republicanism."[20]

Housing and the space it occupies

Ascribing to the architects' theory of effective architecture, social critics held that architectural environment was more than a site of dissent. Dwelling place held the power to effect character change, or, at least, solidify character traits. Here again the moral uprightness of the middle class, inscribed in their houses, was brought into contrast with the life of the lowly. Late in the century, Elgin Gould, a housing reformer who considered commercial enterprise a solution to housing problems, suggested that a home in the suburbs encouraged its inhabitants to be "wedded to order and rational conservatism . . . and turn a deaf ear to specious isms." Others suggested that eruptions of disorder could be circumvented if tenement dwellers were encouraged to live in detached houses on separate plots of land. Physical separation of immigrant and worker families would encourage them to act independently. They would be less inclined to congregate and collectively form a powerful counterpoise to those beliefs integral to Americanization.[21]

Reformers indeed campaigned to improve the immigrants' plight. Architects were exhorted to design more habitable multiple dwellings, and enterprising entrepreneurs were offered compelling arguments for investing in such improved housing. Changes directed toward bettering safety and health were implemented but the benefits of financial speculation in housing for the poor were also disputed. These arguments against providing housing were often directed toward the social character of the prospective inhabitants rather than any economic impediments to building. While reformers, social scientists, government officials and authors of popular books and articles promoted improvement, they as earnestly raised questions about the tenement dwellers' actual desire to live in different surroundings, even given the opportunity to do so. As early as 1873, nearly two decades prior to the Gould report to the same effect, F. W. Draper proffered the image of a house in the country as a prototypical contrast to the tenement. After studying the tenement poor he concluded for the Massachusetts Board of Health that "the chief obstacle to suburban homes for the working classes is the disinclination of the laborer—the very poor and unintelligent class—to accept such an opportunity when it is offered. . . ."[22]

Tenements became an omnipresent symbol of resistance to American social identity, and a detached house on an individual lot became the architectural symbol of Americanization. The living environments of the middle-class exemplars and those not yet Americanized were contrasted just as their differing characters were contrasted. The discourses about representative character and architecture converged in the process, and the internal strengthening of national ethos was located in specific architectural sites—tenements in the city and detached houses in the suburbs. Opponents of American "progress" were conceptually confined to cramped urban spaces while the middle classes were allocated larger geographical spaces, rendered through mental images of communities sprawling over the vastness of the extra-urban landscape. However, as we found above, while the ideal of suburb was readily incorporated as a sign of middle-class values, suburban spacial identity was not yet fully actualized. Promotion of the suburb as a site of detached homes in the country became a strategy of middle-class cultural empowerment. While popular periodical articles with such titles as "The Suburban House" broadcast the advantages of living in a home with a spacious lawn, railroad companies intent on expansion and selling land advertised the ease of commuting to urban jobs.[23] Developers and individual landowners sectioned lots to sell, and architects and builders offered "suburban" homes.

The pattern of middle-class life

Owning a home was no mere option. According to the Palliser brothers in their popular pattern book *Model Homes* (1878), living in a home not owned by oneself would cause one to live a life "destined to be fraught with all that lacks an interest in practical things, and leads to a life which is sure to warp and run into the quicksands of nonchalance and don't careism for all occupation and responsibility of the home pleasures and comforts that surround the happy possessors of homes."[24] The Pallisers had introduced this passage by asserting, "There are few persons who do not intend to build." Thus with firm certainty home ownership was formulated as a common interest that made departure from that goal socially unacceptable. In 1885, pattern book producer Samuel Reed stressed ideological associations with those who had succeeded by claiming "almost every man prominent and successful in professional or business callings" was a happy homeowner.[25] The lack of a home was an inadequacy associated with the lack of ambition daily typified by those who in newspaper reports were depicted as devoid of reason: the unemployed, tenement dwellers, immigrants. The now-familiar polarity was completed as homeowners were defined as "thrifty," "sensible," "industrious," and "intelligent." Further, the patriarchal component of the definition of American character was enforced with the observation that if a male head of household was a "true man" he would work toward owning a home.[26]

In unspoken, but very apparent, opposition to the political aspirations of the radical elements that had found their way to American soil, it was firmly avowed that an individually owned home was a right provided by democracy. As stated by Samuel Reed in a description of one of his small pattern book cottages, "every industrious man, starting in life, has a right, and should be encouraged, to anticipate property. . . ."[27] "Encouragement" to own a home became, in other pattern books, an exhortation that home ownership was a "duty." Not only was it a duty to provide a safe residence for the family, but it provided inspiration for others to follow suit.[28] The industrious man would express his belief in the possibility of improving his condition, his "progressive character," and that of America by purchasing land and building a house. Home ownership exhibited the rewards of American social mobility and was the foundation of national progress.

The assumption of individual progress was instrumental to the promotion of home ownership as a component of American identity. From *McGuffey's Reader* to Russell Conwell's tract, *Acres of Diamonds*, self-help was a common theme in late-nineteenth-century literature. The titles of four successive tracts by British author Samuel Smiles, published decades earlier but still best sellers, convincingly represented the relation of individual initiative to character: *Self Help, Thrift, Duty*, and *Character*. By late century, the clergyman Conwell preached that it was the duty of every man to secure wealth, while the Social Darwinist William Graham Sumner titled a chapter in his 1883 *What Social Classes Owe to Each Other*, "That it is not Wicked to be Richer than One's Neighbor."[29] Internal class competition was necessary to the functioning of a capitalist society, and believed an admirable mode of practice.

While the rhetoric implied a monolithic definition of the middle class, differentiation began to become obvious as the conception of the middle class was expanded to include poorly paid clerks as well as doctors, lawyers, and proprietors of small businesses. Prior to the Civil War the core middle class had consisted of shopkeepers, merchants, and similarly independent business people. Following the War the nation's social structure was significantly affected by the forces of an economy inexorably changing from an agricultural to an industrial and commercial base. As technological development brought more efficient methods of industrial production, the increasingly abundant manufactured goods were dispersed through an extended mass market. New divisions of labor were required to organize production and the transportation of commodities from the manufacturer or grower to the wholesaler and consumer. The constitution of the work force changed with the addition of jobs that ostensibly allowed for social mobility upward from the laboring to the middle class. Salespeople and clerks, especially, began to be needed in numbers not imagined before.[30] But differentiated positions within the middle class itself began to crystallize at the same time. Many of the white collar positions, especially those in sales and clerical work, paid poorly, and it was understood that the jobs with lower pay were appropriately directed to those whose backgrounds already positioned them lower on the scale of middle-class success. In a review of an 1878 government report published in the *American Builder*, it was noted that young men with sufficient financial backing entered the professions, while young men without the same financial means became "teachers, clerks and bookkeepers."[31] Five months later the editorial staff of the *American Builder* complained that parents insisted on sending their sons to schools to become clerical workers rather than skilled workers in the trades.[32] White-collar occupations had become the career choices for many young Americans. Although the income was low in these entry level jobs, the positions held an element of prestige not shared by blue collar jobs. Becoming a clerk was commensurate with taking a first step toward the ultimate goal of becoming an independent businessman and entrepreneur. But prestige notwithstanding, wages often were too low and jobs too insecure to assure financial security and investment in homes.

Contrary to the messages of social mobility suggesting, and even insisting, that America was a nation of homeowners, home ownership was not an easily attained goal. An individually owned home built on its own plot of land was beyond the immediate financial means of many, making it necessary for the pattern book authors to convince their audience that they should build homes despite all obstacles. Homes were indeed being built, but statistics indicate that more of the middle class were renters than owners. Ironically, studies have shown that a larger percentage of the employed working class purchased homes than did the middle class.[33] As an example, even by 1900, fewer than forty percent of the native, white heads of household who were employed in white-collar jobs and lived in the suburbs of Detroit owned their own homes, but over one-half of the residents of the ethnically distinct neighborhoods had become homeowners.[34] In the United States, individual homeowners were more often the blue-collar workers and the wealthy than the middle class. Although large numbers of potential workers were unemployed, at the same time changes in the structure of the labor market were bringing a number of relatively well-paying jobs in industry. Perhaps more significantly, laborers customarily lived closer to the city in ethnically distinct neighborhoods. Often, they were more likely to be first or second generation immigrants who still had a sense of kinship with their neighbors of similar origin. Family and friends joined together to build modest houses for one another.

Most pattern book authors recognized the lack of a viable market for house plans among laborers and the very wealthy who had the financial means to employ architects to design their large homes, and they concentrated on selling homes to the middle classes. This concentration, however, was not without its subtleties. The dominant characterization of the expanding middle class was a monolithic definition in terms of similar qualities sustaining a uniform expression of national character. Yet economic disparities within the middle class had to be recognized, and a favorable characterization of the disparities had to be found. Consequently, the disparities were linked with the salutary narrative of American equality through social mobility, and the disparities were glossed as manifestations of differential progress by individuals toward the realization of the American dream. In this way, inequality and ideal equality were mediated. For entrepreneurial pattern book authors this mediation became a strategy to sell homes, and they translated differential access to architecture as a national art into differences in taste and status. They found a language appropriate for all buyers of their "artistic" products by introducing aesthetic taste as a mark of intelligence and social distinction. House designs and/or their future owners were described as "intelligent," "cultured," "dignified," "elegant," "noble," "refined," "genteel," "tasteful," and "tasty," all signifying educated artistic sensibilities.

From the eighteenth century, "taste" had become a concept available for the relative determination of admirable, but difficult to define, qualities in the arts. Within the British aesthetic formulation of the picturesque, the sensibility sufficient to recognize aesthetic qualities was possessed by a knowledgeable few, usually the landed gentry who were the legitimated arbiters of taste for the society as a whole. This emphasis on aristocratic class distinction of course required a bit of manipulation for an American audience. The difficulty was evident early in Calvert Vaux's *Villas and Cottages* (1857 and 1864). He asked, "Why is there comparatively so little beauty in American buildings?" He then posited an absence of taste as the reason, and he lamented that since Americans were such prolific builders this defect was particularly evident. Alluding to American social structure in his commentary, Vaux identified the problem with the "industrious classes" because they funded most of the construction in the United States. These active workers determined national standards of building. Americans surely appreciated beauty, but the majority of the population was not sufficiently educated to have acquired taste. Here Vaux was caught in the dilemma of how to apply a hierarchical judgment while retaining the premise of an egalitarian democracy.

In the eighteenth century the wealthy had been regarded as the arbiters of taste because, as people of leisure, their minds were unencumbered with quotidian details, hence open for abstract thought. Vaux adroitly found a similar place for the new American leisure class—comprised, as the ideology of mobility required, of the sons of men who had worked hard to become wealthy. The contribution of this new leisure class to a society in which the work ethic prevailed was to establish a level of discernment in the arts. They could become "earnest laborers striving for a higher national excellence." It could not be forgotten, however, that America was a land of upward mobility, and citizens of lesser means could strive to become wealthy themselves. They could also be educated, but, for the time being, because they had little free time from the labors, they were urged not to form taste, but, rather, to recognize the taste established by the leisure class.[35]

In contrast, readers of the late-century pattern books were supposed not to be impressed with the sense that taste was the entitlement of the select few, but were persuaded that new artistic standards came from themselves—of course following the authority of the architect and/or pattern book authors. The old aristocracy or those born to wealth were rejected as the sole arbiters of taste and appreciators of beauty. Now, prospective homeowners were to be cultivated members of the middle class who knew and valued beauty, and it was their duty to educate the lesser endowed American citizenry through properly designed and built houses. As early as 1875, readers of G. B. Croff's pattern book were assured that houses such as his contributed to "elevating and refining influences" in the communities in which they were built.[36]

Later, the more aggressively entrepreneurial pattern book authors forwarded more explicit distinctions of taste in concert with varying steps on the scale of American success by explaining the appropriateness of a house design for the future owner's social status. Occasionally, designs were directed to distinguished professionals such as doctors and lawyers, but the most esteemed professional appellation, one that could appeal to the largest number of clients, was "businessman." For the Pallisers in 1887, the businessman's home in the suburbs, presented as the first design in their book, would serve to "educate the public taste to appreciate the sensible and artistic treatment that is so satisfying. . . ." (Fig. 31)[37] Further, the owner's taste was to be prominently displayed with a house visible to passers by. Although homes were to be surrounded by spacious lawns, they were not to be tucked away and hidden from view or pushed to the back of the lot. The Pallisers patently spoke to their clients' pride in this matter when they related how a house they had built in Bridgeport, Connecticut, became the site of pageant and "stimuli" for hundreds of people, some traveling a hundred miles to see such "beauty" of the "cultivated."[38]

A display of social status

The language used by pattern book authors, however, indicated that there were varying degrees of expressive appropriateness and capacity. Tasteful display must be coordinated with social status. With an application of gendered language, tasteful homes whose costs were appropriate for the lower to central middle classes were described as "pretty," "attractive," and "cheerful" (Fig. 32). The larger homes of

Fig. 31. Houses were to be placed in public view to educate the public in good taste as well as inspire others to build their own homes. Businessmen often were addressed as model prospective homeowners. (Palliser, New Cottage Homes, *1887)*

Fig. 32. Houses were described with words that correlated the designs with the socio-economic status of the owners. Gendered connotations are frequent in the use of language. A "pretty cottage." (Hopkins, Cottage Portfolio, *1889)*

the more affluent upper middle class, such as Robert Shoppell's "mansion" in his 1883 pattern book, and his "suburban residence" in 1884, respectively had "commanding" and "rich and striking" exteriors (Fig. 33).[39] Descriptions accompanying the house designs implied that a cottage affably attracted attention, whereas a large villa or mansion commanded the regard of the community. In contrast, the home of a farmer whose income was strictly limited and whose buildings were "situated upon an unfrequented road" was described as "plain." Similarly, little decoration was applied to a home for "plain and sensible" people (Fig. 34).[40] As did others, Shoppell's 1883 pat-

Fig. 33. A "rich and striking villa." (Shoppell, Modern Low-Cost Houses, 1884)

tern book included a "farmer's cottage," but his home was built with vertical siding typically used by local builders in the decades leading to the 1880s, thus marking it as unfashionable.[41] As expected, then, houses for farmers, mechanics, or skilled laborers were included in pattern books, but less frequently. Within the context of a sales market for house plans, their less-frequent inclusion was justified because workers and farmers were most likely to follow just those building customs the authors and architects were attempting to displace. Typically, as noted, local carpenters were hired to construct homes—a practice that seldom required purchased books, plans, or other products offered by the pattern book companies. In the context of a defining discourse, however, images of the unassuming homes registered important contrasts further legitimating middle-class values.

Fig. 34. Farmers who were not among the progressively affluent and whose homes were not in public view were assigned simple, relatively unadorned homes. A home for "plain and sensible people." (Hussey, Home Building, *1876)*

House designs for those at the perimeter of the defined middle class strengthened the ongoing representation of differences, and they were a symbolic affirmation of American opportunity. They conjointly served to further social norms, for they provided other groups symbolic access to the culture being defined as American. Consequently they had an important didactic role to play in recruitment to the middle class. Because pattern books were inexpensive and circulated widely, skilled laborers and farmers indeed had access to them, and pattern book authors encouraged them to identify with the prevailing ethos by subscribing to the ethic of home ownership, and by building tasteful homes. Shoppell and the Pallisers, both highly successful in the pattern book market, informed the public that mechanics too must be industrious, save money, and deny themselves tempting luxuries in order to achieve this goal. In 1887 the Pallisers could find no reason why farmers should not have well-designed homes. Here,

FRONT.

Fig. 35. Larger and more elaborate homes were suggested for farmers who participated in the new trend toward agri-business. A house with a home office for a "large farmer, politician or medical man." (Palliser, New Cottage Homes, 1887)

too, was a model for transition to the middle class, for the Pallisers could hold up, as an exemplar, the "large farmer" who had taken advantage of current developments in commercialized farming to bear comparison with the "politician," "medical man," and "businessman," each of whom needed a home office, dutifully included in the accompanying house plan (Fig. 35).[42]

Many pattern book authors were clear that the home's appearance should be suitable to the owner's financial and social status. A family of moderate means should not entertain pretensions for a large home; nor should a small home have too elaborate decoration. S. B. Reed's homes for families of taste ranged from a $1,500 cottage described as "sufficiently trim and neat" to the more elaborate "suburban villa" and "free style" residence for a "genteel family" (Figs. 36, 37).[43] Pattern book authors also explained an obvious and practical reason for building small houses with less ornamentation. Because decoration made the house more expensive, the owner's investment was better directed to a convenient plan than to ostentatious display. In G. B. Croff's book of designs for the "middle classes," published in 1871, he introduced houses of moderate cost and warned his readers, "A highly ornamented design of artistic execution in connection with affluence can never fail to please, but any attempt at gay ornamentation in the humbler styles of domestic buildings . . . is unpleasing."[44]

Nonetheless, many of the entrepreneurial pattern book authors and their clients continued to elaborate their homes irrespective of the modesty of the basic structure. For a house with ornamentation communicated a financial and social position that contrasted with the purely functional home of the common laborer. Houses across the United States were built with exterior moldings, gable ornamentation, and turned posts—sufficient in numbers to prompt the highly conservative Wilson Flagg to argue against such decoration in 1876 in the *Atlantic Monthly*.[45] In Flagg's estimation, ornament was too frequently being applied to conceal lower socio-economic status. His observation of the prevalence of decoration was not inaccurate, for homes became ever more elaborately decorated as scroll saws and mass-produced wood trim made it possible for home builders of even modest means to encrust their homes with trim. Gothic revival, Italianate, and French roof (later called Second Empire) houses set the scene for such decoration, but with developments from the new Queen Anne fashion as a vehicle, it became more widespread. Pattern book author David S. Hopkins, in 1891, rejected the elaborate late-century homes, and reviewed the situation with, "Here it is in a nut-shell. . . . We often see houses overloaded with gingerbread or

Fig. 36. A "sufficiently trim and neat" home. (Reed, Dwellings for Village and Country, 1885)

cut work, and the party who built it thought he had accomplished a beautiful thing."[46]

Another view, however, held that this masking of socio-economic status was necessary. For the distinguishing marks of wealth changed as wealth itself began to take on new meanings and new ambiguities began to arise about the morality of wealth. While the middle class supported an economic system structured on competition, the system had serious consequences for them as the disparity between wealth and poverty broadened. In addition to the contrast in values and status distinguishing them from the poor, new

Fig. 37. A "free style" home for the affluent suburban resident. (Reed, Dwellings for Village and Country, *1885)*

contrasts became evident. In particular, as industrial magnates gained power and their collusion with unscrupulous late-nineteenth-century politicians became evident, the wealthy became identified as a group undermining American values, and the lavish display of their pala-tial city homes became a sign of moral decay. The middle classes were caught in an economic bind believed to have been fostered largely by the greed of the wealthy, who were evidently impeding their progress toward affluence. In fact, many of the middle class, although work-ing in white-collar occupations, experienced financial uncertainties similar to those of the working class. In 1873, Ira Steward, an advo-cate for the eight-hour workday for laborers, inserted an essay entitled "Poverty" in a report for the Massachusetts state government. In it he turned from the problems of the workers to those of the idle-class poor. Distinguishing them from immigrant laborers by identifying them as the "native middle classes," he estimated that they were "a large majority of people," often in debt, whose poverty "consists in the fact that they have only barely enough to cover up their poverty."[47] Robert Shoppell seemed to be responding to this situation when in the 1880s he offered his clients a design for a "double house," half of which could be rented to a tenant. With rent as income, plus a gar-den and a flock of chickens made possible by living in the country, the owner "need not be troubled about loss of employment."[48]

While the loss of wages constituted a general threat to economic security, Steward also reported that the poverty of the lower middle classes was not solely a result of uncertain employment. Nor was it merely due to lack of thrift. He astutely recognized that outward pretensions to a higher status were an expensive requirement in a society that increasingly defined the middle class by its material con-sumption. Middle class expansion was a concomitant of a broadened consumer market. As the century progressed, department stores modeled after John Wanamaker's assemblage of shops in Philadel-phia began to compete with the small specialized stores, and mail-order companies began to be able to ship any manner of item a client would need or desire. Material consumption as a display of wealth became, along with occupational title, a signifier of an individual's position in society.[49] According to Steward, dressing in fine clothing and filling one's home to overflowing with decorative items were necessary, but sometimes debilitating, social investments:

> To betray or confess the secrets of one's destitution, is also regarded, in some measure, as a sign of incapacity; for, as the world goes, the poor man is an unsuccessful man. . . . The more expensive and superior style of living adopted by the middle classes must therefore be considered in the light of an investment, made from . . . motives even of self preservation.[50]

A house became the largest, most desirable and expressive material "investment," and pattern book authors frequently invoked the word. George F. Barber advised his clients in 1891 that well-designed houses increased the value of the owner's property, were resalable, and raised property values in the entire neighborhood.[51] Although references to investment were often couched in language appropriate to the fledgling "capitalist," an often-used term referring to a businessman whose income included more than earned income, pattern book authors at the same time offered means other than mere decoration to enhance the image of status for the wage earner as well. If a man could not afford to build a house by himself, he could build a house to share with a friend or relative. Pattern books included, in addition to the houses with rental units mentioned before, numerous double houses to be owned and occupied by two families. An important feature of these houses was their resemblance to large, single-family homes, and Robert Shoppell offered an alluring simulation of wealth with a double house that had the "appearance of a large mansion."[52] The fact of their double occupancy was hidden by the architect's skillful positioning of doors, porches and ells. The dual entrances posed little problem because single-family houses frequently had two front-facade entrances, and pattern book houses for doctors, lawyers, and other professionals with home offices also required two distinct exterior doors. Both the Pallisers and Shoppell explained to the prospective owners that these houses would conceal the fact of shared ownership until such time that one of the owners could purchase the other side of "his" home. The Pallisers straightforwardly told their clients that one of their double houses did not look like a two-family house. Samuel Reed carefully described the steps toward converting the interior of a double house into a single-family home (Fig. 38). Thus the pattern books were an important part of the discursive negotiations over the contradictions between a belief in equality through social mobility and the historical reality the belief encountered. They gave visual form to the architectural means for displaying *and* concealing status.

Then as now, house selection was more than a matter of owning adequate shelter. It was a question of self-identity as an individual and as a participant in cultural practices. As we have seen, the desire to own a home was indeed shared by a broad spectrum of the American population, but the hegemonic middle class, with its lower success rate in achieving the dream, most trenchantly promulgated the association between self-owned detached houses and national character. For them, home ownership became a rallying cry. And few made the

FRONT ELEVATION.

Fig. 38. Pattern book authors included "double houses" that enabled an owner to pay the mortgage by renting out one-half of the house. This fact of double tenancy was disguised from public view. "The Oaks." (Reed, Dwellings for Village and Country, 1885)

matter more pressing than the businesses that provided house designs, built homes, sold their lots, developed communities, and offered financing. Pattern book authors, especially, drew together the issues that had been localized to architectural sites. They verbally integrated the rhetoric of nationalism, the search for national architecture, and the definition of American character, and with their house plans provided a means to physically implement these beliefs.

The domestic consumer

For the most part, the entrepreneurial pattern book authors' use of pronouns and adjectives defined their buying audience as male. They directed their books to members of the building trades, male heads of household, or males investing in speculative housing. Although families as occupants of the homes were frequently noted and the readers were advised to consult their wives, references to women, the other half of the prospective-client couples suggested a less public role. When women were noted, they often were described in phrases that echoed passages from John Ruskin, eminent author on the arts, architecture, and domestic life. We could imagine Elisha Hussey, in his *Home Building* (1876), having Ruskin's popular tract *Sesame and Lilies* in mind when he praised woman in her kitchen as an "enthroned fixture." And perhaps with interpretations drawn from Catherine Beecher, Hussey's description for Plate 9 expanded the theme by hailing the mother as indispensable, one whose daily activities were centered in a home which was a "workshop for mother and her helps."[53] Robert Shoppell's book, *How to Build, Furnish and Decorate* (1883), offered a similar home-centered idealization with the words, "Woman is the queen of the ideal Home. . . ."[54] Although women from communities where pattern book houses were built actively participated in village improvement societies, competitive drill teams, and other organizations, pattern books contributed to the late-nineteenth-century's separation of public and private spheres for men and women. This separation was firmly planted in the "cult of domesticity," which joined with the ideology of social mobility and home ownership in the formation of American identity to deny the reality of women who worked in factories, fields, and in businesses independently or with their husbands.[55]

This is not to suggest, however, that pattern book authors did not recognize the more active and public lives of late-nineteenth-century women, but they emphasized home-centered lives for their female clientele. Shoppell was among the more ambitious with specific references to female clientele, and he demonstrated contemporary variations in the socially legitimate spaces defined for women's activities. Descriptive text that evoked a visual image of the "homemaker" standing at a window, looking out to her husband's world of work for one design defined the delimited world of a woman living in the country. Shoppell had altered the typical nineteenth-century configuration of rooms so that both the kitchen and living room were placed at the front of the house with windows facing the road. With this plan, the woman of the home would "not be secluded and shut out from the little variety and amusement which may be derived from a sight of highway travel."[56] Another design was entitled, "A Woman's Plan of a House," and was an exterior and plan that had been submitted by a woman who introduced her letter to him with, "My husband and I are in partnership," for she was one of the growing number of women who were employed outside of the home. She, a "school marm," and her husband, a printer, had worked together to save money to build a house. Although Shoppell suggested an architect's improvements for the plan, acknowledgment of submitted designs by readers of either gender was not customary in pattern books.[57]

Pattern books, popular periodicals and architectural journals frequently pointed out that women may know best what was required of a house plan. Shoppell told his readers of *Modern, Low-Cost Houses* (1884), "And last, but not least, show your wife the selections you have made. If her good sense—particularly acute in anything which concerns the home—approves, then go ahead."[58] A. W. Brunner, in his *Cottages* (1884), addressed "Mr. and Mrs. Client" and wrote of the couple's discussions about floor-plan arrangements, and others following him suggested as well the woman's role in house selection.[59] However, their sales custom depended upon a support of the model nuclear family, and they reminded readers of the separate duties of husband and wife. Indianapolis architect Louis H. Gibson titled his book *Convenient Houses with Fifty Plans for the Housekeeper* (1889).

"Housekeeper" was not a gender-specific term at all times in the nineteenth century, although it more often suggested the husband. To include men and women in his audience, he added below his title the chapter heading, "Architect and Housewife." Following, he introduced woman's concern for convenience and beauty in the home, then concluded with an explanation of the male wage-earner's duties and means to provide a home for the family.[60]

Pattern books also offered advice from women authors on the subjects of convenient planning, but more emphasis was placed on interior decoration. Detroit architect Almon C. Varney allotted almost one-third of his book, *Our Homes and Their Adornments* (1882), to chapters having instruction for needlework, embroidery, door hangings, screens, pillows, and other handmade items. He also instructed clients on wallpaper and other floor and furniture coverings.[61] Robert Shoppell included a lengthy treatise on home decorating in his 1883 book that presented advice to enable the woman of the house, with her "quick feminine perception and good sense," to translate the more elegant examples of interior decoration to her humbler situation. At the same time, he stated, "the carpets, wall-papers, furniture, and probably the pictures and other art ornaments, are the product of other peoples' minds."[62] His estimations were drawn directly from Ruskin's *Sesame and Lilies*. Literature by men for women, such as Ruskin's work, pattern books, widely sold home decorating manuals, and women's magazines, advanced a need for artistic home decoration for all families.[63]

Following the example of Charles Locke Eastlake's *Hints on Household Taste* (1868), numerous books, such as Clarence Cook's *The House Beautiful* (1878), Harriet Spofford's *Art Decoration Applied to Furniture* (1878), and Robert Edis' *Decoration & Furniture of Town Houses* (1881), promoted the image of artistic homes owned by the cultured to one of popular appeal.[64] Magazines directed to the more affluent middle-class readers published works by these authors as shared information among the knowledgeable. Women's magazines published articles to instruct their readers on the elevation of home life and home decoration, and pattern books joined in this energetic print culture that transformed a social practice to unquestionable common sense. Women's magazines, especially, were a voice of authority. In addition to *Godey's*, there were *Frank Leslie's Ladies Journal*, the *Home Companion*, *Domestic Monthly*, *Women's Home Journal*, *Ladies Home Journal*, *Good Housekeeping*, and many others. *Ladies Home Journal*, introduced in 1883, reached a circulation of two hundred thousand by 1885 and had doubled that number by 1888. When architectural pattern book authors inserted chapters on home decorating, the "housewives" already were prepared as readers. Being defined as reading subjects in women's magazines, decorating manuals, even etiquette manuals, women viewers of pattern book designs became readers who were addressed with a socially valid identity.

One of the most powerful motivating forces for decorating homes was its moral cast. Ruskin's ideal woman was placed on a pedestal of "queenliness." She was an object of virtue and beauty within the home, always wise, always lovely. Above all, she was the "soul-maker" of her children and her husband, which she accomplished by making the home a "place of peace" and a "sacred place" through the order and beauty she produced.[65] Stemming largely from the arts and crafts movement in England, a moral aesthetic was applied to home decoration which gave objects placed in the home a use value beyond physical function. Decorative items, including paintings, engravings, vases, decorative screens, and an amazingly vast array of handmade items, were valued as objects of aesthetic and moral education. Clarence Cook instructed readers in a series of articles in *Scribner's* (1875–1877). The living room, which he favored over the parlor as a room for family activity, should be decorated ". . . as an important agent in the education of life; it will make a great difference to the children who grow up in it. . . ."[66] On the shelves over the fireplace, which was the spiritual and intellectual center of the home, there should be a few beautiful things "to lift us up, to feed thought and feeling . . . because they belong alike to nature and humanity."[67] To this selection the woman of the home should contribute her own skills. She could paint china, cut pictures from books and paste them to screens, and embroider furniture coverings. Harriet Spofford told readers of her book on interior decoration, "Provided there is space to move about, without knocking over the furniture, there is hardly likely to be too much in the room."[68] Women's magazines were filled with articles on handcrafts for home decoration, and the seriousness with which this notion was taken is verified in diaries and photographs of interiors from the late nineteenth century, as well as today's museum collections of embroidered work, lace, woven hair, and hand painting. An 1878 satirical comment on the new aesthetics and its promotion of decorative arts described the popularity of handcrafts and, in doing so, suggested that it kept women at home. He observed, "I have noted that the ladies are less given to roaming about; and you should see the happy faces bent over canvas and jugs."[69]

Although women's handcrafts were raised to the status of social mandate, the literature on decoration stressed the importance of a woman's careful selection of objects for the home more than her making the objects. In addition to making "homely" items, women determined which items should be bought for display in the home, and they were encouraged to study to improve their tastes by reading inspirational books and periodicals that helped them become familiar with the finest of arts. In this way they would understand the profound secrets of high art and the differences among the arts and crafts. According to Cook, speaking as one among many male and female authors, of first concern for the woman's discriminating eye were the "great things," such as the casts and engravings made from fine art. Then "at the feet of greatness" were those lesser things which "cannot derogate from the master's dignity." These were the items of decorative functional arts—for example, a Japanese bronze, an Etruscan vase, Venetian glass. The casts, engravings, and objects were purchased items to accompany the housewife's offerings, which could include a tumbler filled with roses and a chair covered with her needlework tapestry.[70] Shoppell, again, drew from this view using passages directly from Robert Edis' book, to join in its production. Women could understand fine art even if they could not produce the same themselves.[71]

The attribution of morality to art legitimized the practice of filling one's home with fashionable objects, but with women's handcraft belonging to a lower social and cultural status, it was necessary to complete the home's artistic decoration with purchased goods. While woman's space of creativity was largely confined to adorning the home, the education of women as purchasers of artistic objects inserted them into the public realm of economic activity and altered their place in the social matrix as consumers of mass-produced goods. An unprecedented grouping of decorative objects was displayed at the Philadelphia Centennial Exhibition and they were remarked upon in popular periodicals, home-decorating treatises, and decorating chapters in pattern books. The public saw a variety of objects from Europe, Britain, Asia, and the Middle East that were designated as beautiful. There were exhibits of high art and handcrafted arts, but, overall, the exhibition highlighting American industry was more a celebration of mass-produced culture than of high culture. A number of reviewers judged the event as a large sales exhibition. William Dean Howells called it a display of democratic art that would bring "splendor to every home though mass production."[72] The following year, a commentator on the new aesthetic doubted the moral contribution, but he believed that "improved taste in the consumers of the products of those arts" would develop.[73] In the context of a moral aesthetic, the mass-produced objects exhibited as decorative art suggested that machine-made goods, too, contributed to the family's moral, intellectual, and artistic education, and they were legitimized for consumption. As with building a house, decorating its interior was a means to practice the new morality of spending. Not only was it a project of status-building, it was instrumental to the family's well-being, and ultimately a contribution to the industrial progress of the nation.

Women were formulated as shoppers, and through the nineteenth century, the act of shopping was transformed from a matter of selecting necessary dry goods and foodstuffs to a social activity given social and moral purpose. The home was a woman's sphere, but a consumer culture adumbrated that sphere. The interior of the home signified the spaces of activity for women, but their arena of activity became less precisely circumscribed as they became facilitators of consumption and became integral to the American economy. By the 1870s women who lived within suburban commuting distance shopped in city stores for clothing, home accessories, and personal effects. From a male author's point of view, these women shoppers showed "a spirit of imperativeness and supremacy . . . and the men among whom she moves drop into a sort of nebulous inferiority."[74]

Department stores became a new gender-specific space of shopping activity by the late 1890s. Their more sumptuous interiors, tea rooms, and elaborate displays of household finery structured a refined domain for the domestic consumer.

Women living farther from city centers purchased their functional and artistic necessities by mail. Hundreds of mail-order magazines with nominal subscription rates joined with advertisements in magazines to bring an enticing assortment of mass-produced clocks, fabrics, beauty aids, craft supplies, framed engravings, vases, and other dream-fulfilling articles of contemporary culture. Their articles and advertisements sold the items, as they sold the notion that they were leaders in democratizing information and consumption.[75] Mail-order catalogues, too, entered the broadened market. Montgomery Ward's catalogue, introduced in 1872, was two hundred forty pages by 1883, and Sears, Roebuck soon followed with their catalogue. The nation's wealthy were not the only Americans to enjoy material goods of leisure and beauty. Women living in communities without day transportation to commercial centers now had the opportunity to share in the progress of the nation. It was not necessary to leave their homes to fulfill their function as consumers, for mail-order purchasing was a part of American life. By the end of the century, mail-order catalogues reached almost every community in the United States, making material consumption more efficient, and not least, more exciting as the number of pages in the catalogues grew.[76]

If we consider this conception of the "American" woman, it is not difficult to understand the attention paid to women as clientele in pattern books. As the formulation of woman as consumer emerged, more pattern book authors began to recognize the profitability of addressing women in the household. Even the Pallisers, whose posture allowed for less discussion of the female gender, offered occasional references. But women were defined as buying subjects while the trajectory of traditional gender relations was sustained. Women were defined as consumers, and the development of the collective social function made them an integral part of the economy of the American middle-class social structure. However, they were consumers who were artistic curators of the home. Their economically productive task was to select, purchase and decoratively arrange

products that often had representative value more than practical function. The objects they purchased were defined as objects of moral value
within the home, and the symbolic value of their activity rested on
conceptions of the home as woman's sphere. In the words of Almon
C. Varney in his book on exterior and interior decoration:

> The object of this, our labor, is to link—as in a *mar-
> riage tie*—this venerable and comprehensive word,
> *"home"* with that other word of classic mold, but of
> modern application,—*"adornment."* And with the
> whole-hearted enthusiasm of "match-makers," we
> sincerely hope and believe that they will be found to
> be not "unequally yoked."[77]

NOTES

[1] Elisha Charles Hussey, *Home Building* (New York: By the Author,
1876), iii.

[2] T. J. Jackson Lears, *No Place of Grace: Antimodernism and the
Transformation of American Culture 1880–1920* (New York: Pantheon
Books, 1982).

[3] "Nebulae," *Galaxy* 21(April 1876): 580.

[4] "Characteristics of the International Fair, III," *Atlantic Monthly*
38(September 1876): 359.

[5] Philip S. Foner, p. 33; and Herbert G. Gutman, *Work, Culture, and Society
in Industrializing America* (New York: Alfred A. Knopf, 1976), p. 242.

[6] Turlington W. Harvey, "Letter to a Friend," 17 November 1888, from
the Harvey File, Moody Bible Institute Library, Chicago, Illinois. Quoted in
James Gilbert, *Perfect Cities. Chicago's Utopias of 1893* (Chicago: University of
Chicago Press, 1991), p. 180.

[7] Josiah Strong, *Our Country: Its Possible Future and Its Present Crisis* (New
York: Baker & Taylor, 1885), pp. 170 and 57.

[8] Quoted in Gutman, p. 72.

[9] William G. Swinton, *Elementary Course in Geography* (New York: Ivison,
Blakeman, Taylor and Co., 1875), p. 114; in Ruth Miller Elsen, *Guardians of
Tradition* (Lincoln: University of Nebraska Press, 1964), pp. 162–63.

[10] John D. Quackenbos et al, *Physical Geography*, Appleton's American
Standard Geographies (New York: D. Appleton and Co., 1887), p. 109; cited
in Elson, p. 163.

[11] Gutman, p. 40.

[12] Ibid., p. 72.

[13] Strong, pp. 58–61.

[14] See Daniel Horowitz, *The Morality of Spending: Attitudes toward the
Consumer Society in America 1875–1940* (Baltimore: Johns Hopkins University
Press, 1985), pp. 13–24.

15 Charles S. Hoyt, "The Causes of Pauperism," *Tenth Annual Report of the State Board of Charities* (New York, 1877), p. 287; and Michael B. Katz, *Poverty and Policy in American History* (New York: Academic Press, 1983), p. 103.

16 Jacob A. Riis, "How the Other Half Lives," *Scribner's Magazine* 6(December 1889): 645; William T. Elsing, "Life in New York Tenement-Houses," *Scribner's Magazine* 11(January-June 1892): 699.

17 From the Ohio Bureau of the Statistics of Labor, 1887, 1881, 1883; in David Ward, *Poverty, Ethnicity, and the American City, 1840–1925* (New York: Cambridge University Press, 1989), p. 61.

18 *Chicago Tribune*, 29 June 1877; in David John Hogan, *Class and Reform School and Society in Chicago, 1880–1930* (Philadelphia: University of Pennsylvania Press, 1985), p. 3.

19 Helen Campbell, *The Problem of the Poor: A Record of Quiet Work in Unquiet Places* (New York: Fords, Howard and Hulbert, 1882), p. 117; and *Darkness and Daylight: Lights and Shadows of New York Life* (Hartford: The Hartford Publishing Company, 1895), pp. 99 and 109–10.

20 Lyman Abbot also wrote the introduction to Helen Campbell's 1895 volume.

21 In Ward, pp. 61–67.

22 F. W. Draper, "The Homes of the Poor in our Cities," Massachusetts State Board of Health, *Fourth Annual Report*, 1873, p. 399; in Ward, p. 64.

23 The article by architectural critic Bruce Price, "The Suburban House."

24 Palliser, *Model Homes*, p. 15.

25 Samuel B. Reed, *House Plans for Everybody* (New York: Orange Judd, 1878), p. 121.

26 *Scientific American Builders Edition* 2(September 1886): 53.

27 Reed, p. 10.

28 Robert Shoppell, *How to Build, Furnish, and Decorate* (New York: The Cooperative Building Plan Association, ca.1883), Des. 59.

29 Russell Conwell's tract was republished as a "Christian Heritage Inspirational Classic" in 1992 (Lake Wylie, South Carolina).

30 In 1870 there were 154 stenographers, many of whom were women; by 1900 there were 112,364 stenographers and typists. The number of bookkeepers, cashiers and accountants grew from 38,776 to 254,880. Alba M. Edwards, *Population: Comparative Occupation Statistics for the United States, 1870–1940; Sixteenth Census of the United States, 1940* (Washington, D.C.: U.S. Government Printing Office, 1943), p. 112.

31 "Industrial Education," *American Builder* 14(December 1878): 272.

32 "Too Much High Education," *American Builder* 15(May 1879): 114. The article also spoke against teacher-training for women because it led to the dislike of housework.

33 See Robert G. Barrows, "Beyond the Tenement: Patterns of American Urban Housing, 1870–1930," *Journal of Urban History* 9(August 1983): 395–420.

34 Oliver Zunz, *The Changing Face of Inequality: Urbanization, Industrial Development, and Immigrants in Detroit, 1880–1920* (Chicago: University of Chicago Press, 1982), p. 169 and 171.

35 Vaux, 1864, pp. 26–27, 39 and 44.

36 Croff, n.p.

37 Palliser, *New Cottage Homes*, Plate 1.

38 Palliser, *Model Homes*, pp. 44 and 46.

39 Shoppell, "A Gothic Mansion," Des. 76 and "A Suburban Residence," Des. 159.

40 Hussey, *Home Building* , Plates No. 10 and 1.

41 Shoppell, *How to Build*, Des. 47.

42 Palliser, *New Cottage Homes*, Des. 145. On the commercialization of farming in the nineteenth century, see Robert McGuire, "Economic Causes of Agrarian Unrest," *Journal of Economic History* 41(December 1981): 835–45.

43 Reed, pp. 20, 84 and 102.

44 Gilbert B. Croff, *Model Suburban Architecture* (New York: By the Author, 1871), Introduction.

45 Wilson Flagg, "Rural Architecture," *Atlantic Monthly* 37(April 1876): 428–43.

46 Hopkins, 1891, pp. 4–5.

47 Ira Steward, "Poverty," *Massachusetts Statistics of Labor, House Document* 173 (Boston: Wright and Potter, 1873), pp. 413–15; also in Stuart Ewen, *All Consuming Images: The Politics of Style in Contemporary Culture* (New York: Basic Books, Inc., 1988), p. 66.

48 Robert Shoppell, *Artistic Modern Houses at Low Cost* (New York: Co-operative Building Plan Association, ca.1887), Des. 545.

49 On department stores and consumption, see Leach.

50 Steward, p. 413.

51 George F. Barber, *Cottage Souvenir, No. 2* (Knoxville, TN: S. B. Newman, 1891), p. 3.

52 Shoppell, *How to Build*, Des. 108.

53 Hussey, Plate No. 9.

54 Shoppell, *How to Build*, in "Furniture and Decoration," supplement, p. 5.

55 Margaret Purser demonstrates that the cult of domesticity in its actual workings in a community is more complex than the ideology would suggest. In "Keeping House: Women, Domesticity, and the Use of Domestic Space in Nineteenth-Century Nevada," in Thomas Carter, ed., *Images of an American Land* (Albuquerque: University of New Mexico Press, 1997).

56 Shoppell, *How to Build*, Des. 47.

57 Shoppell, *How to Build*, Des. 83.

58 In his chapter, "Getting Ready to Build–Helpful and Practical Hints," n.p.

59 Arnold William Brunner, *Cottages or Hints on Economical Building* (New York: William T. Comstock, 1884).

60 Louis H. Gibson, *Convenient Houses with Fifty Plans for the Housekeeper* (New York: Thomas Y. Crowell & Co., 1889).

61 Almon C. Varney, *Our Homes and Their Adornments* (Detroit: J. C. Chilton & Co., 1882).

62 Shoppell, *How to Build*, "Furniture and Decoration," p. 5.

63 Martha Crabill McClaugherty includes an annotated bibliography of nineteenth-century books on the decoration of artistic houses in "Household Art: Creating the Artistic Home, 1868–1893," *Winterthur Portfolio* 18(Spring 1983): 1–26. She also points out the intersection of discourses on art and science in household decoration.

64 See McClaugherty. The artistic home in the context of the aesthetic movement is examined in a book produced by the Metropolitan Museum of Art, *In Pursuit of Beauty: Americans and the Aesthetic Movement* (New York: Rizzoli, 1987).

65 John Ruskin, *Sesame and Lilies* (Boston: Dana Estes and Company, 1900), p. 87. This small but phenomenally popular publication was a collection of essays written from 1864 to 1869.

66 Clarence Cook, "Beds and Tables, Stools and Candlesticks," *Scribner's Monthly Magazine* 10(June 1875): 174.

67 Cook, "Beds and Tables . . .," *Scribner's* 10(January 1876): 352.

68 Harriet Spofford, *Art Decoration Applied to Furniture* (New York: Harper & Brothers, 1878), p. 222.

69 John Trowbridge, "Imaginary Dialogue on Decorative Art," *Atlantic Monthly* 40(June 1878): 696.

70 Cook, "Beds and Tables . . .," Jan. 1876, pp. 352–53.

71 Shoppell described Edis as "a gentleman well known as a writer and lecturer on domestic art." Shoppell, "Furniture and Decoration," p. 6.

72 William Dean Howells, "A Sennight at the Centennial," *Atlantic Monthly* 38(July 1876): 100.

73 "Art," *Atlantic Monthly* 39(May 1877): 641–44.

74 William H. Rideing, "Life on Broadway," *Harper's New Monthly Magazine* 56(December 1877–May 1878): 235 and 238.

75 Ellen Gruber Garvey examines the strategies used by advertisers to normalize consumption for women in *The Adman in the Parlor: Magazines and the Gendering of Consumer Culture, 1880s to 1910s* (New York and Oxford: Oxford University Press, 1996).

76 Richard Ohman, *Selling Culture: Magazines, Markets, and Class at the Turn of the Century* (London and New York: Verso, 1996).

77 Varney, pp. v–vi.

◿ 5 ◺

The American Architect *and Categories in the Profession*

When the *American Architect and Building News* began publication in the centennial year of 1876, it was introduced as the first professional journal for American architects. Produced in Boston as the official organ for the American Institute of Architects, with an editorial staff headed by Harvard graduate W. P. P. Longfellow, the journal represented the East Coast architectural establishment.[1] From the outset, the vision for the organization and its journal was not limited to the urban centers where A.I.A. chapters already had been formed. The contributing architects were embarking on an enterprise with national scope in which they advanced themselves as authorities in architectural matters for the entire nation. When respected architect and A.I.A. fellow Henry Van Brunt announced the coming journal at the 1875 convention, he proudly reported the organization's growth during the past six years from sixty-five members in 1869 to one hundred fifty-seven members in 1875. The American Institute of Architects, he added, was already recognized by comparable architectural groups throughout the "world" as the only "organized body of architects" in the United States. He envisioned the pending journal as a venue for architects to exchange information and as a means to circulate knowledge about architecture to both architects and to a broader public. With crowd-stirring words to draw his "new world" audience of architects into the common cause, the prominent speaker advised the audience that it was their "sacred duty," "responsibility," and, not least, "opportunity" to educate the building community and public in the matters of "good architecture." "This enlightenment," he asserted, "it is clearly within our power to bestow."[2]

Henry Van Brunt's speech advanced a program of action for the *American Architect* and its readership. But their undertaking was not

posed simply as an articulation of architectural standards. It was a program of professionalization in the building trades in which the logic of professional authority was projected beyond the immediate American Institute of Architects membership. The journal was launched as a setting for establishing a ranked separation of employment in the building trades. An implicit point in Van Brunt's address was the characterization of his audience and their peers as an exceptional group whose knowledge could amend the nation's lack of sophistication in architectural concerns. According to Van Brunt, their group's sort of knowledge was not general to the building trades but was peculiar to experts—professional architects—who produced buildings with greater cultural value. The agenda was clearly stated in a subsequent journal article: "There ought to be a distinct line of demarcation between the profession and the rest of the world. . . ."[3] With the journal presented as a medium of textual exchange, standards for the practice of architecture were proposed and the words "architecture" and "architect" were defined with hierarchical social meanings that were carried forward within the next decade by other journals, most notably the *Inland Architect,* Chicago, and the *Califor-
·ia Architect and Building News,* San Francisco. Many of the distinctions ι in force today, over one hundred years later.

ſhe journal's staff proposed national norms for architectural ʌice—the architect's education, moral responsibilities, business duct, building designs—and introduced strategies to persuade members of the building trades as well as the public who commissioned buildings. The editors' selection of articles published in the *American Architect,* however, was calculated upon a recognition that direct dictation of the criteria would not be acceptable to a group of independent-minded readers. Articles and unsolicited letters offered differing opinions and introduced a general impression of open debate among the contributors. Disagreements were made evident, but they were subordinate to an overall inference that areas of consensus were being negotiated.[4] Using the subtle yet persuasive strategy of implying common consent, the editors worked out areas of mutual accord and translated them into prescriptions for the legitimate conduct of architects and for appropriate criteria in building design. Through the first years of the new journal, the heretofore indiscriminately used title "architect" was persuasively argued as a discrete category in the building trades. Architects, frequently contrasted with carpenters, other mechanics, and many pattern book authors, were articulated as an elite group who merited the power to determine the shape of America's architecture.

However, the members of the American Institute of Architects and their compatriots cannot be seen to have influenced others in the building trades to conform unconditionally to their outlook on professional categories and attributes of beauty in architecture. Carpenters, builders, and their clients, from their various social positions, interpreted differently the issues of well-designed buildings. Not only did the carpenters' and builders' livelihoods depend on differing articulations; their reputations and their clients' identity as respected community members called for making the discourse relevant to their social perspectives. We find in building journals, pattern books, and in the built houses of middle-class America that they took on notions of distinction but made them their own. By so doing, the middle and lesser classes were agents in forming the built landscape of the United States. Here, and in the following chapters, the spaces of architectural jurisdiction mapped out in the *American Architect and Building News*, in pattern books and responses to pattern book publication, will be explored.

The field of competition

Cultural ownership of the title "architect," as well as its suggested economic and social privilege, was argued by Henry Van Brunt and his colleagues in the American Institute of Architects because the word "architect" was a broadly used term which did not hold today's distinctions. As young New York architect A. F. Oakey bemoaned, anyone occupied in building fabrication could, and often did, take on the title.[5] Distinctions between professional architects and those builders judged to be less qualified by these architects were not generally known to the American public. Nor were the differences recognized in the building trades. Local carpenters and contractors advertised themselves as architects. Pattern book authors of widely varying degrees of respectability purveyed themselves as qualified architects. As it stood, with such universal application, the label "architect" was too all-embracing to hold much prestige or commercial clout for the self-declared professionals.

The *American Architect* introduced standards for "architecture" and its practitioners, and in doing so, it devalued the work of those who were operating differently—especially the "unprofessionals" who were most active in building the homes of the working and middle classes. Such a strategy was critical because custom worked against the architects' prerogative. As they clearly recognized, the United States was essentially a carpenter-built nation, and further, the difference between "architecture" and ordinary buildings was recognized by few. When A. J. Bloor launched his address to the 1876 American Institute of Architects convention, appropriately for that historical moment, he assessed the past and present condition of American architecture. After admitting to many excellent colonial period buildings, most of which were houses of the wealthy, he concluded that a larger majority of America's existing buildings resulted from local carpenters' and homeowners' poor interpretations of architects' work.[6] In another discussion of the matter, president of the Baltimore A.I.A. chapter, E. G. Lind, submitted that architecture and the profession suffered from the public's misunderstandings about the architects' duties. Recalling his earlier days in practice, Lind explained that people in years past placed their trust in the practical builder rather than the architect because they regarded architects as mere draftsmen who prepared drawings for the builder.[7] In effect, the architect was perceived to be the builder's assistant, and misguided prospective clients consequently turned to builders rather than to architects.

These arguments were common to the discourse which defined the professional architect, but more compelling arguments for instating professional authority were needed. It would not have been politic to assign responsibility for the abundance of poorly designed buildings in the United States solely to the ignorance of the nation's citizens. A. J. Bloor introduced a more cogent rhetorical device to establish differences between professional and lay building practices and aesthetic tastes by tapping into societal fears. He recast growing alarm about the detrimental effects of mass immigration into fears about the future condition of the nation's architecture. Simply, the nation's inferior architecture was a natural outcome for a country carved out of the wilderness. It was an architecture developed "amidst the war-whoops of savages and the incessant influx of crude material from the overstocked populations of the Old world."[8] Alexander F. Oakey, a frequent contributor to the *American Architect*, kindled similar convictions when he deplored the increase in a population who were uneducated, and perhaps uninterested, in the finer arts, especially architecture. Journal editorials did not belabor this point, but, then, it was not necessary in the current climate of Americanization. Their subtle uses of language were sufficient to intimate that uncultured immigrants contributed to the national practice of building homes without use of professional expertise. And in the process, both builders and clients were categorized.

The categorization was a form of one-upmanship in business in order to garner a clientele for their "architect's" work, but we need to be aware that the competition was over cultural authority as well as commissions. Economic competition from carpenters and builders factored into arguments for professionalization, but for most part, the carpenters who built homes in the nation's small towns and for the less affluent did not constitute strong market competition for the architects' commissions. The *American Architect* contributors were accurate in their estimation that the majority of the nation's buildings were designed without professional assistance, but local carpenters competed for only a portion of the jobs which the architects pursued. Builders, if defined as contractors, were more legitimate competitors, for they frequently gained commissions for homes for the more well-to-do and houses for speculators developing rental properties. But, again, the number of buildings commissioned was not the only issue, although economics constitute power. Carpenters and builders, because of the large numbers of buildings they constructed, were strong contenders for the cultural authority over defining societal norms for architectural design. The *American Architect* was very clear about their purpose. Already in 1876, "The profession began to work together; a distincter demarkation was established between building and architecture; a better standard of design and more uniform practice grew up."[9]

Among the more problematic forms of competition over who would define national taste was the pattern book. The popularity of pattern book design was firmly established by 1876. Several of the architects involved in defining professional status published their own pattern books filled with house plans and instructional information which echoed their journal's goals. Among others, the well-established New York architect Henry Hudson Holly published *Modern Dwellings* in 1878, and the younger architect A. J. Oakey published *Building a Home* in 1881. Pattern books brought their architectural designs to a much broader public and aided them in defining their professional status, but there were problems as well. As A. J. Bloor had noted, many of the nation's homes were poor imitations of architects' works. The common practice of using architectural pattern books as source books for sometimes unrelated architectural forms rather than for designs to follow with exactitude contributed to idiosyncratic interpretations and the development of vernacular architecture. In an 1878 study of American architecture, the author explained that "vernacular architecture" was "another kind of American architecture" differing from that enjoyed by the "cultivated classes" of clients and architects.[10]

There were, of course, many pattern books published by builders not considered professional. But these older types of builder pattern books could be more easily marginalized in the pursuit of categories of distinction. There were more worrisome challengers to "architecture." While the self-proclaimed professional architects' pattern books offered models for America's homes, they were introduced into a new and developing arena of competition. In the late-century escalation of publication for mass audiences, pattern books by more entrepreneurial authors, who adopted the polemics for professional architects for their own use, entered the market. They not only more forcefully competed for cultural authority over forging the visual character of the nation's domestic architecture, but they tended to erode arguments for paying professional architects' commissions. Addressed to the nation's mobile middle classes, the entrepreneurial books deviated from the traditional pattern book format and content that the new professionals continued to endorse. As recounted above, they modified traditional pattern book formats and sold their books at lower prices in order to promote their architectural services and products. Their books of designs served as advertisements for their practice and, in some, the offer of mail-order house plans and architectural services contested conceptions of architectural practice promoted in the *American Architect*. Not only did the new pattern books compete for business in a fluctuating building market, they more forcefully intersected in the struggle of power over ownership of the title "architect."

Mapping out the difference

From its January 1, 1876, issue, the *American Architect* editorial policy was directed to mapping out boundaries to define the notion of a professional architecture as a means to rectify this status-damaging situation. However, the program was given an altruistic character as the journal's founders worked to bring together a program of architectural practice which would establish differences between professional architects and non-professionals. In articles and a discretionary selection of letters to the editor, this body of architects representing the American Institute of Architects considered professional qualifications, education, certification examinations, responsibilities, and fees in order to constitute architects as conscientious representatives for the building of America.

From the outset, the endeavor was based on moral imperative. Henry Van Brunt urged, "Let us, then organize a crusade against ignorance and indifference. Let us cultivate the mutual devotion and the discipline essential to soldiers engaged against heavy odds in a holy alliance for the sake of civilizations."[11] Architects implemented the language of Christian missionary zeal, calling the architects' enterprise "missionary work," and in essence, these professional architects assumed it their duty to lead the nation from the perfidy of false taste.[12] With their aspirations given a righteous cast, the readers of the journal were exhorted and given authorization to work for the public good. There was no question that the A.I.A., with its journal, must function as a leader in organizing a national crusade to ameliorate the current state of affairs. According to the author of a leading article in the inaugural issue, the nation faced imminent danger if the general population continued to build without the architect's assistance; even the belief in distinctions between good and bad taste would be lost. Already American towns were characterized by "tumultuous incoherence" because architects were "not yet accepted as arbiters in all matters of design."[13]

When the journal architects presented this judgment, however, they had to explain their proposed relation to conventional building practice. Raising the status of the architect involved proving that the new professionals did not supersede the mechanic's role but were necessary intermediaries between their clients and the carpenters and masons who provided the physical labor to construct buildings. In order to convert the American public to a belief that architects were necessary, not just desirable, the *American Architect* gave substance to the word "architect" by establishing a polarity between the new professional and the long history of carpenter, or non-professional, dominance in building the nation's homes and businesses. Contrasts between suitably trained architects and the nation's past and present would-be architects were couched in a variety of articles. On the other hand, the shortcomings of the nation's carpenters were not belabored. Instead, it was suggested that workmen had their place in the architects' program. Belying fears of unemployment that were recognized as real by the journal authors, carpenters would not be eliminated from the work force and their role would be more clearly understood by all. Architects were to supply managerial, intellectual, and creative work. Carpenters and masons were to provide the physical labor. They, classified as mechanics, were important to the realization of the architect's design, but they were assigned a conceptually subsidiary role. In the August 12, 1876, issue of the journal: "An architect . . . supplies the mind; the builder is merely the bricklayer, or the carpenter. The builder is in fact the machine; the architect, the power which puts the machine together, and sets it going."[14] Proponents of John Ruskin's and William Morris' craft aesthetic maintained the distinction but suggested that the laborers be given sufficient variety of work to maintain interest and pride in their labors.[15]

A verbal articulation of the architect's distinctive role was not difficult, but convincing the public of its need held some problems. Foremost, there was the fact of the added expense for architects' commissions. Lind had concluded his commentary on American architecture with a succinct statement of the fundamental matter at hand: "It has been too much the custom for clients to consult with carpenters instead of the regular practitioner, for the sake of saving the commission."[16] The architects' claim for the prerogative to design the nation's buildings not only challenged familiar routine in communities throughout the United States, but it faced economic constraints of a boom and bust economy. Although building continued through the economic fluctuations of the 1870s, many carpenters were unemployed. The building market was highly competitive, and arguments for paying additional architectural fees needed to be convincing. From the "professional" architects' perspective, self-proclaimed architects who sold books of "ill-conceived designs" also enabled the public to avoid paying commissions. Further, the practice encouraged by these books denigrated the profession. Such buildings were constructed without supervision, and the sorry results reflected on architects as a whole.[17]

Using these arguments, the professional architects attempted to cultivate a following and ensure that prospective as well as previous clients would not be tempted to hire their competitors who were not professional architects. Once again, the strength of the architects' case depended greatly upon a collective effort. The American Institute of Architects was a small organization with a fledgling journal and it was necessary to exhibit a unified commitment among growing numbers of architects as well as external approval by respected authorities in the field. If the new professionals were to serve as experts in architectural affairs, it was necessary to gain the confidence of the public as well as the building trades. Generally understood signs of legitimacy were needed to persuade the public that the architects' claim for authority was not only moral but publicly legitimate. One salient strategy was to declare kinship with famous architects from abroad who were known to the "cultivated classes." When Henry Van Brunt reviewed the Institute's membership in his address, he proudly informed his audience that there were 30 to 40 honorary members from abroad. Among them were such renowned architects from France and England as Eugène Emmanuel Viollet-le-Duc, Gilbert Scott, William Burges, G. E. Street, and James Wyatt.[18] For the convention audience, sharing an organization with these practitioners who were already accepted as authorities, even luminaries, held significant prestige value. The *American Architect,* too, needed the sanction of higher authority and frequently included essays from foreign architectural journals, suggesting common aims.

But in the fervor of nationalism brought by the centennial year, American models were implemented to help validate the architects' case for professionalization. Because they were embarking on a public program to elevate national architecture and American identity, comparative examples which were more relevant and adaptable than foreign models were necessary to their quest. American professionals outside of architecture were found to fill that role. Comparisons between the architectural and the medical and legal professions were standard in the journal, as well as in other architectural literature. Lawyers were brought forward as voices of authority who facilitated moral and ethical judgements. Indeed, when Henry Van Brunt reported that court decisions had upheld schedules of charges for architects, he was also reporting the legal profession's approval of the architectural profession. Doctors and their unprofessional counterparts, the "quacks," provided an especially colorful, and perhaps more readily grasped, comparison. Doctors were perceived as "progressive," a most praiseworthy nineteenth-century distinction, because they exchanged new information that would advance their mutual work.[19] The nation's qualified doctors shared a growing, unified body of esoteric knowledge. Medical doctors provided their patients with an expertise gained from long experience and study, just as architects held the secrets to artistic and scientifically sound building design. The comparisons implied that both the doctor and the architect selflessly entered their professions with an intent to help others. Both professions also were plagued with pretenders. Quacks who practiced sham medicine and hawked their miracle elixirs were well known. From the architects' standpoint, now the public must be aware that, similarly, there were "empirics" in architecture who turned out sham buildings that did not embody the mind of the architect.[20]

Architects attempted to legitimize their activities by association with those who had already gained some vestige of professionalism in the United States. They targeted criteria that publicly identified their counterparts as professional, then applied them to architecture.

Among the recurring themes through the early years of the journal was the matter of remuneration—money equaling value. In a society that equated the amount of earnings with ability and prestige, a higher level of income helped to project the architect's professional standing. The journal architects argued that consistent and appropriate fees were a publicly recognized mark of professional, thus proper, work and were beneficial to both architects and their clients. Young architects and unemployed architects in acute need of work notwithstanding, charging less than the current rates nullified one of the client's "strongest guarantees for honorable practice" because "diminished fees mean diminished service, if nothing worse."[21] The journal articles argued for standardization of architects' fees, especially since it was generally agreed among architects themselves that they were not sufficiently paid for their services in the first place.[22] However, agreement on fee schedules required more negotiation, for determining charges on a qualitative rather than quantitative basis was difficult. Many argued for consistent fees, and a charge of five percent of construction costs as recommended by the American Institute of Architects, the journal's sponsoring organization, was largely accepted. Although there were some arguments that young architects should not charge as much as those who were more experienced and that some jobs required more supervision than others, there was a consensus. Above all, maintaining a standard for sufficient fees for architectural services identified unanimity among a group of professionals.

But in light of the architect's occupation as "missionary work," the issue of remuneration was presented in the journal as moral more than pecuniary. In this way, the public could be assured that they were the actual beneficiaries when they paid the higher fees commanded by professional architects. Not least significantly, professionals were characterized as members of the building trades who accepted it as their duty to be honest. Too many builders and contractors accepted kickbacks and too many unqualified architects underbid jobs, whereas the professional architect, implied as a model of moral rectitude, did not succumb to these temptations. He was distinguished by his good business practices. From the inception of a project, he was responsible for making reliable cost estimates, and he hired qualified laborers or contractors to complete the agreed-upon construction. Befitting his position of authority, the professional architect supervised all stages of planning and construction even while it was a most disagreeable task. In short, by hiring a professional architect, the client was ensured his/her money's worth, a point clarified in the *American Architect* when contrasts were posed with unscrupulous would-be architects and mechanics in the trade. One published correspondent went so far as to claim that about one-half of the carpenters and masons in his community were irresponsible and required his supervision.[23] From the journal's perspective, both safety and aesthetics were at risk without the professional's intervention.

Dishonesty and errors resulting from the ignorance of carpenters, builders, and contractors were suggested frequently enough to establish a clear distinction between carpenters and architects, but journal criticism paid more attention to clarifying the subtle differentiation between architects and non-professionals who called themselves architects but did not accept the formulated obligations of the title.[24] Pattern books were again a target. Cost estimates in these pattern books were suggested as too often misleading, with figures frequently lower than actual building costs would be. And A. F. Oakey warned that architects who sold their drawings permitted contractors to take advantage of the client by using inferior materials and workmanship.[25] In other words, fees paid the architect were offset by monies saved because of the architect's expertise and character.

The professional's client

The efforts by American architects to secure relevance for professional status at this time did not mark an entirely new course. A quest for differentiation between knowledgeable arbiters of taste who set the standards for American building and those who followed their lead was widespread in building journals and books from early in the nineteenth century.[26] But by the last quarter of the century, circumstances converged that brought an unprecedented potency to the enterprise. As Robert Bledstein has shown in his study of the late nineteenth century, Americans had "committed themselves to a culture of professionalism." The public began to rely on professional expertise and a remarkable number of professional schools and organizations emerged to fulfill the demand for experts. The discourse on the professional defined the expert as one who had the wisdom and education needed to meet complex modern-day problems, a task which was beyond the capability of ordinary citizens. From undertakers to university professors, and leading to today's "tree surgeon" and "sanitation engineer," classifying titles were adopted to distinguish those with superior expertise. Distinctions were made among the levels of subsidiary positions leading to the professional, and task specialization began to replace broadly based proficiency.[27]

The resultant proliferation of experts did not go unnoticed and was a frequent topic in satire. One *American Architect* contributor was prompted to suggest yet another to the American mix—instead of the myriad of experts now needed for home upkeep, one extraordinary specialist. In a rather tongue-in-cheek letter, the author united the medical and architectural professions to call for a "house physician" whom a homeowner could hire for life to handle all of the maintenance problems accompanying home ownership. With the house physician's services, such inevitable vexations as faulty heating, ventilation, plumbing, even insect infestation, would be corrected as they occurred. The new professional was presented in jest, but the author had an important point to make. The typical homeowner did not understand the complicated "contrivances" that served "a great variety of luxuries, comforts, conveniences, necessities" which were a product of modern life.[28] Homeowners faced swiftly changing technology as advances were made in the design of water closets, plumbing to eliminate the accumulation of sewer gases, heating systems, lighting, and appliances. The architect, who orchestrated their installation by drawing up specifications and contracting the labor, was presented as a necessary facilitator.

Contributors to the *American Architect* considered professional architects essential for solving the practical problems of building, but they recognized an equally pressing need for their services. The public were even more helpless when they confronted the complexities of artistic judgment in architecture. Deep-rooted feelings of American cultural inferiority were becoming acute as reviews of foreign arts at the Centennial Exhibition were published in a variety of popular journals, and improving standards in literature, music, and the arts was regarded as a national concern. Enlarging on that sensitivity, the architects argued that their clients did not have sufficiently refined taste and gravely needed their assistance. Alexander F. Oakey gave the matter a national cast in his article about relations between architects and their clients. He blamed the public's poor taste for much of the nation's unsatisfactory architecture. To fortify this generally agreed-upon point for his peers, he posed a contrast between painting and architecture in order to suggest that artistically designed architecture was more difficult to recognize. Anyone could have an opinion regarding whether or not an object in a painting was rendered with veracity, but for architecture, evaluation based on opinion was not acceptable. Architecture, like music, was not a representation of natural objects. Architecture was an "artificial art" that did not replicate nature. This made it more complex and necessitated specialized study. Essentially, he argued that architecture was one of the more esoteric arts because it was produced with a knowledge of the underlying principles of nature more than from a familiarity with the external guise of nature. Personal points of view were not valid judgments of buildings because architecture was a product of scientifically founded combinations of form and color. With an obvious slight toward popular taste, he lamented that just as people without musical training may neglect Beethoven's Seventh Symphony for tunes from the hand-organ, an architect's uneducated clients were unable to recognize tasteful architecture.[29]

The *American Architect* proposed that the American public needed education and it was the professional architect's duty to instruct them to recognize the differences between good and poorly conceived buildings and their builders. Architects had a responsibility, but in Oakey's view, architects could not assume to dictate taste. Their task was more subtle; by their works they could influence taste. Following prevalent convictions that architecture held the power to modify thought and behavior, he proposed that people who were surrounded by well-designed buildings would spontaneously acquire more refined judgment. Oakey admitted that anyone had the right to make a fool of himself, although he continued with a probing question for the client, "But does not a man inflict a lasting injury upon society when he builds a hideous structure, staring good taste out of countenance?"[30] Other members of the American Institute of Architects were more forceful as they maneuvered between the implications of dictating taste and guiding it. Henry Van Brunt told the 1875 convention audience, the American public must be taught how to "read" architecture.[31] He, and others following in the journal, urged members to take it upon themselves to educate clients as well as aspiring architects and others employed in the building trades. By bringing lectures, tracts, competitions, and exhibitions to the public and contributing carefully selected books to libraries, the professional architects' taste would soon predominate.

The professional's credentials

Amidst the enthusiasm, however, the task was challenging. The American Institute of Architects had existed for some twenty years, but, even within their own membership, American architects remained a disparate group with widely varied education, methods of practice, and compensation. Each local chapter was independent and member architects served functions particular to their respective communities. A balance between organizational unity and prerogative for individual architects to accommodate specific local concerns was essential. America was a nation with a belief in individualism, and the notion that personal initiative was fundamental to the structure of a democratic society had gained hegemonic currency. While solidarity was desired among architects, an attempt to impose too much conformity would alienate prospective members and readers. The organization was aware of arguments against their claims for authority and negotiated between their readers' and the public's perceptions of consensus and individualism, as well as between leadership and exclusionary control over architecture. While some architects spoke in favor of standardized qualifications, one went so far as to suggest that such formalization was analogous to "writing their own obituaries."[32]

Architects on both sides of the qualifications issue spoke against intimations that they were taking control to the exclusion of architects who may wish to enter their professional category. Henry Van Brunt assured his audience at the outset of his convention address that the A.I.A. worked to establish fee scales and systematize competitions, but the organization was no trade union. His reference to unions would not have been lost on his audience, for he spoke at a time of union growth. This was a matter addressed by the journal following the violence of nationwide strikes in 1877 and during the continued unrest in 1878. Early in 1878 an article which concluded with a linkage between public assistance and communism criticized those who were "out of work simply because they will not work for what wages are offered them."[33] The journal continued to introduce editorials against strikes and communism and convincing arguments that the American Institute of Architects bore no similarity with trade unions.[34] As a projection of their agenda to establish differentiation, it was suggested that some carpenters who faced worries about jobs and wages in this difficult time had begun to entertain political thoughts considered too closely allied with socialism.[35]

As strategies for professionalization developed in the *American Architect,* formal education to provide publicly recognized credentials became a prominent issue. Following the general understanding of an American professional in the hierarchy of the work force, professional architects did not sell specific products nor did they engage in physical labor. A profession was a level of occupation that required theoretical knowledge gained through education, and in the opinion of architects themselves, their fees were justified because they delivered benefits of their education and experience to the client. In the second of a six-part series of articles titled "Architectural Students," readers were informed, "The time is happily past, except in remote and uncultivated districts, where the ability to make a clean line-drawing and to frame a timber house, with the possession of a book of orders or of cheap designs, was thought to make an architect."[36]

Many of the nation's established architects had received training as apprentices in architectural studios, but institutional education was becoming a more highly favored point of distinction. Following Richard Morris Hunt, who in 1848 was the first American architect to begin study at the Ecole des Beaux-Arts, many aspirants traveled to Paris for formal study. In centennial-year America, architectural programs had been introduced at M.I.T., Cornell, and more recently at the University of Michigan.[37] And, hand in hand with emphasis on academic training, the body of information relevant to architecture expanded to make attainment of professional status more difficult. Acceptance into the architectural profession now required education in art theory, scientific theory, and applied scientific knowledge, as well as familiarity with practical building skills.

Conflict between the proponents of a scientific emphasis and the advocates of artistic priority in a field of study that integrated the two marked the last quarter of the century. But in the first years of the journal's publication, artistic training took precedence. The introductory article in the "Architectural Students" series flatteringly told the readers, ". . . success truly professional, not worldly, that is—requires a peculiar and rather a rare kind of mind." The author continued by acknowledging that an architect must be able to meet practical needs and know building construction, but he must, above all, be an artist. Without the instinct of the artist, he was merely a builder, not an architect. The author then turned to the familiar subject of architect's fees, noting that architects earned less than doctors, lawyers, businessmen, and, significantly, builders with business acumen. Adding to the impression that architecture was a calling more than a calculated choice of profession, he did not deny that an architect must be part businessman, for architecture required business transactions, but he again reminded the readers that art must be their priority. Building "substantially, conveniently, economically" was not enough. Those who did not practice as artists were not necessarily architects; nor were their buildings deserving of the designation "architecture."[38]

The number of pages allotted to the articles on architectural education is evidence of the subject's importance. Circumscribing educational requirements was a fundamental strategy in the process of professionalization, for it accomplished more than establishing professional qualifications to distinguish between qualified and unqualified persons. Education established a future for the authority of the profession by inculcating upon students the model of professional status. In this case, the author's emphasis imprinted America's future architecture with a mark of Beaux-Arts priorities. With support from numerous articles on illustration techniques in the journal, and using the French school as a model, the exposition on education suggested that training as an artist began with courses in drawing because an architect must be able to communicate visually the work of his mind. Developing mechanical drawing skills, as builders did, was necessary but was a mere rudimentary stage in the progress of an architect's education. Artistic drawing was an indispensable tool used to develop the architect's creative ideas, then the language to express his artistic conception.[39] When the perspective views and elevations of the architect's "creation" were rendered with color and placed before the public eye, educated artistic abilities afforded an impressive means by which the public could readily distinguish between professional and unqualified architects.

Artistic illustration brought an unambiguous separation between professionals and those being defined as non-professional, but in actual practice it was problematic. A relatively small number of architects met the requirements of such education. Too, building trade journals such as the *American Builder*, through their much broader circulation, testified to the importance of pragmatic concerns. The *American Architect* editorial staff elected to publish articles and correspondence that questioned their apparent de-emphasis of practical concerns. Earlier in the year, the author of a letter from Cleveland had argued for better practical knowledge among architects as a means to gain respect from the mechanics who worked for them. He envisioned a purpose for the existence of the *American Architect* that was closer to building journals than a professional journal. He foresaw it as a vehicle for exchanging technical information. From his point of view, rather than "talking Ruskin" and giving lay sermons on taste, architects should be able to understand such practical things as building materials.[40] The journal's insertion of arguments against theory in the midst of the larger narrative on professionalism shows that careful negotiation of their authority was warranted. Modification of the distinction was necessary as well. The author of the articles on education apparently deflected criticism mid-way through his series by clarifying his definition of the architect's creative faculties. Because architecture was a constructive art, he explained, an architect's artistic expression was not the same as a painter's creativity. An architect's imagination was not necessarily "poetic or inventive imagination"; rather, it was "clearness of conception." The architect who was trained in art had a greater ability to retrieve images from memory and recreate them in line, form, color, and shading.[41] Training in artistic drawing took on a more functional rationale with this disassociation from invention.

With some distance from the non-constructional arts but with further discussion of the need for art education, the journal continued to inscribe the difference between architects and mechanics. The proponents of education in drawing and artistic illustration suggested that it enabled one to develop an ability to remember the extensive variety of buildings from the history of architecture. By drawing the orders of ancient classical buildings, then adaptations of the orders to medieval buildings, the architect could gain an understanding of proportion, detail, and composition. Perhaps more important to a nation of undisciplined builders, these repeated exercises enabled the young architect to know which of the many architectural forms now in his vocabulary could be appropriately combined.[42] It was essential that an architect be able to distinguish between good and bad forms and, referring to the classical-medieval separation, to avoid "coarse, vulgar, or feeble forms" that were not in the categories of early Gothic or Greek.[43]

But knowledge of historic forms brought dangers of temptation as well. With the skepticism of established architects toward adventuresome youth, some feared that young architects were too "progressive" and lacked self-control.[44] Learning the broad variety of world architecture could lead to an undisciplined eclecticism which would carry forward, if not exacerbate, the current state of affairs. As noted above, while the new architectural freedom that allowed architects to extricate themselves from the strictures of designing in one narrowly defined style provided them with a means to adapt buildings to diverse populations, geographies, and functions, the profusion of historic models made discipline brought by education mandatory. From the perspective of the journal architects, education became more imperative as eclecticism became more prevalent. The author who was quoted above explained, "the details are picked up anywhere, ill-assorted, the carving incongruous, the mouldings mean and unstudied. . . . The temptations of eclecticism to neglect of serious study are as obvious as the tendencies of American desultoriness."[45] A later article asked, "As for expression of character, . . . vainglory, ostentation, restlessness, irreverence, haste, commercial unsoundness, and a general want of substance—are they not written on the fronts of a million of our buildings?"[46]

A professional's buildings

Criticism of America's own carpenter-built vernacular buildings was inevitable. Circumscribing boundaries for acceptable design was a process of establishing norms for architectural practice and education. As the number of publications designed for mass-market consumption increased dramatically in the late nineteenth century, carpenters, would-be architects, and their clients had ready access to illustrations of historic buildings and a broad range of contemporary architecture and architectural details. The American building public exploited this knowledge with an enthusiasm that the architects considered unfortunate, if not ruinous. Architecture was becoming too freely eclectic.

For the architects taking on the mantle of professionalism, America's propensity for indulgence was too readily visible. It was especially apparent in the new and growing communities which were, for the most part, outside of the purview of the architectural establishment. Chicago and the Pacific West were prime examples. A correspondent reported that architecture in Chicago after the fire of 1871displayed "rather an exuberance of ornament in many buildings, which is not in keeping with the objects for which they are intended." Amid the "cheap and showy buildings," however, the author found some good examples, especially Gambrill and Richardson's modern thirteenth-century French-style building for the American Express Company. Although the author did not belabor the point, Gambrill and Richardson, as Boston architects whose work was illustrated in the *American Architect*, represented a professional contrast. The contrast was even greater when juxtaposed with a vision of San Francisco, a city where "'gingerbread' architecture" was already popular. And with a striking prediction of the city's future devastation, he mused, "It is pleasant to think that in its western course it bids fair to be drowned in the Pacific, which may literally be the case some day; for our western rival may yet have an earthquake which will rival the

fame of our fire."[47] Although eclecticism was broadly accepted as
ineluctable in the progress of modern architecture, architects who were
defining the profession needed to restrain its application in order to
establish an authority that would be impossible if an "anything goes"
policy became prevalent. Taking a direction that would soon turn
toward a "scientific eclecticism," journal contributors spoke of a
need for methods to systematize the combining of different architectural forms.[48]

The concern, which would continue to the end of the century,
was fostered by a number of timely intersections that also affected
the early mutations in the discourse on professionalism: a growing
middle-class housing market, increased mass-media circulation of
designs, centennial nationalism, and the introduction of the new
Queen Anne and allied fashions from England. Each brought eclectic
design, plus house design, to the forefront of architectural concerns.
In the early years of the *American Architect* the process of professionalization encompassed negotiations which concerned ownership
over who should determine the norms of design for residential building. The editorial staff's selection of materials for publication suggests
some irresolution regarding the importance of domestic architecture
to their own professionalization, and reports and editorials on new
developments in housing design were limited in scope and number.[49]
However, essays on broader topics frequently introduced commentary about domestic architecture. Historic domestic architecture of the
United States was also of interest in feature articles, and in the
journal's early years, illustrations of new houses predominated. New
public and commercial buildings were illustrated less frequently.[50] As
noted, domestic architecture was given greater validity as a professional concern within the centennial-era search for symbols of national
identity and was argued to comprise an American vernacular.[51] With
eminent associations, the house was legitimized as one of the sites of
the architects' struggle to gain authority, not to mention economic
prestige, as professionals. But the architects' editorial position in relation to vernacular design, the form of building they so highly
criticized, also required negotiation.

The Queen Anne style and vernacular building

An analysis of the negotiations leading to the emergence of professionalization cannot be accomplished without examining the role played by the so-called Queen Anne style. When the *American Architect* was introduced, such up-and-coming American architects as Henry Hobson Richardson, Charles Follen McKim, and Alexander F. Oakey already were experimenting with Queen Anne, or free classic, formulations on eastern seaboard summer homes. Although this new difficult-to-define fashion was being adapted to buildings serving a variety of purposes in England, it was a mode of design which became more strongly associated with coziness and domesticity, qualities more appropriate to housing than to public or commercial buildings. In the United States, too, it took prominence as a housing fashion. The style's introduction was propitious. The writing of American architectural history sought beginnings, and with a small amount of manipulation, the name Queen Anne conjured images of an ancestry for modern American houses. That this style had ties to national history was important to a country celebrating a centenary of nationhood. Even while the modern fashion's name was agreed to be a misnomer and was typically amended as "so-called Queen Anne," the new buildings' antecedents were recognized to include architecture spanning the English queen's reign (1702–1714). Proponents of the new fashion argued that the original Queen Anne style, an early-eighteenth-century blend of classic and medieval architecture, was among the styles adapted to demands of the new land. As such, colonial-era Queen Anne was argued as a foundational component of American vernacular architecture, and following, modern Queen Anne was an inheritor of the original national characteristic of architectural adaptation to climate and geography more than modern gothic or the recently fashionable French roof house. As an eclectic integration of medieval and classical forms, with embellishments from numerous historical and contemporary sources, the freedom of design inherent to the so-called style continued to permit unlimited accommodation to site and function.

Arguments giving American historical legitimacy to Queen Anne were presented in the *American Architect* from 1876 to the end of the

decade and were generally accepted, but the contemporary consequences were not necessarily hailed by all. From the perspective of
the architectural establishment, Queen Anne's potential for manipulation, the trait that permitted the nation's architects to take ownership
of the fashion for the United States, constituted both its appeal and
its menace to American architecture. It was a fashion enthusiastically
embraced by younger architects, and with customary wisdom of age,
some members of the Boston chapter of the A.I.A. admonished the
new generation of architects for their lack of self-denial and discipline.[52] It was a fashion that allowed too much liberal interpretation,
and its applied decoration, an important component of the fashion,
was particularly problematic. Charles A. Cummings, secretary of the
Boston chapter of the A.I.A., left no doubts about his position when
he criticized modern Queen Anne's "puerility and feebleness of
ornamentation."[53] Earlier, the architectural critic Montgomery
Schuyler had pronounced the decorations applied to Queen Anne
buildings as the fashion's major flaw. Further, classical ornament on
buildings derived from medieval sources did not follow constructive
principles.[54]

Promotion of so-called Queen Anne seemed to imply an endorse-
ment of a more broadly inclusive form of eclecticism than many could
accept; yet, it was the latest fashion from England. The journal's
editorial staff responded with a monthly visual display of appropriate housing design that both mediated the issue and worked to
separate architect from mechanic. Illustrations of modern houses
showing changes in design conception, but not given precise stylistic
designation, were regularly published. Most of the designs were
characterized by a comparative simplicity and suggested that the
gingerbread found on the nation's provincial houses was, for the most
part, not a part of the new professionals' architectural vocabulary
(Fig. 39).[55] The illustrations were not explained with commentary
about the stylizations, but articles that were published concurrently
with the illustrations fostered worries that provincial builders who
lacked educated restraint in their work may be getting out of control.
Although the new fashion that sanctioned the broadened eclecticism
of intermingled medieval and classic had yet to reach most American carpenters in 1876, contributors to the journal lamented that the

advent of the scroll saw and "moulding machines" already had encouraged the "fancy carpenter" to have "his wicked will" with houses
in towns everywhere.[56] With gendered language firmly in place to
describe a loss of architectural purity, so-called Queen Anne, with its
"wriggling gables," soon became perceived as a fashion to fuel undisciplined imaginations.[57] In point of fact, by the end of the decade,
the fashion was enthusiastically expanded upon by carpenters, builders, pattern book authors, and their house-building clients. As the
architects being designated as non-professional began to enlarged the
definition of so-called Queen Anne's eclectic mode of design,

Fig. 39. The American Architect *published many designs in the new
fashion inspired by English Queen Anne. Robert Peabody, "House at
Medford, Mass." (*American Architect, *1877)*

architects who considered themselves the nation's professionals began to dissociate themselves from it and began to turn to other
colonial-inspired houses, including the shingle house, as more appropriate vernacular interpretations.

The professionals on vernacular building and pattern books

With connections made between colonial and such contemporary
houses, architects were compelled to deduce that the overly decorated
houses of the nation's carpenter-built towns and villages were emanations of vernacular design just as their own designs in the new
fashion were. But vernacular architecture as it had been developed
by the uneducated and their clients in the United States was not the
stuff of pride. A correspondent from New Haven, Connecticut, who
contributed one of the frequent reviews of local architecture, encapsulated the widespread professional attitude toward America's
housing with sharp humor. He did not directly critique New Haven's
houses in his article on the community's buildings. Instead, he admired the plant-filled baskets hanging from the house fronts. He was
most grateful for these displays because they drew attention from the
ubiquitous scroll-sawn and molded decorations. The author was dis-
mayed because he saw only one architect-designed house in the entire
community (although he admitted that he had not seen all of the
houses). He could, however, offer a note of encouragement. Happily,
plants could not be subjected to mistreatment by carpenters and their
machine tools![58]

Jig-saws (scroll saws) and lathes, planing mills and factories
made "coarse ornament" readily available to the American public and
the result was frequently criticized. The architectural establishment
frequently incriminated carpenters and their clients, but they granted
additional culpability to pattern books and their power to dissemi-
nate such architectural transgressions. The author of a lengthy article
on the history of American architecture in 1876 characterized the
books, their designs, and their users with words that unequivocally
established an otherness for propagators of the popular vernacular.
The "vulgarity" of American building was largely due to the "cheap

books of designs" available to carpenters and other "amateurs."[59] His implied censure of Andrew Jackson Downing's long-enduring pattern books was unusual in the *American Architect* but his pointed criticism of "cheap" pattern books was common to the journal's enterprise. Brief but harsh references to objectionable pattern books were often couched in articles on a variety of subjects related to professionalization. In essence, there were too many books of bad design whose use encouraged the uneducated to consider themselves architects.

By 1878, intersections among the issues of vernacular architecture, pattern books, and the new expanded eclecticism were becoming more pronounced. In September 1877 the first of a series of five articles titled "American Vernacular Architecture" was introduced. After an eight-month hiatus, the series was continued with regular installments. Each article was a review of a recently produced pattern book. Until that time, only a pattern book by Isaac Hobbs, whose house designs had been published in the highly popular *Godey's Lady's Book*, had been formally reviewed—and subsequently dismissed as "trash."[60] The journal's choice to examine vernacular architecture through reviews of pattern books was a subtle, yet vital, stratagem. It enabled them to modify a general interest subject to a more direct undertaking. While the titles of the essays suggested expositions on vernacular architecture, the subsequent reviews became a means to clarify those divisions within the building trades which were less straightforward than the simple distinction between the architect and mechanic. The books selected for review were by authors whose names had been brought to the public eye through previous publication. The books also represented traditional formats—educational, having an abundance of text, or visually informative, having pages of designs and little text. The *American Architect*'s selections were: two reviews of the initial and final segments of George F. Woodward's second volume of the *National Architect* (1877), Amos Jackson Bicknell, *Specimen Book of One Hundred Architectural Designs* (1878), Henry Hudson Holly, *Modern Dwellings* (1878), and Samuel B. Reed, *House Plans for Everybody* (1878). Each comprised a different aspect of pattern book practice which, in sequence, qualified degrees of difference among builders, pattern book authors, and architects who were working in the vernacular mode.

The first two articles on vernacular architecture examined portions of Woodward's book-in-progress, which the author had submitted to the journal. Woodward's book was reviewed with an admission that the widespread use of such books in the North and West rendered them important. In the reviewer's estimation, the *National Architect* was a praiseworthy undertaking, but praiseworthy only as a work of its type. He approved of the author's "mechanical execution," and the plans and elevations were of "the better sort of builders' work" found all over the country.[61] With Woodward's book now summarily separated into a lesser class of books, the reviewer developed the article as a medium to iterate distinctions between professional and unqualified practice. The popularity of pattern books notwithstanding, he patently assured his readers that Woodward's work was not in competition with work by architects. Nor was the book written for architects; it was to be used by builders for "inspiration." The type of architecture in Woodward's book was "machine architecture," a descriptive phrase most likely alluding to copyist mass production as well as balloon-frame construction, in contrast with traditional framing and wood crafting. An architect's work, on the other hand, was "art," produced by an architect who adjusted the building to the client's needs, adapted it to the site, and applied his knowledge of plumbing, heating, and ventilation. The review did not nullify Woodward's book but justified it for general use as a portrayal of "American vernacular architecture" and the "American style" of building with a "certain grammatical coherency."[62]

The architects who claimed professional status recognized that they could not eliminate the use of pattern books produced by those they considered unqualified. They could not wholly defy customs, nor current economics, that ensured the importance of carpenters and books of designs to the continuing development of America's domestic architecture. But they could attempt to circumscribe the appearance and cultural value of vernacular architecture produced in the books. As the articles on architectural education had done, the review of Woodward reserved the right of creative, yet disciplined, thought for professional architects. Builder-authors such as Woodward were cautioned against exercising "original thought" even while they were criticized for a lack of creativity. As the *American Architect* author explained, true vernacular, or "American," architecture meant restraint. If Woodward was to remain "truly national," he "must keep a vigorous curb upon his resources of imagination."[63] He, too, must participate in his appropriate sphere for the good of the nation.

A model example of an architect remaining "national," whose house designs were characterized by restraint, was offered in the third review. *Modern Dwellings*, by Henry Hudson Holly, another New York architect and one of the A.I.A.'s own, was produced in the traditional educational format and was introduced as a gauge for evaluating the other books in the series. The illustrations were described as a record of the nation's vernacular house architecture in somewhat similar terms as Woodward's book. But, in contrast with Woodward's designs, Holly's houses were defined as having constituted an unbroken line of change and adaptation from the past to the future. This assessment more closely aligned Holly's work with current architectural theory and desires for an appropriately formed national architecture. The reviewer judged Holly's designs for country homes as exemplars of contemporary vernacular design and, as such, they were a "safe point of departure for architectural development" (Fig. 40). Applying language of evolutionary adaptation and art, Holly's houses were also forwarded as contributions to the advancement of art in vernacular architecture. Of course, the fact that Holly had suggested so-called Queen Anne as the basis for contemporary development of an American vernacular could not be ignored. The reviewer noted Holly's revival of features of eighteenth-century Queen Anne and granted that this may have saved Holly from current design hazards. Holly had incorporated vernacular wood construction, verandas, extended eaves and "workmanlike roofs" with Georgian balustered porches, paneling, chimneys, even sunflowers (whose popularity as a motif was usually attributed to the "aesthetes" in England) to produce houses that were not English but American. With an affirmation from American history, the reviewer found them a "sublimated derivative from the Dutch or Yankee wooden farmhouse."[64]

Although faults were found in Holly's book, the reviewer's praise of the architect supported a rationale for publishing pattern

Fig. 40. The American Architect *published a series of pattern book reviews under the heading of "vernacular architecture." A book by A.I.A. member H. H. Holly, with the new fashion claimed as a new American vernacular, was praised. (House from Holly,* Modern Dwellings in Town and Country, *1878)*

books authored by professional architects at a time when their use-fulness could be questioned from many fronts.[65] Holly's book was supported as a contribution to professional practice because it assumed a reading public who would consult architects when they decided to build. *Modern Dwellings* was more than a book of designs; it was considered an educational tool to inform prospective clients about the architect's functions. Respected mid-century pattern books, such as those by Downing, presupposed a clientele who would hire a local builder to interpret the enclosed house designs, but in the process of professionalization, pattern books by professional architects needed adjustment to their newly defined clientele. The *American Architect* recognized that it could not prohibit the public from freely interpreting published and built designs. But the public's enlighten-ment to their need of architects to bring the nation proper design was a crucial component in their program. Pattern books written by pro-fessional architects, already an accepted medium, were a contribution to the public's education.

Holly's houses were granted an originality due a professional's work, but A. J. Bicknell's houses were vilified. Bicknell compiled and published designs by other architects in a book called by the reviewer "a disjointed and illiterate collection of wood-cuts mostly blurred by long usage" taken from other pattern books by "minds . . . working on the dead level." These designs, too, were emanations of the ver-nacular and were expressions of national architecture, for they, too, had developed from adaptations to American material and climatic conditions. But it was a vernacular that had been "developed by untrained hands into painful absurdities and exaggerations" involv-ing bracketed cornices, "bastard" French roofs, finials, crestings, compound gables, dormers, towers, architraves over windows of varied shapes—an array he found unique to America (Fig. 41). The author clearly feared the incursion of free-rein eclecticism. With ech-oes of nationalism, he encouraged architects to avoid foreign elements which were not fitting for American building and develop a national heritage which would influence builders. Once again, self-discipline, the positive element in American character, was extended as a rem-edy. With an interesting blend of the current language of sexuality and moral restraint to accompany the gender distinctions made with regard to highly decorated buildings, it was argued that architects must take responsibility, for it was their duty to practice self-denial in order to "correct this national exuberance of fancy" and mold "vernacular architecture into shapes consistent with the higher civilization."[66]

Following the review of this insupportable type of pattern book, the articles on vernacular architecture turned again to a pattern book which could be used as a source for ideas, as well as a modicum of education, by the public and their carpenters. The final selection was a book of rural houses presented by Samuel Burrage Reed whose designs had been published regularly in the *American Agriculturalist*. Reed's designs were examples of carpenter's architecture, but they

Fig. 41. The designs in A. J. Bicknell's compilation were described as "painful absurdities and exaggerations." The reviewer urged pattern book authors and local carpenters to practice self-denial to "correct this national exuberance of fancy." (House from Bicknell, Specimen Book of One Hundred Architectural Designs, *1878)*

were ranked higher in the scheme of hierarchy developed under professionalization. His designs were "crude," "illiterate," and "vulgar," but they were at the same time the roots to "pure language." According to the reviewer, who also classified their future inhabitants, they were for the most part simple, practical designs for "frugal country people." In other words, the house designs were appropriate to the class of people for whom they were intended (Fig. 42).

DESIGN I.

Fig. 1.—EXTERIOR OF COTTAGE.

A COTTAGE, COSTING $250.

Fig. 42. Reed's designs were "crude," "illiterate," and "vulgar," but their simplicity was appropriate for "frugal country people." The reviewer took this opportunity to argue against machine-made decoration. (House from Reed, House Plans for Everybody, *1878)*

The common sense exhibited in them made them valuable to carpenters as well as to architects who wanted to learn about "cheap architecture" and the historical foundations of rural or suburban architecture. Again, elaboration was targeted. Although Reed had taken advantage of machine-produced details, the reviewer considered his houses better because he had introduced fewer "wild jig-sawed brackets, gingerbread eavesboards, gorgeous but cheap dormers, bastard mansards, top-lofty finials and other peculiarities of our more ambitious vernacular. . . ."[67]

The *American Architect* was not the only journal to review these pattern books. Charles Lakey's *American Builder* regularly reviewed pattern books and served as a vender for them. The *American Builder* was published in New York and presupposed an audience who would benefit from reports from other periodicals. Reviews, excerpts, and condensations of articles from *Scribner's, Harper's,* and *Atlantic Monthly* accompanied news from English building journals and articles on building technology. Illustrations of houses by a variety of architects were an important feature, as they were in the *American Architect*. That the journal favored the use of pattern books in general was made clear. Charles Lakey's goal was to make the *American Builder* a "pattern magazine."[68] In fact, in 1875 he compiled designs from the journal in a book titled, *Lakey's Village and Country Houses, or Cheap Homes for all Classes*. The stated purpose of the book was to provide prospective home builders with a variety of ideas to inspire them more than with designs to copy.[69] Although the *American Builder* was forwarded with the authority of an educational enterprise, as was the professional journal, it was directed to a broader audience, the "hundreds of thousands who are practically engaged in building operations."[70]

The *American Architect*, too, claimed to be a journal for builders and carpenters, but it worked more coherently to marginalize them in the quest for professional status for architects. This difference between the journals notwithstanding, the editorial position of the two journals coincided in their estimations of books by Isaac Hobbs and Henry Hudson Holly. The *American Builder* surpassed the other in criticism of *Hobbs's Architecture*. The designs were not drawn well, and worse, the author was guilty of "insufferable egotism" and of being a "charlatan under the masque of the architect." The houses were "clap-trap" and "sensationalism."[71] What provoked such sharp criticism of a book by an architect who evidently had a successful practice and whose work was popularly known? It is not unlikely that the publication of Hobbs' house designs in the immensely popular *Godey's Lady's Book* brought some derision, but it is also possible that it was not the mere fact of that feminine audience. Rather, Hobbs and Sons appear to have crossed boundaries of propriety. Both journal reviews refer to the editorial pretentiousness of the pattern book, evidently seen as a claim for status that was not deemed appropriate by their colleagues nor was evidenced by their clientele.

Agreeing in praise for a book, Charles Lakey strongly recommended Holly's *Modern Dwellings* to his readers, saying that "a most valuable feature of this work is the number of plans for small but cozy houses. . . ." What most appealed to the reviewer, though, was Holly's use of the "so-called Queen Ann [*sic*] style." Following a synopsis of the historical antecedents of the new fashion, he concluded, "The author has attempted, and in our opinion succeeded, in adapting this style of building to the wants of the American citizen. . . ." For the readers of the building journal, excerpts from Holly's book defined the new fashion as simple, honest, expressive of domestic needs, and "conserving truth far more effectually than can be done with the Gothic."[72] Lakey was clearly a fan of the Queen Anne fashion and it was noted frequently. The readers, too, had been given news of work by Holly. His Hamlin Mansion in Orange, New Jersey, was both "genuine revived Queen Anne" and "modern art."[73]

Some divergence in opinion appeared in the review of Reed's 1878 pattern book, although the *American Architect* did offer favorable commentary, albeit half-hearted. The *American Builder* reviewer was most impressed with the practical tenor of the designs and editorial content. The designs were easy to interpret and Reed had provided information for making material cost estimates. The houses could be built without incurring extra costs for the owners and the contractors would still be paid their usual fees. But rather than judging the designs as "crude," he found aspects to praise. For example, the house on page fifty-five was described as "a neat and very comfortable house" (Fig. 43). A practical approach to housing design inevitably brought favorable commentary in the journal, and was the

Fig. 43. In contrast, American Builder reviews praised both Bicknell's and Reed's books. The reviewer noted Reed's Des. X, a "neat and comfortable house" in the Italian fashion. (Reed, House Plans for Everybody, *1878)*

basis for a clear departure in the *American Builder* review of Bicknell's *Specimen Book*. The reviewer found the one-dollar book "neatly bound . . . a compilation of designs from various published works . . . of great practical value to those contemplating building or remodelling, and its low price places it within the reach of everyone."[74] In the editorial estimation of the journal for professionals, designs in Bicknell's book epitomized the unleashed creativity of ill-informed eclecticism. This criticism was not brought forward in the journal for builders. From earlier articles in the *American Builder*, we find that Lakey encouraged freedom to experiment with design for the larger public, especially for local carpenters whom he credited with building one-half of the nation's country homes. Because prospective rural and small-town late-nineteenths did not customarily consult with architects, the condition of domestic architecture in the United States was improved ". . . by placing in the hands of the country carpenter designs which, if not always of the highest order of merit, in an artistic point of view, have nevertheless, set him thinking, and led him to aspire after something beyond the dull monotony to which his eye had become accustomed."[75]

The *American Architect* and the *American Builder* agreed that local builders and carpenters needed practical and artistic guidance, but the latter allowed for their creative interpretation of architectural forms and decoration. Nonetheless, pattern book and new building reviews in the *American Builder* also demonstrated parameters. Decoration for decoration's sake was unacceptable.[76] Models for good design were established with illustrations of new buildings and with lengthier book reviews. Holly's book with so-called Queen Anne houses received much more attention than Bicknell's and Reed's books, and reviews of the Palliser brothers' *American Cottage Homes* was positively adulatory. Common features of the admired homes were their association with the picturesque and their appearance of greater restraint in the use of decoration. The exterior silhouettes of the homes were picturesque—the Pallisers' roof configurations, much like Holly's, were remarked upon—and the interior planning made possible by picturesque massing responded to the needs of their occupants. They were developments from the new English fashion. Queen Anne was the latest style of consequence to be brought across the Atlantic Ocean and was being turned over rapidly to popular consumption and, of course, manipulation. As the houses became quintessentially "modern" and "suburban" in mind and practice, pattern book authors, local carpenters, and their clients continued to expand upon them. As they did so, many architects claiming professional status correspondingly separated their collective professional identity from this genre of residential design.

NOTES

[1] The most thorough study of the *American Architect and Building News* to date is Mary Woods, *The "American Architect and Building News" 1876-1907*, diss., Columbia University, 1983. As she points out, with few exceptions the *American Architect* published works by East Coast architects. It wasn't until the 1880s that midwestern architects were better represented, and even then, visual presentations of their work were limited. Nonetheless, the editors of the journal claimed their national status as a periodical. See, Woods, pp. 245–57.

[2] Henry Van Brunt, "Opening Address before the American Institute of Architects (November 17, 1875)," *American Architect* 1(January 29, 1876): 34–36.

[3] "The Qualifying of Architects.-II.," *American Architect* 3(April 27, 1878): 143.

[4] Mary Woods also reveals the editors' contradictory claims that they were reporting current architectural conditions rather than attempting to direct them. Woods, pp. 219–20.

[5] Oakey, "Architect and Client," p. 278.

[6] A. J. Bloor, "Annual Address: Tenth Annual Convention of the American Institute of Architects, held at Philadelphia, Penn., Oct. 11 and 12, 1876," *American Architect* 1(March 24, 1877), Supplement, p. ii.

[7] "Report of Meetings. The Baltimore Chapter," *American Architect* 1(February 19, 1876): 63.

[8] Bloor, "Annual Address,", p. i.

[9] "American Architecture.-Past," *American Architect* 1(July 29, 1876): 243.

[10] "Archaeology and American Architecture," *American Architect* 4(October 5, 1878): 115. The term "vernacular" was used frequently by contributors to the journal. Although it was applied to criticisms of buildings designed by local builders and carpenters, vernacular also more generally referred to the particularly American character found in the unpretentious houses built by the American public from the earliest colonial days to the present.

[11] Van Brunt, "Opening Address," p. 36.

[12] Bloor, "Annual Address," p. xiv.

[13] "The Need of Unity," *American Architect* 1(January 1, 1876): 2 and 3.

[14] "An Apt Reply," *American Architect* 1(August 12, 1876): 264.

15 See, for example, "The Workman Again," *American Architect* 1(February 12, 1876): 50–51.

16 "Report of Meetings," p. 63.

17 Ibid.; also A. F. Oakey, "Architect and Client," p. 276–77.

18 Van Brunt, "Opening Address," p. 34.

19 "The Need of Unity," p. 3.

20 "A Word with Clients.-I," *American Architect* 1(July 8, 1876): 223.

21 "Summary," *American Architect* 1(February 12, 1876): 50.

22 "Architectural Students.-I," *American Architect* 1(September 23, 1876): 307.

23 "Sub-contracts," *American Architect* 1(April 8, 1876): 120.

24 Definition of the term "builder" alternated between carpenter and contractor.

25 Oakey, "Architect and Client," p. 276. Oakey called supervision "onerous."

26 See Upton, "Pattern Books and Professionalism."

27 Robert Bledstein, *The Culture of Professionalism: The Middle Class and the Development of Higher Education in America* (New York: W. W. Norton and Company, 1976). See especially his chapter, "The Culture of Professionalism."

28 "A New Profession," *American Architect* 1 (April 1, 1876): 109–10.

29 Oakey, "Architect and Client," p. 277; these passages were incorporated into his 1881 book.

30 Ibid., p. 278.

31 Van Brunt, "Opening Address," p. 35.

32 "The Qualifying of Architects," *American Architect* 3(April 20, 1878): 135.

33 *American Architect* 3(January 26, 1878): 26.

34 *American Architect* 3(January 26, 1878): 25–26 and (April 20, 1878): 134. "The Qualifying of Architects," p. 135 and "The Qualifying of Architects. II," p. 142.

35 "The Workman Again," pp. 50–51.

36 "Architectural Students.-II," *American Architect* 1(September 30, 1876): 315.

37 The University of Michigan program was announced August 12, 1876, p. 258.

38 "Architectural Students.-I," pp. 307 and 315. Henry Van Brunt offered similar sentiments in his "Opening Address," p. 36.

39 "Architectural Students.-IV," *American Architect* 1(November 11, 1876): 362–63.

40 "The Necessity of Individual Research," *American Architect* 1(April 8, 1876): 119–20.

41 "Architectural Students.-III," *American Architect* 1(October 17, 1876): 323.

42 "Architectural Students.-IV," p. 362 and "Architectural Students.-V," *American Architect* 1(November 18, 1876): 370–73.

43 "Architectural Students.-V," p. 370.

44 Ibid.

45 "Eclecticism in Architecture," p. 19.

46 "American Architecture—with Precedent and without," *American Architect* 3(October 26, 1878): 139.

47 "Correspondence," *American Architect* 1(April 1, 1876): 110.

48 See also Richard Guy Wilson, "'The Decoration of Houses' and Scientific Eclecticism," *Nineteenth Century* 8, no. 3/4(1982): 193–204.

49 Gwendolyn Wright's chapter, "Populist Visions," in *Moralism and the Model Home: Domestic Architecture and Cultural Conflict in Chicago 1873–1913* (Chicago: University of Chicago Press, 1982), is a seminal discussion of this matter.

50 Mary Woods' review of illustrations shows that "country and suburban houses" predominated for the first thirty-one years of the periodical. Woods, p. 223.

51 This argument was carried into the next decade by architectural critics in popular periodicals. See Van Rensselaer, 1886, Price, 1890.

52 Bloor, "Annual Address," p. x.

53 "American Institute of Architects, Boston Chapter," *American Architect* 2(February 17, 1877): 53–54.

54 S. (Montgomery Schuyler), "Concerning Queen Anne," *American Architect* 1(December 16, 1876): 404.

55 An example is Peabody and Stearns, "House at Medford, Mass.," *American Architect* 2(February 17, 1877), n.p. This is not to mean that all prominent architects eschewed elaborate decoration. Frank Furness, who trained in R. M. Hunt's studio, took full advantage of the current eclecticism his work. One of his more well-known projects was the Pennsylvania Academy of Fine Arts, Philadelphia, completed in 1876.

56 "Building in New Haven," *American Architect* 1(November 25, 1876): 380.

57 "American Institute of Architects. Boston Chapter," February 17, 1877, p. 54.

58 "Building in New Haven," p. 381.

59 "American Architecture.-Past," p. 243.

60 "New Books," *American Architect* 1(September 16, 1876): 303. A review of Isaac R. Hobbs & Son, *Hobbs's Architecture*, 2nd ed. rev. and enl., (Philadelphia: J. B. Lippincott & Co., 1876). His houses in *Godey's* often were built designs, and through the years they included homes in Indiana, West Virginia, Pennsylvania, Missouri, Virginia, Ohio, New York, Connecticut, New Jersey, Illinois, and in 1880, Texas. In Mary Culbertson, comp., *American House Designs: An Index to Popular and Trade Periodicals, 1850–1915* (Westport: Greenwood Press, 1994).

61 "American Vernacular Architecture," *American Architect* 2(September 1, 1877): 280.

62 "American Vernacular Architecture," p. 280.

63 "American Vernacular Architecture. II," *American Architect* 3(May 25, 1878): 182.

64 "American Vernacular Architecture. III," *American Architect* 3(June 8, 1878): 198–99.

65 The journal also published criticisms of Holly's book in an anonymous letter to the editor who did not consider Holly's designs original in any sense. See "Mr. Holly's Modern Dwellings," *American Architect* 3(June 15, 1878): 212.

66 "American Vernacular Architecture. IV," *American Architect* 4(July 4, 1878): 5. Interestingly, Bicknell's *Cottage and Villa Architecture*, 1878, contained designs by A. J. Bloor, Richard Upjohn and other architects associated with the A.I.A. He also inserted a full-page copy of the Institute's schedule of charges.

67 "American Vernacular Architecture. V," *American Architect* 4(September 21, 1878): 101.

68 "Publisher's Circular," *American Builder* 12(December 1876): 283.

69 Charles Lakey, *Lakey's Village and Country Houses* (New York: American Builder Publishing Co., 1875), n.p.

70 "Publisher's Circular," p. 283.

71 "New Publications," *American Builder* 12(August 1876): 192–93.

72 "New Publications," *American Builder* 14 (July 1878): 162.

73 "Important New Buildings," *American Builder* 14(April 1878): 92.

74 "New Publications," *American Builder* 15(March 1879): 59. The *California Architect and Building News* praised Bicknell's publication, too, in recognition of the numbers of carpenter builders working in California. Immediately following, however, the editorial position was directed more toward concerns for professional architects.

75 "Country Building," *American Builder* 12(January 1876): 7–8.

76 A review of a Palliser cottage praised it as a brick building without "gewgaw and gingerbread work . . . stuck on for mere ornamentation." "Plate 37. Handsome Brick Cottage," *American Builder* 15(October 1879): 232.

⊿ 6 ⊾

Defining the Modern House: Seeds of Disagreement, 1876-1881

Although many types and styles of houses may fulfill needs for cultural and individual self-identity at any moment in time, frequently
a design genre will emerge as the fashion of the moment and it will
serve more actively as a nexus of material reality and beliefs. Typically, it is ready for popular consumption as the most recent "modern"
home. At the beginning of the last quarter of the nineteenth century,
when images of national character were being sought and home
ownership was being promoted, the public chose from a wide variety of house styles. Gothic revival homes had been extremely popular,
with meanings of the moral home, picturesque nature, and high fashion brought together in a variety of interpretations. Although not fully
supplanting the gothic, French mansard-roof houses were in the 1860s
and 1870s popular statements of up-to-date housing design. Italian
fashions for villas and cottages had been introduced earlier in the
century and were later transformed into a more elaborated wood
Italianate rendition that extended its popularity. Each of these styles
retained some currency in community building through the end of
the century. Plus, an "Eastlake" fashion, derived from the writings
and furniture designs of Charles Locke Eastlake, had emerged shortly
after the Civil War to join "stick" and other stylizations that were
among the public's selections (Fig. 44). "So-called Queen Anne" had
its public debut at the time of the centennial, but the fashion already
was being cultivated by architects in Boston, New York, and other
East Coast cities, and was soon to be taken up by other designers of
homes and their clients. Within a decade, Queen Anne connoted a
genre of design that was quintessentially middle class: suburban,
modern yet with old-fashioned comfort, a secure haven for the nuclear

family and an excellent choice for a display of status and participation in the ideology of social mobility.

Houses were called "Queen Anne" in the late nineteenth century, and use of the name continues today. Nevertheless, the housing fashion that developed as a model for late-century suburban homes cannot be explained as a seamless development of the Queen Anne style. From its first application in the United States, it was a loosely used style and name. The most significant aspect of its introduction was its physical affirmation of an eclecticism that in many ways was already in practice. It did not offer a complete shift, but provided a highly versatile grouping of architectural features that could be adapted to and merged with current styles. When this new fashion was introduced, homeowners, local carpenters, and some pattern book authors were freely interpreting old and new fashions, even

Fig. 44. An "Eastlake" house. (Smith & Robinson, Art in House Building, *1890)*

intermingling the architectural vocabulary of the classic and medieval. And as remarked upon by nineteenth-century critics of American domestic architecture, exterior applied decoration was already abundant. Overall, those who built houses in this new fashion were genuinely interested in what it had to offer, but they did not copy slavishly. Whether in massing or decoration alone, so-called Queen Anne was adapted to existing housing design. It was used as an impetus for expanding the vocabulary of architectural forms suitable for picturesque suburban homes.

What resulted was not so much a popular style as a prevailing mode of design—a *modus operandi* for designing contemporary houses. This mode of design was most notable for its absence of specific style as well as its cross application to existing fashions, for example the wood-frame Italianate and Eastlake houses. At the same time, certain features of suburban homes were repeated across the country. The exteriors were an inventive interplay of features and a type of picturesque silhouette that, from this nineteenth-century perspective, permitted a natural adaptation of house and plan to site and function. With nature foremost in notions of national character—and with developments in paint manufacture that expanded the variety of colors available for house paint—these modern houses were painted in a rich palette of colors, allowing not only an artistic prerogative but encompassing a basis for national style. The range of manipulation was great, for the new fashion legitimized the penchant for eclectic design. Housing fashion now was officially removed from the limiting moral sanctions of design implied within the gothic. The new direction also permitted a complex massing of exterior shapes that was made difficult, even theoretically inappropriate, in the French roof and Italianate houses. By the 1880s, a general schema evolved into a picturesque, vertical-silhouetted home with bays, dormers, and chimneys. Working with its signifying features was a means for home builders and owners to communicate their being up-to-date, while its possibilities for creative manipulation insured that individuality could be communicated.

But architects who argued for professional credentials were concerned about uncontrolled eclecticism and elaboration. As colorfully painted houses having complex plans and silhouettes were popularized in pattern books from the 1870s to the end of the century, architects allying themselves with the professionals countered the trend with arguments for simplicity. Just what American houses should look like and who should cultivate the frontiers of American taste was contested territory. Members of the American Institute of Architects put themselves forward as cultural authorities, but they, too, debated the course of modern domestic architecture even as they delimited the range of its interpretation. Pattern book authors, some of whom pushed the limits of eclecticism, also presented themselves as leaders. Chapters six and seven will examine the textual and visual negotiations among the discussants indicating the range of their positions. As the self-defined professional architects attempted to structure a polarity, they and non-conforming pattern book authors made use of the nationally shared configurations of American identity to legitimize their claims. But interpretations included colonial shingle-clad homes as well as indescribable celebrations of decorated eclectic design.

Queen Anne introduction

The new Queen Anne architecture was not completely unknown to centennial-year America. Architects who read the English professional architectural journals had seen illustrations of these buildings by the leaders of contemporary English architecture since 1871. Examples of "Queen Anne" began to be noted in the journals in 1872, and in 1873 London's *Building News*, which was read in the United States, reviewed the Royal Academy exhibit of new buildings that were known as "Queen Anne" and continued to publish articles, including some vitriolic criticisms, on the subject. Among the group of American East Coast architects who adapted the information to their own work in the early 1870s were Henry Hobson Richardson, his draftsman, Charles Follen McKim, and William Rutherford Mead, an architect who joined McKim in practice in 1872. Richardson and McKim interpreted work by Norman Shaw, a leader in the development of English Queen Anne, as early as 1872, by translating Shaw's application of tile to the upper stories of his brick houses into shingle superimposed over wood siding. The upper stories of Richardson's William Watts

Sherman house, built in the wealthy summer community of Newport, Rhode Island (1874), were clad in shingles and its large interior hall and overall spatial planning were modeled on Norman Shaw's work (Fig. 45). Some of the early designs were published. One by Mead of a board and shingle hotel at Cayuga Lake, New York, was published in the *New York Sketch Book* in April 1875.[1] And for the builders and contractors of the nation in 1875, the *American Builder* published elevations and plans for the English architect J. M. Brydon's houses at Spring Bank, Haverstock Hill (near Hampstead Heath), that had been published in the London *Building News* (Fig. 46).[2]

When the *American Architect* began publication in 1876, features drawn from modern British buildings were incorporated into many of the designs by the American architects. For the next decade, freely interpreted applications of the fashion appeared regularly in the journal's weekly issues, although they were not identified as such. Reportage of the so-called Queen Anne also was brought into a broader public realm in the years leading to the centennial. English designer Charles Locke Eastlake previously had brought attention to modern yet antiquarian trends for furniture and interior decoration in his *Hints on Household Taste* (1868). New fashions in interior decoration inspired by England's Elizabethan, Jacobean, and eighteenth-century Queen Anne history were introduced by *Scribner's Magazine* in a series of eleven articles titled "Beds and Tables, Stools and Candlesticks" by Clarence Cook. Published from June 1875 to May 1877, Cook's articles were later compiled as *The House Beautiful*.[3] Queen Anne furniture at the Centennial Exhibition was described by both the popular and professional press throughout 1876, as were Britain's buildings at the Centennial. Although the buildings were not in the recognized Queen Anne style, their half-timbered exteriors were drawn from the important "old English" component of Queen Anne (Fig. 47). In May 1876, *Harper's* introduced Henry Hudson Holly's interpretation of the latest British architectural fashion in the first of a series of articles titled, "Modern Dwellings: Their Construction, Decoration and Furniture." Holly proposed to the readers of that popular periodical a new model for American domestic architecture and interior decoration known as "Queen Anne," or "Free Classic."[4]

Fig. 45a. Exterior. H. H. Richardson, William Watts Sherman house, 1874, Newport Rhode Island. (Newport Historical Society, P946)

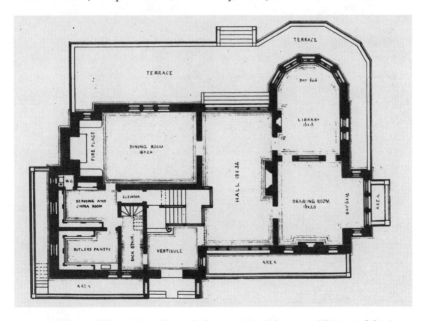

Fig. 45b. Plan. William Watts Sherman house, 1874. (Newport Historical Society, C-70 detail)

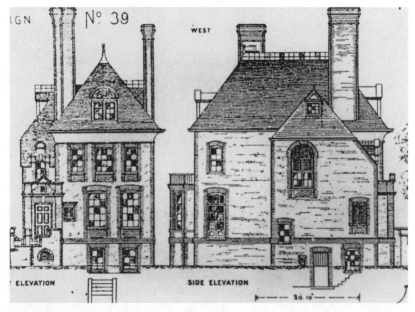

Fig. 46. J. M. Brydon design, Spring Bank, Haverstock Hill, England. (American Builder *1875*)

Fig. 47. British Buildings, Centennial Exhibition, Philadelphia, 1876. (McCabe, History of the United States, *1877*)

There can be no question that Holly's series of articles was timely. The Centennial, especially, exposed a keen awareness of America's inferiority in the arts. The Exhibition put the nation in the international spotlight, and while American industrial accomplishments were readily apparent, artistic accomplishments were not. Professionals and non-professionals alike aspired to be informed and looked to reports from abroad for the new fashions. Visitors to the event thronged the British Government displays, where they saw rooms resplendent with domestic accouterments from the craft and artwork of what would become known in 1882 as the "Aesthetic Movement." This latest fashion was modern, but all appeared to be overflowing with old-fashioned comfort and domesticity, which was a blending of old and new to be repeated in pattern book houses.[5] While the arts from France and Germany were equally admired, the British exhibit was more poignantly consistent with the expanding American definition of home as a center of artistic education and a haven from the exigencies of contemporary events. Drawing from this moment, Holly's attempt to present a cohesive vision for an American domestic architecture encompassed social ideals as well as architectural concerns expressed by the American Institute of Architects. Holly's articles and subsequent book cannot be claimed as the source for the developing housing fashions of the late nineteenth century, but his works were known from coast to coast. Visual and textual references to Holly were frequent in pattern books, although without giving credit to Holly.

Holly's publications are important to our understanding of later debates and publications on middle-class housing because he drew together the current issues in housing design that would be developed in pattern books for the coming decades. His avowed purpose was to translate the subjects of contemporary architectural theory for an untrained audience, and his articles provided a synopsis of pertinent architectural issues, most particularly those related to the development of an American vernacular. Several of these issues have been introduced in previous chapters. The public's need for expertise in matters of house building was an underlying theme in Holly's book, and this theme became a selling point for most pattern book authors, whether they published books to advertise their services or to sell plans. Holly also dwelt, as did most pattern book authors, on the importance of site selection for the house. More than an aesthetic choice, knowledgeable site selection guaranteed good soil drainage, fresh breezes, and overall a more healthy home. Architects and pattern book authors also stressed the importance of a house plan that served the needs of a family. Plans were to be functional, meeting modern requirements.

One important symbolic component of Holly's designs was a large entry hall complete with an old-fashioned inglenook, the warm glow of a fireplace and an elegant staircase (Fig. 48). Often called a Queen Anne hall, this configuration was introduced with the fashions from England and was shown repeatedly in magazine articles, home decorating books, and pattern books. The hall, with special emphasis on the fireplace, was a symbol of family domesticity, a place where mother and children shared a moment of quiet. As with most symbols of American life, the fireplace was given practical value, too. Fireplaces no longer were primary heat sources, but they were explained to contribute to heating and to facilitate good air circulation. When placed in modern open-house plans, they functioned as "giant radiators" for surrounding rooms and drew fresh air to the center of the house.[6] The halls also made a public statement—of domesticity, coziness, and social status. Their decoration was a guest's first introduction to the family's taste. Because some houses were too small for such halls, Holly introduced other validating interpretations. One design had an enlarged hall that served both as a hall and a sitting room. It opened to adjoining rooms on the first floor and all were separated by folding doors that could open to permit free movement and unimpeded views from one room to the next (Fig. 49).[7] In subsequent built interpretations in suburbs and towns across the United States, the hall was made smaller and served solely as a reception entry. Hall trees and other items of furniture substituted for the fireplace.

Holly's houses were houses in nature, but they were not isolated country houses. They were suburban houses designed for a park-like setting, again, as most pattern book houses would present. Holly, supporting beliefs in social mobility and home ownership, told his readers that with "rapid transit" by rail and steamboat, "all classes, from the humblest mechanic to the wealthy banker," could have

Fig. 48. A large entry hall with an old-fashioned inglenook, warm glow of a fireplace, and elegant staircase was a feature of the new fashion. Staircase hall. (Holly, Modern Dwellings in Town and Country, *1878)*

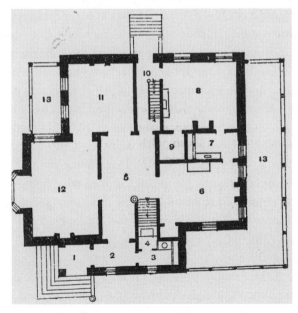

Fig. 49. Floor plans were opened with sliding doors between rooms. (Holly, Harper's Magazine, *1876)*

"picturesque and cheerful" homes in the country. Among the steps toward owning such a home, he explained, site selection was the first, for the most important consideration of location was its amenability to sanitation requirements. But prospective homeowners should then select the site for its scenery. Holly's settings were not houses situated alone in the wild, natural state of forest and mountain frontiers but groups of homes in parks of "shady nooks or pleasant streams."[8] Readers of Harper's were presented with houses that expressed both community and a love of the nation's unique, bountiful nature. As others had done and would continue to do, Holly merged familiar themes, making suburban life the most suitable for the nation's citizens. Although city houses were included in late-nineteenth-century pattern books, the suburban house predominated.

The needs for authoritative advice, healthy siting, functional planning, and a house in groomed nature were generally agreed upon by traditional and entrepreneurial pattern book authors, though with some variations. With other issues found in Holly's works, seeds of disagreement are found. Holly directed his writings to a popular public, but as a member of the American Institute of Architects who was a protagonist of Queen Anne he also wrote for his skeptical peers. His first article subtly introduced a dialogue with professional architects and addressed their hesitations about the fashion. Holly had determined England's modern architecture eminently suitable for American use, and he legitimized his claim by briefly situating Queen Anne developments in the mainstream of architectural practice and theory. As a response to the general concern that a distinctive style of architecture had not yet been achieved in the United States, he applied the theory of evolution in American domestic architecture to claim that "idiosyncrasies of building" indeed were being developed as architects continued to respond to the unique requirements of the land and climate.[9] Following, he addressed the subject of the nation's search for a distinctive style and grounded it in a discussion of middle-class housing. By doing so, he took part in the ongoing professional debate about the relative prestige for an architect to design houses rather than public buildings. As an architect who focused on domestic architecture, he unsurprisingly found domestic architecture more distinctively American. Because houses were designed with constructional and functional considerations foremost in mind, American house design developed with forms uncommon to British and European architecture. The ground floor of a typical American home contained a kitchen joined to the body of the house with a butler's pantry. It was not necessary to build the kitchen as a separate structure because the nation's pure air eliminated cooking odors. Second, implying a homogenous American climate, he explained the veranda, which was inappropriate to England's dampness, as a particularly American feature generated by architectural adjustments to climate. This point was repeated frequently in architectural literature. Third, different materials were appropriate to the United States. American houses were more frequently built of wood because it was in abundant supply. Few pattern book authors would disagree with these suggestions, but when Holly commented on decoration, he was critical of current practice by less knowledgeable builders. From his point of view, architects were finally learning to value the intrinsic properties of wood and were turning from "stupidly" copying original masonry details in wood.

Holly added support to his arguments for the new architecture by featuring a brief history of its English sources. A group of English architects, including Shaw and Stevenson, he noted, had found the new style fitting for their nation's domestic architecture, and he found it equally suitable for American houses. For the English proponents of the style, he explained, Queen Anne expressed truth in architecture for domestic building more effectively than gothic, for it was "the most simple mode of honest English building worked out in an artistic and natural form. . . ."[10] But Holly was aware of the irony of validating a new style of American buildings with foreign sources. Essentially, he asserted that Americans had no other choice but to adapt foreign architectural styles to their needs, and among all styles at their disposal, this seemed the most appropriate model for contemporary building. He also found a very practical reason. American builders were already familiar with constructional methods of the style because the sources of this "free classic" mode were found in the same forms of architecture brought to the colonies in the eighteenth century. Here, without explicitly pointing out negative aspects, he waylaid expected arguments against the imported fashion. There was indeed valid ancestry. It was not too complex to be built in local communities. And with a distinct separation from popular building techniques, the method of construction appropriate to Queen Anne was traditional timber-frame construction, not the quickly built balloon-frame method so readily accepted by local carpenters.

Then exercising his faculties to confront Queen Anne's problematic stylistic definition that vexed architects schooled in the custom of more precise categories, he clarified the sources of the composite style by quoting British architect Lacey W. Ridge:

> The Queen Anne revival shows the influence of the group of styles known as the Elizabethan, Jacobite, and the style of Francis I., which are now, indeed, to be arranged under the general head of "free classic," but the Queen Anne movement has also been influenced by what is known as the "cottage architecture" of that period.[11]

From the beginning, "Queen Anne" was loosely defined and referenced by a number of related names. The introduction of swags, garlands, and other forms associated with the nineteenth-century definition of "classic" to domestic architecture caused "free classic" to become a designation synonymous with Queen Anne. At the same time, medieval sources were equally important to the development of the style and gothic was at its foundation. Modern Queen Anne overlaid the opposing stylistic categories, classical and medieval. All of the building styles that Ridge had distinguished in the grouping were characterized by a merging of northern medieval with Italian interpretations of the Greco-Roman lineage. Italian ornament mixed with French dormers, chimneys, and towers on the chateaux of Chambord, Chenonçeau, and Blois built during the reign of Francis I. Henry VIII had brought French craftsmen to England toward the end of his reign, and French translations of Italian architecture continued as a source for English building during the reign of his daughter Elizabeth. Under James I and James II, contemporary Italian design and Flemish decorative forms introduced by Flemish craftsmen blended with traditional English architecture. With a legitimate history accounted for, he turned to English vernacular custom. Cottage architecture also integrated nineteenth-century conceptions of medieval and classical. "These cottages are partly timbered," Holly wrote,

> partly covered with tile hangings, and have tall and spacious chimneys of considerable merit. They have really nothing to fix their date. Their details partook strongly of the classic character, while the boldness of their outline bore striking resemblance to the picturesque and ever-varying Gothic.[12]

English models for the modern style were of a vaguely discernible lineage, and Holly's houses added an American gloss. The six designs which followed his introduction to the new fashion were not emulations of modern English Queen Anne houses. They were modifications of contemporary American houses, for his concern was finding a contemporary American vernacular. Overall, he presented the fashion as flexible, with an architectural vocabulary that permitted individual interpretation. Among his design features: clapboard exterior sheathing for the first floor of a house and shingle for the second, sash windows with the upper sash sectioned into small square lights, two-story bay windows, shingled gables, and floral decoration. The picturesque skyline was formed by a "tent" roofing configuration that organized balconies, dormers, verandas, and other projecting forms under one enveloping roof (Fig. 50).

Holly not only proposed design features; he convincingly argued their effective power of communication as a rationale for their implementation. Readers were instructed that with the assistance of an architect "one of the most important aesthetic ends" of the art of house building would be achieved. The house would be imprinted with the owner's character. These houses conveyed values of home and family, of social and cultural refinement, graciousness and hospitality, and (a love of) nature. Open floor plans, for example, suggested the owner's generous hospitality and social nature. The fireplace was described as "that ancient symbol of domestic union and genial hospitality." Important associations of hearth, home, and taste, which were already fundamental to the literature of home-building and domesticity and would continue to be promoted in subsequent

pattern books, were interwoven with his description of the homeowner. Holly also explained the library as means to communicate the
owner's character, and in a reference designed to appeal to the male
householder, the library was presented as the "gentleman's growlery"
and a sign of his literary taste. Projecting an image combining a verdant site, exterior detail, and interior planning, such a house would
directly communicate that an educated and refined gentleman lived
within, a man whose delicate sensitivity to nature sought a physical
and visual integration of the trees and rocks of the site with the
materials and silhouette of the house.[13] Holly established meaningful
correlations between the new fashion's interior planning and its prospective owners that would grow with the proliferation of the fashion
in entrepreneurial patterns books. Robert Shoppell, the strong competitor to the Palliser Company, was but one pattern book author to
use Holly's terminology when he described a private retreat for the
man of the household as the "growlery."

   Although interior planning for function and meanings of association was fundamental to late-nineteenth-century housing design,

*Fig. 50. Holly termed the type of roof on this home in Bellingham, Wash., 1890s,
a "tent roof." (Photograph by Barbara Plaskett)*

the exterior was a matter of great significance because it was a public proclamation of the owner's character. Holly was less informative than the more entrepreneurial pattern book authors would be regarding specific attributes of the house exterior as a display of its owner's character. Nonetheless, he assured his readers that the new houses exhibited American roots. With Design No. 5, a "Jacobite" variation with half-timbering on the upper floors, readers of *Harper's* were furnished with theoretical and historical validation of his overall scheme for the new vernacular (Fig. 51). It met the criteria of modern functional aesthetics. With gables, hips, crests, and chimneys, and "fair acknowledgment of all constructive obligations," the exterior expressed the plan. And it had a common parentage with American colonial-era architecture, for houses in this Jacobite version of Queen

Fig. 51. Holly and others used English colonial history to validate the adaptation of modern English fashions for an American style of architecture. A house in the "Jacobite style." (Holly, Harper's Magazine, *1876)*

Anne were reminiscent of colonial houses of New England, revolutionary period Dutch farmhouses, and plantation houses of Maryland and Virginia. Looking back to the past with a nostalgia that was to become progressively important to the American consciousness, he found in them an "Old-World expression." Houses from the nation's past were "free of pretense" having "truth and solidity in their construction." For Holly, this quality had been lost to American architecture. That he claimed the colonial houses expressive of "the solid energy, determination, and great-heartedness of the founders of the new empire in the wilderness" and identified the owners as esteemed men of the "colonial aristocracy" added most convincing arguments for adopting his proposal.[14]

Holly's 1878 publication of the articles in book form was presented as an educational resource for prospective homeowners and builders rather than a source for plans and building specifications. By producing a traditional format pattern book, he positioned himself with the East Coast architectural hierarchy. However, many of his contemporaries were turning from Queen Anne to other variations allied with American colonial building, and in fact, Holly had allied himself with their promotion of colonial architecture in a letter to the *American Architect* in 1877. With no mention of Queen Anne in the letter, he argued for an "American style of architecture" drawn from the "Dutch and Puritan" examples.[15] Yet, Holly's popular publication remained an exposition on adaptations of the new British fashion for American soil. Holly embodied the ambivalence regarding the merits of design associated with the new fashion. His praise for "Dutch and Puritan" architecture argued against the extravagance of the developing vernacular Queen Anne; yet he appears to have been a pragmatic business person. The idea of Queen Anne, and the more eclectic, unnamed fashions developing from it, sold to middle-class homebuilders.

The *American Architect* and Queen Anne

The editorial staff of the *American Architect* did not endorse Holly's exposition of Queen Anne architecture but, on the other hand, they did not discredit the author's claims either. Although the style was familiar in name in the spring of 1876 and would be reported in the autumn as an English "madness," it was evidently too recent and problematic a development for a conclusive editorial position.[16] American architects were, if not skeptical about the ramifications of this new importation, at least uncertain about their own theoretical positions regarding modern Queen Anne. Articles and letters to the editor in the 1876 *American Architect* began a lengthy debate among architects on both sides of the Atlantic concerning the definition of the new Queen Anne architecture and its architectural validity. Because "Queen Anne" was a misnomer from the beginning and the forms of the style were not necessarily drawn from the reign of the eighteenth-century queen for whom it was named, authors more commonly referred to the new fashion as the "so-called Queen Anne." As Holly had noted, the style known as modern Queen Anne was, in fact, an amalgam of stylistic elements widely defined as medieval and classical. Eclecticism had become accepted as inevitable in contemporary architecture, but the new repertoire of forms seemed to include an unprecedented number of sources. Definition became even more complicated in America as architects recognized a relationship between Queen Anne and colonial architecture.

In December of 1876, critic Montgomery Schuyler set the editorial tone for the professional journal in his article, "Concerning Queen Anne." Schuyler immediately asserted in the introductory sentence, "The pretensions that are made for Queen Anne as an architectural style are very lofty." He was adamant that modern Queen Anne architecture did not constitute a style. Not being built on constructive principles, it was merely a fashion. With the enthusiasm of an avowed gothicist, Schuyler could not find in the Queen Anne fashion what had become understood as a vital principle in the modern gothic buildings. From the perspective of biological analogy popular at the time, buildings were organisms which expressed their "functions and conditions." Without such a principle, architecture could not be considered a style. The critical flaw of modern Queen Anne architecture was the non-constructive application of decoration, and Schuyler's major difficulty with Queen Anne was its classical detail which could not develop naturally from a medieval architectural body. Very seldom could buildings that developed from plans adapted to natural and architectural conditions be decorated with classic details. Patterns stamped on the stucco walls, which were characteristic of the new fashion, did not constitute organic decoration. With reference to English architects Norman Shaw and Thomas Colcutt he pointedly concluded, "But of the work of its practitioners it may be safely said, that what of it is good is not Queen Anne, and what is Queen Anne is not good. . . ."[17]

More moderate views were expressed by some of the participants in a discussion on the subject of Queen Anne recorded in the minutes for the February 1877 meeting of the Boston Society of Architects, the local chapter of the American Institute of Architects. However, the report in the *American Architect* began with a more negative version of the proceedings than recorded in the Society's minutes, bringing an edited account to the journal's readers. At the meeting, Henry Van Brunt began the discussion in generally favorable terms. He explained that what was called Queen Anne in contemporary practice was actually from the Stuart period when "the classic predominated but retained some of the freedom of the mediœval." Van Brunt was optimistic about the style's future and submitted, "It is this that the young architects of Great Britain abandoning the Gothic, are now taking up & practising with so much vigor and skill. We are living in the midst of an epoch, which may hereafter turn out to be as memorable as the Gothic revival of twenty years ago."[18] The editor (or reporting Society secretary) did not share Van Brunt's positive opinion. He added a pejorative interpretation of the style's history by claiming that the characteristics of Queen Anne had developed with Stuart architecture "and had run into extravagance and decline before the time of Anne" and, following a variant of the epochal theme, he lamented, ". . . the Gothic is now abandoned by a considerable number of the younger architects, who are doing their best to revive the style known as the Queen Anne style. We are living in what may be called an epoch. We know every style as well as the generations did in which they were first known and practised. But our general knowledge prevents us from having strong convictions."[19]

Remarks by other members of the Boston Society were also subjected to editorial revision in publication to bring a more negative view to readers of the journal. Edward C. Cabot's criticism of

Queen Anne stepped gables as "a showing after the picturesque at the expense of the practical" was expanded in the *American Architect* to read, "and most of the external peculiarities of the Queen Anne style are open to the suspicion of a certain straining after picturesqueness, at the expense of good sense and good construction."[20] Similarly, trenchant criticism of the Queen Anne raised by the secretary, Charles A. Cummings—"extravagant affectations of broken pediments and lank pilasters and ridiculous little obelisks & balls and pot-hooks . . . unworthy of thoughtful & serious architects"—was amplified with editorializing that showed the growing interest in French architecture:

> The Secretary condemned the puerility and feebleness of ornamentation which characterizes this style—the wriggling gables, the little pyramids and balls and scrolls stuck about on every shelf and corner—as unworthy of serious imitation; and contrasted all this nonsense with the grace and dignity and real picturesqueness of the style which prevailed at about the same time in France." [21]

A week later, the *American Architect* carried a report of buildings completed in England during 1876, most of which were Queen Anne. While the correspondent determined that no great architectural monuments could be recorded for the year, he observed that changes were underway in England which deserved attention. The "so-called Queen Anne style" was rapidly becoming more than a domestic style and in recent competitions was replacing "Gothic" as the chosen style for public buildings. The modern Queen Anne was more "Stuart" than Queen Anne, and the author concluded, ". . . the age of medievalism seems past, and a modified Renaissance seems taking its place".[22] His definition corresponded with the one that had emerged in the Boston Society of Architects discussion. With a conclusion that would lead to greater interest in colonial and classical stylizations for housing, he observed that Queen Anne partook more of the classic than the gothic.

Later that spring, the journal published a paper on Queen Anne that had been given at the April meeting of the Boston Society of Architects by Robert S. Peabody. A pragmatist regarding this issue,

Peabody urged his fellow professionals to pay heed to the English developments because, as a matter of course, American architecture quickly reflected English work. But Peabody was also an apologist regarding its historical intersections with American buildings. The new style not only accommodated the eclectic tendencies of American architecture, but its eighteenth-century sources were the foundation of colonial architecture as well. Adhering to the architects' search for legitimizing antecedents, he found that the most favorable characteristics of the style were those drawn from the past:

> Of all this work the distinctive feature is beyond all its pleasant, homely, hospitable warm color, that should be backed up by the green of old English trees. . . . Then its careful brickwork is to be noted, and the extraordinary affectation of cut brick; mouldings, carvings, garlands, all being cut in the bricks after they have become set in the wall . . . , the only worthy material in which to carve the mysterious pot of sunflowers. Again, its white frames and sashes near the face, giving deep interior recesses, its turned wooden posts, and any eccentricity in general design that one can suppose would have occurred to designers one hundred and fifty or two hundred years ago.[23]

Peabody renamed Queen Anne the "bric-a-brac" style. It appears not to have been meant as a completely disparaging term, although later writers applied it in that sense. Rather, it was a glib, tongue-in-cheek critique of the taste for a new and highly eclectic fashion that had come from changes in interior decoration brought by William Morris and company and the Pre-Raphaelites. According to Peabody, the old, crude "medievalism" had been replaced by "gods and goddesses, Earthly Paradise and Chaucer and Old Kensington, sunflowers, sconces, blue china, turned work instead of notches and chamfers, and above all Japanese screens, fans, stuffs, papers, pictures, bronzes and china." The exterior architecture, too, borrowed from many sources and became a suggestion of the "wealth of bric-a-brac" within. Although classical was an important element in the overall conception of Queen Anne, the new architecture was neither strictly

Queen Anne nor Stuart nor Italian. What was called Queen Anne was in practice "odds and ends, beauty in any form, cosiness, comfort, picturesqueness." In short, the essence of the "bric-a-brac" style was the architectural freedom implied by the variety of sources allowed the architect. In his estimation—and suggesting the vagaries of the fashion—pointed arch or lintel, the choice made little difference as long as the architect was artistic.

Professional separation

Peabody referred to the growing enthusiasm for the arts of the English Aesthetic Movement and its relationship to the new fashion. Perhaps the professional separation from Queen Anne was inevitable at this moment in time because it tipped the theoretical balance toward art and away from science. As we are aware, so-called Queen Anne was introduced at a time when the belief that science offered solutions for sorting out the complexities of modern life was taking prominence. The *American Architect* contributors actively applied this conception of science as an objective ordering agent, and as the late-century penchant for an eclectic mixture of architectural forms grew, they sought a method, or system, to control it. Science represented the assurance of classification systems and inherent formulae, and when the established architects yearned for "a body of rules" to control the eclecticism that characterized Queen Anne, they were speaking of perceived needs that had become common truth.[24] Both heterogeneity in evolutionary science and in architecture required a governing principle. Even when clear priority was given to architecture as an art, a shift in theoretical evidence was becoming evident. Architectural art was being formulated as the "science of art." By 1878, both the practical and theoretical sides of science were brought forward more strongly. In response to dramatic construction failures, technical expertise began to take prominence over art as a professional attribute. Articles proposing legal certification for architects suggested construction and construction theory for qualifying examination subjects and paid less attention to art.[25] When architect Leopold Eidlitz wrote to the *American Architect* with an argument for "artistic expression," he expressed the altered direction by declaring, "Artistic expression in architecture is to be attained by the modeling of inert matter in its relation to other matter. This relation is construction [that] forms the groundwork and keynote of all architectural effort."[26]

The developing genre of design was, and would continue to be, problematic for the architects seeking underlying scientific principles for architectural design. It was too firmly defined as a predominantly "artistic" fashion. Popular associations with what became known as the English Aesthetic Movement and its decorative emanations in the United States made it difficult to construe modern Queen Anne as "scientific." The impact of the aesthetic movement in the United States cannot be denied. The Boston architects of the American Institute of Architects, especially, introduced interior and exterior architectural design associated with the aesthetic movement when they experimented with the early derivations of nineteenth-century Queen Anne.[27] At the same time, the nation's prominent architects began to reveal their discomfort with the architectural license implied by Queen Anne's relationship to the growing popularity of aestheticism. By the early 1880s, the aesthetic movement had become such a phenomenon that it was formally named and defined. Through media coverage of the activities and dress of such notorious enthusiasts as Oscar Wilde and James McNeill Whistler, it had become associated with effete dandyism as well. In the United States, the languid, lily-bearing Oscar Wilde spoke to overflowing crowds while Gilbert and Sullivan's *Patience*, a satire of the Aesthetes that parodied Wilde as the poet Bunthorne, packed the house night after night. The association of Queen Anne architecture with libertinism, which was prevalent in the descriptive language used by the architects who argued against its use, further complicated its acceptance as a professional style. For architects who defined their program of professionalization in paternally moralistic terms, so-called Queen Anne was difficult to mediate.

The dominant strains in American architectural theory were in opposition to art for art's sake because artistic freedom, although necessary, could become artistic abandon in the hands of the uneducated. The A.I.A. architects in Boston inquired into the boundaries of the architect's artistic responsibilities at a February 1878 meeting of the Boston Society of architects, and secretary Henry Van Brunt read a paper on the subject. His words stimulated a vigorous discussion and exposed how difficult it was to articulate the relation between art and moral design in modern society. A portion of the debate was reported in the *American Architect*. Without deviation from the belief in the architect's moral duty to the nation, the speakers agreed that freedom of design was an opportunity contingent on Van Brunt's call for a "conscienscious [*sic*] spirit."[28] William Robert Ware, Van Brunt's partner in business, responded first, ". . . the greater freedom must beget the greater responsibility; hence follows that moral element in design. . . ." Avowed gothicist Russell Sturgis then observed that the new catholicity was "creating among architects a very marked mental peculiarity in their work," that prompted a comment on England's modern architecture. Ware considered modern Queen Anne and Jacobean architecture "a national recoil or revolt of the artistic mind from the undue control exercised over it by Mr. Ruskin, Mr. Pugin [both leaders in forming the conception of moral architecture] and their followers in the interest of the medieval revival." He continued with an emphasis on moral architecture, which was fundamental to such English "medieval revival" architects as Ruskin, G. E. Street, and William Burges, but he also recognized some interpretation. Ware concluded, "It seems to be a matter of feeling and impulse, justified by the occasion, indicative of greater catholicity of spirit and inconsistency with the moral instincts of the new culture."[29]

But while these discussions were carried on, popular associations between Queen Anne, housing design, and the aesthetic movement were being forged. In 1876, adding another intersection of events in that American centennial year, the conception of modern Queen Anne as a style for an artistic and middle-class public materialized when construction of a new suburb at Turnham Green station outside of London was begun. Entrepreneur Jonathan Carr first employed English architect E. W. Godwin, then Richard Norman Shaw, both practitioners of the new fashion, to design inexpensive houses for his garden community named Bedford Park. The British architectural journal, *Building News*, reported on December 22, 1876, that eighteen houses by Godwin had been completed for the "middle classes" (although perhaps more precisely upper middle classes) and praised the designs of the houses with phrases that would become widespread in American pattern book literature. The houses were "well planned, conveniently arranged, and constructed with regard to both stability and comfort and architectural character." The community became so popular that by 1881 over 300 houses had been built and prospective homeowners were waiting for more to be completed.[30] From its inception, Bedford Park, with its Queen Anne houses, was perceived as a stronghold of artistic and refined taste. It was presented as an affordable taste for the American middle class when *Harper's* in 1881 published a report by Moncure Conway who, in this and other articles, helped fuel enthusiasm for English domestic fashions. According to his romanticized vision, Bedford Park was "a little red town made up of quaintest Queen Anne houses," a "dream of old-time homesteads," and "an antique townlet," a "Utopia in brick and paint in the suburbs of London"(Fig. 52). The houses also fulfilled a modern need for "persons of moderate means," for they were a venue that offered them an opportunity to communicate cultivated taste in a way that was formerly possible for the wealthy alone.[31] Although these houses bore little visual similarity to the fashion developing in the United States, the conceptual image of Queen Anne

Fig. 52. An "antique townlet" of modern Queen Anne houses in the London suburb of Bedford Park. "Queen Anne Gardens." (Conway, Harper's Magazine, *1881)*

as high fashion signifying cultural status and domesticity was taking hold in the minds of American builders, carpenters, and their clients. And while the name "Queen Anne" was attached less frequently than the descriptive words "suburban" and "modern" to houses in pattern books, it evidently sustained a marketable mental image through the end of the century. In 1895, one cynical critic observed,

> When a person is at loss for a suitable name by which to convey an ideal of the beauty and charm of his home, it is "Queen Anne." Of course, when there is "love in a cottage," that cottage can be none other than "Queen Anne." When the ubiquitous speculating builder wishes to lure an intended victim he baits his hook with "beautiful Queen Anne cottage. All modern improvements." [32]

The "American" interpretations

Again, the architects who were intent on formalizing national professional standards were confronting the nation's preferences in residential design. They saw that the middle and working classes had taken possession of gothic, Italian and French stylizations, and their use of decoration had transformed them into popular fashions having the stamp of "exuberance." Queen Anne was the latest style of consequence to be brought across the Atlantic Ocean and was sure to be turned over rapidly to popular consumption and, of course, manipulation. With its evocations of vernacular simplicity, as well as being the most up-to-the-minute fashion, it was at first a point of departure for many members of the "new profession." But as a housing fashion whose features were simultaneously positive and highly problematic, it was not taken on as a mode of design signifying architectural professionalism. Its eclectic make-up rendered it unreasonably open to appropriation by the masses. So-called Queen Anne could not be held secure as a professionally articulated national style. Instead, it served a crucial role in the formation of professional status as a site on which professional priorities could be mediated, and these were integrated into house designs. Some visual results were closely allied with the English Queen Anne and others were not.

Illustrations of homes in the *American Architect* show a wide variety of stylistic interpretations, but two general directions emerged in pattern book debates. On one hand, the architects and pattern book authors turned to the nation's colonial past to devise and validate a new fashion. Others explored an eclectic use of British and European sources admitted into the vocabulary of domestic architecture by the freedom of so-called Queen Anne. By 1877, the preoccupation with national identity, the Centennial, and a need for a retreat to an idealized, untroubled past converged with beliefs in progress. For professional architects in the *American Architect*, America's colonial and revolutionary period history became a source of vision for the present and future. In the estimation of some, such as Holly, interest in so-called Queen Anne should be diverted to a study of the nation's own past. Among the articles on colonial architecture, the *American Architect* published "Georgian Houses of New England," accompanied by drawings of "Old Houses at Lennox and Little Harbor." The author, Robert S. Peabody, under the pseudonym "Georgian," had by this time come to conclusions about Queen Anne that criticized the outgrowth of the fashion. The presumed freedom from style brought by studying sixteenth-century architectural precedents was in actual practice resulting in yet another antiquarian revival commensurate with "Eastlake chairs, the American rococo mantel, and the Puginesque sideboard." Warning his readers against imitation, he offered an alternative brought by the Centennial—colonial, "our only native source of antiquarian study and inspiration."[33] Speaking in 1887, W. P. P. Longfellow observed, "The 'Colonial' fashion has divided our attention with [Queen Anne]."[34]

A. F. Oakey, Charles McKim, and William Ralph Emerson were among the architects who developed an idiom for eastern seaboard houses that developed from colonial-Queen Anne formulations. These houses were typified by large halls, expanded plans, broad horizontal rather than vertical massing of forms, and shingle cladding. This interpretation of colonial (via Queen Anne) housing was termed the "shingle house" by New York architect Bruce Price in an 1890 article on contemporary suburban houses (Fig. 53). Using terminology prevalent in pattern book descriptions as a critical device, Price compared the new shingle-clad houses with the modern houses that were frequently called "quaint," "novel," and "picturesque." The contrast between the two types of houses was not illustrated, but the image of the less desirable home by its ubiquitous presence could readily be called to mind. Price advocated a better inspiration for modern houses, and a national style, in the "architectural" buildings from America's past.[35] The use of the word to denote true architecture as a contrast to mere buildings would not have been missed by many of his architect readers.

The *American Architect*, while including some shingle houses, chiefly published drawings of houses characterized by verticality and a perpendicular assemblage of rectangular volumes that was associated with gothic tendencies of the Queen Anne fashion. These represented the type of house that would be developed as the modern fashion of the middle classes. Features included tent roofs, dominant ribbed and molded chimneys, dormers, clapboard and

Fig. 53. Colonial and new republic architectural heritage was identified in contemporary shingle house designs, which many East Coast architects saw as more appropriate representations of national character. (House by Rich, Short Hills, N.J., in Price, Scribner's Magazine, *1890)*

shingle siding, half-timbered gables, turned posts, jettied second floors, chamfered or canted bays, shutters, vertical bands of windows with upper sashes having small panes, and sunflower-decorated panels. Towers, which became an important feature in built pattern book houses, were common to contemporary gothic houses but infrequent on the *American Architect* houses showing so-called Queen Anne features. They appeared more frequently on contemporary houses drawn from French sources. As previously noted, modern Queen Anne was recognized as having features comparable to French seventeenth-century architecture, but discussion concerning the style's definition emphasized its classical characteristics with few references to France. The confusion caused by the presence of French sources for the English style was noted by an American correspondent who went to London to search out the true Queen Anne. When he went to a reputable book shop to search for information that could lead him to an understanding of the style, he was told that English architects were now referring to Sauvageot's book on French chateaux. Indeed, Claude Sauvageot's well-known *Palais, châteaux, hôtels et maisons de France* (1862–1867) brought French domestic design to British and American architects. But the mixture of styles was too frustrating for this researcher. He decided to call the new fashion "the anonymous style," and turned to lengthy and lavish praise for the house of gothicist William Burges, evidently something much easier to tackle for someone schooled in the precision of classification.[36]

Pattern book houses 1876–1881

With the exception of Henry Hudson Holly, pattern book author-architects from 1876 to the end of the decade were either more cautious about introducing new fashions or were unfamiliar with them. From the mid-1870s to the mid-1880s, pattern book fashions were a mixture of current and recently popular fashions. The thrust to shape taste through marketing was not as prominent. Book formats and textual content were diverse as well, ranging from compendia of designs with minimal textual information to instructional manuals having only a selected few designs for houses. For the most part, they featured houses for the country rather than the city. Pattern book producers agreed on the public's need for expert guidance in practical matters and questions of taste, but they differed when they described their parts in the program and their audiences. In both the similarities and the thematic variations in this array of pattern books, we find intimations of separation that would become more distinct in the next decades. On one hand, those aligning themselves with the professional architect proponents of colonial and classical design brought a message of discipline and control through simplicity in housing design. On the other hand, pattern book author-architects broke the rules of academic architecture to introduce house designs of increasing complexity.

A comparison of representative pattern books published between 1878 and 1881 demonstrates the early workings of architectural fashion. William Woollett, a fellow of the American Institute of Architects, was typical among the established architect-authors who produced pattern books. His *Villas and Cottages, 1876*, followed the traditional instructional format of mid-century pattern books; it offered neither plans nor other services by mail order. As an architect who worked in the cosmopolitan East, he showed his knowledge of contemporary architectural fashions, but he did not introduce Queen Anne stylizations. Contemporary Italian fashions joined integrations of gothic and classic. Explicitly eschewing the French mansard roof houses still popular in other pattern books, Woollett advocated the modernized gothic currently in vogue, represented by Richard Morris Hunt's house published in the *American Architect* and known today as a stick style (Fig. 54). Two years later, in his 1878 publication that capitalized on the active popularity of remodeling houses, Woollett made clear his low opinion of extant houses and his approval of colonial with, "American houses of any date are not very likely to possess to any great extent those features which we deem desirable to preserve, and it is only in the homes of colonial times that we find much interest or that is in itself is meritorious."[37] Following this justification for modernization rather than preservation, each design demonstrated the sometimes startling transformation of an older, unfashionable house (Fig. 55).

Entrepreneurial pattern book author Elisha Hussey accompanied his lengthy survey of towns with designs in a creative variety of

Fig. 54. A modernized form of gothic, known today as the stick style. (Woollett, Villas and Cottages, 1876)

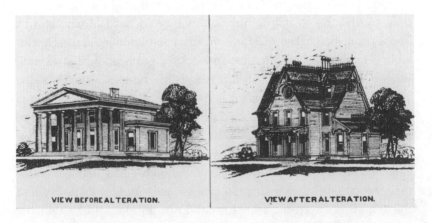

Fig. 55. The ideology of modern progress justified remodeling rather than preserving old houses, although a select number of colonial houses were saved through historic preservation efforts. (Woollett, Old Homes Made New, 1878)

fashionings, some of which may have been directed to the immigrant population with northern European origins who were seen to be adapting to American ways of life. Even though he recognized that French roofs were not as fashionable any more, he included them, as well as Italian interpretations. He favored gothic more, but he noted German influence and seemed to fancy Swiss and Swedish renditions. His observations of a "Swedo-gothic" house and his personal research into the fashions of the time led him to conclude that many contemporary houses showed mixtures of French, Swiss, and gothic (Fig. 56). This array of styles notwithstanding, the first house design in Hussey's book was "sensible," for ". . . it does not pretend to be what it is not." Hussey defined his audience as practical people who were making new lives in new communities; complex houses were too costly for many of his clients to build. At the same time, refined taste was an important attribute of his clients—a point that could not be neglected as a sign of social status. Above all, he recognized his mobile clients

Fig. 56. "Swedo-gothic." (Hussey, Home Building, *1876)*

as home-loving, and his houses provided those home-like qualities they desired. His book's title, *Home Building*, its introduction, and several designs emphasized home and home-loving occupants. Design sixteen was described, with Hussey's customary articulation of gender roles, as a "home . . . where the homely virtues daily grow stronger, and the true, manly acts of kindness, charity and good feeling toward all men are the ruling principle." Another design, he claimed, was recognized without prompting by a gentleman passerby as "home-like." Interestingly, this was one of his more up-to-date designs, made home-like with its "projecting entrance to the broad piazza, the bays and overhanging gables at the second story, the orioled gablet with its hipped roof, the crestings and the slated roofs. . . ."[38]

George Palliser, throughout his publishing career, attempted to align his practice with the architectural establishment. His small plan sales pattern book, *Model Homes for the People* (1876), included gothic, French and Italian stylizations but he exercised more restraint than did Elisha Hussey.[39] The styles of the houses largely were fashions that had been popular for decades but remained current. An "imposing" house (Design 40), costing the large sum of $10,000 to $15,000, had an octagonal tower and "observatory," and his feature house, the "Centennial Villa," was in the newer gothicized style with stick work, having a picturesque silhouette with gables and dormers. He described the houses with little textual exposition, but he did suggest the imperative of suburban home ownership with a house (Design 23) having "plenty of room for the well-kept lawn the pride of every true American." With a message common to the discourse on home ownership, he advised frugality and entrepreneurship to make possible that dream. Design 24 was a small house appropriate for "every mechanic and laborer of small family" and it could be paid for by renting the second story.

When Palliser, Palliser and Company published their 1878 *Model Homes*, there was much more text, and it had a specific intent. A lengthy essay was a polemic for architects who were experts needed by the home-building public. In fact, as noted earlier, the Pallisers plagiarized a large portion of the essay from the *American Architect*. In their newer book, the author-architects accompanied each house

design with a full page of text. Some pages included significant correlations between the home owner's identity and the house fashion;
a larger number were descriptions that concluded with other comments regarding the need for an architect. The house fashions showed,
too, an alliance with architects who were experimenting with English
Queen Anne. The Pallisers did not give stylistic labels to their houses,
although two were described respectively as Queen Anne and
Jacobite, and several houses exhibited features of the fashion. On
larger homes, stained-glass upper sashes, window hoods, sunburst
gable decorations, shingled gables, projecting bays and chamfered
bays with broad decorative brackets, half-timbering, decorative panels with floral motives, and barge boards with molded decoration
expanded the pattern book vocabulary of forms. Several houses were
enclosed with Holly's tent roof as defined in his May 1876 *Harper's*
article. Others represented a less marked change from rural building
configurations.

The Pallisers described Plate III, a cottage built in West Stratford,
Connecticut, at a cost of $1,460, as "a free rendering of what is known
as the Queen Anne style of architecture" (Fig. 57). The Queen Anne
house did not fulfill expectations for Queen Anne exuberance, but was
a simple frame structure typical of village homes across the country.
Nonetheless, it was given the requisite picturesque silhouette with a
gabled roof enclosing an enlarged staircase bay that projected from
one side of the main roof. The front gable was decorated with queen
and king posts embellished with sawn edges in curvilinear patterns,
and the rectangular spaces formed by the intersections of the boards
were filled with a sunburst-floral pattern. The semicircular pattern
was open to individual interpretation as a sunburst, a shell, a Japanese fan, and a flower, usually the ever-present symbol of constancy,
the sunflower. Its variations became typical features on modern suburban homes, primarily by way of factory production. The Pallisers
introduced another feature that was to become familiar: sash windows
decorated with small panes, some of which contained stained glass.
For exterior color, the Pallisers favored schemes drawn from nature,
and recommended that both houses be painted Venetian red with
black details. For the Jacobite house, they recommended a colorful
accent with sash and veranda panel details painted yellow. In the

manner of Andrew Jackson Downing who decades earlier had criticized white houses, the Pallisers exercised their expert authority to sharply chastise one client who had painted a Palliser house white instead of the architect-specified sage with buff and black detailing.

S. B. Reed defined his role, thus his audience, somewhat differently in his *House Plans for Everybody* (1878). He established himself as an authority through his experience in "planning and superintending the erection of country buildings," but he did not stress the need for an architect as expert.[40] This former editor of the *American Agriculturalist* directed his book to farmers, homeowners in small communities, and the local builders of the homes. Rather than use names of known styles he used more general terms—"Southern House," "French Roofed House," "Frame House," "Farm House," "Suburban Residence," and so on. For the most part, his houses were characterized by greater simplicity, which was customary in pattern book representations of farm houses. Although Reed included larger

Fig. 57. "Queen Anne." (Palliser, Model Homes, 1878)

houses in his book, he defined an audience that was less affluent but working toward economic stability, and their house selections communicated their place in this American enterprise. He advised his readers to begin with dreams of a small house saying, "To a certain extent, one's dwelling is an index of his character. . . . Every industrious man, starting in life, has a right, and should be encouraged, to anticipate prosperity, as the sure reward of honest worth; and he may, with propriety, give emphasis to such anticipations in every step, and with every blow struck. His dwelling may well express the progressive character, rather than a conclusive result."[41]

By 1880, "professional" criticism of the new eclecticism represented by so-called Queen Anne had become much more direct. The lack of architectural discipline that had been predicted appeared to be at work. Washington, D.C., architect John L. Smithmeyer published a lengthy diatribe against the style in which he claimed with typical consciousness of status marked by cultured tastes, "Queen Anne has now arrived at the currency to which a new opera attains when its tunes descend to the hand-organ."[42] The *American Architect* published similar sentiments in 1881, claiming, "The term is so loosely used . . . that every builder and furniture dealer can rehabilitate his obsolete designs, or invent new and unheard-of ones out of his own head, and put them boldly forward as examples of the new style without much risk of being repudiated.[43]

Many pattern book authors found this inexactitude a reason for and a means to facilitate the development of a market for their books, plans, specifications, and other services. In 1881, the architectural publisher William T. Comstock produced a compilation of designs by practicing architects with the express intent "to furnish good examples of complete buildings, as well as practical details."[44] His publishing company, formerly headed by Amos Bicknell, was not in the business of selling plans. It was a visual educational tool needed because of the extensive changes in contemporary architecture. Modern fashions formed a group of related styles that were modifications of the gothic to which classic features had been added. Comstock clarified his predilection in the Preface with, "The French . . . has been supplanted by our present modified Gothic, which appears as 'Queen Anne,' 'Elizabethan,' 'Jacobean,' or 'Colonial.'" By his choice of architects from the East Coast who were producing house designs similar to those in the *American Architect*, he defined modern with complex, irregular massing and exterior silhouettes but with decorative restraint (Fig. 58).

In the same year, A. F. Oakey, the Boston A.I.A. architect who frequently contributed essays to the organization's journal, published *Building a Home*, a book containing in the traditional manner both practical and aesthetic instruction. Much in contrast with Comstock's emphasis on visual illustration, Oakey verbalized his expertise on many related subjects. Lengthy text advised readers on such matters as site selection, drainage, house plans, house exteriors and interiors, and construction. Oakey, as we are aware from his participation in the discussions on professionalization, was stridently opposed to the tastes of a carpenter-built America, and he expanded on his earlier articles. Applied decoration was specifically targeted, with his objections to "flimsy ornamentations" on "cheap houses," and "[n]o

Fig. 58. "Queen Anne" by architects Lamb and Wheeler, located in Short Hills, New Jersey. (Comstock, Modern Architectural Designs and Details, 1881)

amount of scrolls and quirks, perched upon any projection that offers, will improve it; much less can such gewgaws improve the
appearance of a meanly constructed . . . building."[45] In his estimation, there were "too many cottages trying to look like villas" with
"sham decoration."[46]

It is evident, however, that Oakey was aware of the seductive
power of the notion of the picturesque for middle-class homeowners,
and he redefined the picturesque house to meet his scheme. Industrial expansion and the manufacture of decoration had destroyed the
picturesque in landscape and in houses, he asserted. But there was a
remedy. His house designs were picturesque "due to the extreme
simplicity of treatment."[47] Most of Oakey's houses had compact rectangular massing. They were box-like configurations in brick or clad
in oiled or unstained shingle that would weather into a patina of gray.
The popular colors recommended by other authors did not conform
to Oakey's criteria of natural fitness, and decoration, of course, was
minimal. Of interesting note is his blending of the exotic and the
picturesque with an interpretation of an East Indian "bangla," which
Oakey considered more picturesque than houses in the United States
because it had a thatched roof. From this example, he introduced a
bungalow in North American building materials to meet the needs
of American homeowners (See Figs. 9 and 10). And his estimation of
his prospective homeowners? Oakey questioned whether they had
taste, and following criticisms of the built landscape, he placed the
blame for diminished beauty by asking . . . is it not your taste that is
at fault?"[48]

Oakey represents a position most opposed to the vernacular and
pattern-book inspired developments in housing design that were
beginning to spread across the United States. From the 1880s to the
end of the century, others took up his cause, although with less stri-
dency. Concurrently, pattern book authors and innumerable
homeowners in villages, small towns, and suburbs relished the modern houses typified by the new eclectic and picturesque genre of
design that had earlier emerged as gothicized Queen Anne. Some
opted for interpretations having less surface decoration; others demonstrated the polarity which was alleged by the proponents of a
nostalgia-defined colonial dignity for residential architecture.

NOTES

[1] Two books have served as foundations for the study of nineteenth-century Queen Anne: British Queen Anne is examined in Mark Girouard, *Sweetness and Light: The "Queen Anne" Movement 1860–1900.* (Oxford: At the Clarendon Press, 1977), and shingle developments in Vincent Scully, Jr., *The Shingle and the Stick Style*, rev. ed. (New Haven and London: Yale University Press, 1971 [1955]). See also Leland M. Roth, *McKim, Mead & White Architects* (New York: Harper & Row, 1983).

[2] *American Builder* 11(November 1875); description, p. 262.

[3] Clarence Chatham Cook, *The House Beautiful* (New York: Scribner, Armstrong and Company, 1878).

[4] Henry Hudson Holly, "Modern Dwellings: Their Construction, Decoration and Furniture. I. Construction," *Harper's New Monthly Magazine* 52(May 1876): 855–67; "II. Color Decoration," 53(June 1876): 49–64; "III. Furniture," 53(July 1876): 217–26; "IV. Furniture," 53(August 1876): 353–63. *Harper's Bazaar* also published an article on the new fashion in furniture. "Household Furnishing: The Queen Anne Style," 9(October 21, 1876): 674–75.

[5] The Aesthetic Movement was defined by Walter Hamilton in *The Aesthetic Movement in England* (London: Reeves & Turner, 1882). Not all reviewers praised the British exhibit and their criticism was often founded in dissatisfaction with the prevalence of items associated with the Aesthetic Movement. See "Characteristics of the International Fair," *Atlantic Monthly* 38(September 1876): 350.

[6] Townsend, p. 38.

[7] Design No. 2. Sliding doors became a popular feature in pattern book houses, even more so than the large reception hall which was often eliminated in favor of a functional passage hall. It was often too expensive to build a seldom-used hall, but sliding doors introduced a fashionable open plan that was suggested by the hall. The sliding door was one of many decorative features interpreted from Japanese architecture and art. Holly specifically praised Japanese joinery.

[8] Holly, "Modern Dwellings. I," pp. 856–58.

[9] Ibid., p. 855.

[10] Ibid., p. 856.

[11] Ibid., p. 856. Quoted from Edward W. Lacey, *Architect* 13(March 1875): 159.

[12] Holly, p. 856.

[13] Ibid., pp. 859–60.

[14] Ibid., p. 864.

[15] Henry Hudson Holly, "The American Style," *American Architect* 2(August 18, 1877): 267.

[16] "Notes and Clippings: Queen Anne," *American Architect* 1(October 21, 1876): 344.

[17] Schuyler, pp. 404–05.

[18] Boston Society of Architects, minutes, February 2, 1877.

[19] "American Institute of Architects. Boston Chapter," *American Architect* 2(February 17, 1877): 53.

[20] "American Institute of Architects," pp. 53–54.

21 Quoted as recorded in the minutes. *American Architect*, p. 54.

22 "Correspondence. An Architectural Year," *American Architect* 2(February 14, 1877): 60–61.

23 "A Talk about 'Queen Anne,'" *American Architect* 2(April 28, 1877): 134.

24 "American Architecture.—Past," p. 242. The French were admired for being the "most systematic, and most academic in training" in "American Architecture—with Precedent and without," p. 139.

25 "The Qualifying of Architects,"; "The Qualifying of Architects. II."

26 Leopold Eidlitz, "The Qualifying of Architects," *American Architect* 3(May 25, 1878): 185.

27 See James D. Kornwolf, "American Architecture and the Aesthetic Movement" and Roger B. Stein, "Artifact as Ideology: The Aesthetic Movement in Its American Cultural Context," in Metropolitan Museum of Art, *In Pursuit of Beauty: Americans and the Aesthetic Movement* (New York: Rizzoli, 1986).

28 Henry Van Brunt, "Growth of the Conscienscious Spirit in the Art of Decoration," paper read at the Boston Society of Architects, February 8, 1878. A summary of the paper was reported in the secretary's minutes.

29 Boston Society of Architects, minutes, February 8, 1878.

30 "Bedford Park, London," *Chamber's Journal* 31(December 1881): 41.

31 Moncure D. Conway, "Bedford Park," *Harper's New Monthly Magazine* 62(March 1881): 482. Bedford Park drew many visitors and sightseers from the United States. Among them was Helen Hunt Jackson who later became known as a chronicler of California Native American life in children's literature.

32 Hobart A. Walker, "Cottages," *Art Interchange* 34(August 1895): 50.

33 Robert S. Peabody, "Georgian Houses of New England," *American Architect* 2(October 20, 1877): 338–39.

34 W. P. P. Longfellow, "The Course of American Architecture," *New Princeton Review* 3(March 1887): 206.

35 Price, "Suburban House," p. 14.

36 R., "Correspondence. So-Called Queen Anne Work.—Mr. Burges's House," *American Architect* 3(November 2, 1878): 148.

37 William M. Woollett, *Old Houses Made New* (New York: A. J. Bicknell & Co., 1878), p. 6.

38 Hussey, *Home Building*, Plate No. 16.

39 Palliser, *Model Homes*, 1876.

40 Reed, 1878, p. 3.

41 Reed, 1878, p. 10.

42 John L. Smithmeyer, *Strictures on the Queen Anne Style of Architecture* (Washington, D.C.: By the Author, 1881), p. 8.

43 C., "The Queen Anne Style," *American Architect* 7(February 21, 1881):73.

44 William T. Comstock, *Modern Architectural Designs and Details* (New York: William T. Comstock, Architectural Publisher, 1881), Preface.

45 Alexander F. Oakey, *Building a Home* (New York: Appleton and Company, 1881), p. 112. The book was republished in 1882, 1883, and 1884.

46 Oakey, 1881, p. 100.

47 Ibid., p. 45.

48 Ibid., p. 98.

⤢ 7 ⤡

The Modern Suburban House
Holds Its Own

A. F. Oakey's *Building a Home* represents a stance taken by the Boston circle of architects who contributed most to the editorial content of the *American Architect*. On one hand, his work was progressive. His houses were new stylizations and were a foretaste of classic box houses and bungalows that would become popular in the twentieth century. Alternatively, Oakey was working from a position of nostalgia for an idealized past, and his goal was to develop a new housing vernacular from a history of colonial and American building, even to the extent of opposing balloon-frame construction in favor of traditional heavy timber framing. Most significantly, he and his compatriots were opposed to elaboration and other ostentation, whether on small homes or mansions. Mary Woods concludes from her study of *American Architect* essays and house designs, "The *AABN* never cared for the French chateaux, Roman palaces, and Italian villas architects built as suburban and country houses in the late 1880s. . . . Perhaps the editors' puritanical background bristled at the ostentatious displays of private wealth."[1] Henry Van Brunt, with the missionary zeal noted earlier, explained the architect's duty: ". . . it is plainly to simplify and purify; to distinguish his work by self-denial and reserved force; to chasten and correct this national exuberance of fancy." An architect must be a leader in developing this good taste, for, "[h]e may be assured that every builder in his neighborhood will have his eye upon the new idea which is thus taking shape, and the lesson will not be lost."[2] They envisioned a nation of houses characterized by refined— or, from another perspective, restrained—taste.

The architects and architectural critics who assumed leadership in bringing refined taste to the masses were a small group who represented established eastern seaboard families or the upper middle-class population who could claim native-born status. For them, family history and extant historical buildings were ever-present reminders of the nation's beginnings, and these reminders gave symbolic coherence to nostalgia for a simpler past. This nostalgic image of colonial life and its production in tourism, historic preservation, and literature helps to explain the urgency for colonial architectural precedents expressed by some of the American Institute architects. Their assumption of authority rested on their notions of professionalism and progressive leadership, but it also stemmed from their cultural position. In their writings on architecture they defined their colonial forbearers with an American character exemplified by perseverance, strength, discipline, and diligent labor, plus a refinement that was traditionally associated with the elite. Henry Hudson Holly, among others, separated these home-building colonial predecessors from the rabble with suggestions that they belonged to the priviliged class of "aristocracy." Architecture characterized by restraint was part of a much larger ordering stratagem to define a singular American character in the midst of immigration and national expansion, as well as unleashed entrepreneurship. For the architects arguing a need for professional credentials, pattern books not only fostered uncontrolled taste among the public but represented business practices that confronted tradition. Built pattern book houses and their kind were visual reminders of the cultural authority of the masses.

The polemics of architectural discipline

The 1880s brought a proliferation of articles and pattern books that structured oppositions between colonial simplicity and contemporary building custom that favored complexity and decoration. In 1884, *Century Magazine* published analyses of contemporary American architecture by Mariana Griswold Van Rensselaer, a respected critic. She was from an eminent New York family with colonial lineage, and she stood firmly opposed to popular manipulations of the picturesque. In her estimation, the demand for picturesque buildings had corrupted American taste by substituting decoration for integrity. Again, the language of simplicity encompassed favorable character traits, and with the free use of racial analogies typical of the late nineteenth century, she likened overly decorated country cottages to "card-board boxes put together by a Chinese child."[3]

The 1884 pattern book compiled by New York architect Arnold William Brunner clearly explained the position held by those agreeing with criticisms such as Van Rensselaer's. *Cottages,* a book of twenty-four designs by well-known East Coast practitioners, was produced in the traditional instructional format of the professional architects. Brunner assumed the role of educator to inform his readers that elaborate ornamentation, which had emerged with builders' interpretations of English architecture, was being supplanted by greater simplicity. The "Queen Anne craze [was] subsiding." Said in this way, readers who were inclined toward decoration were required to re-evaluate the currency of their taste. With the energy of a reformer he pleaded, ". . . the less ambitious of dwellings must not be left to the mercy of those builders whose ideas of beauty are limited to scroll saw brackets and French roofs." As homes decorated with gingerbread, dormers, and turrets were gaining in popularity among strata of the middle class, a modest dwelling should not be pretentious (Fig. 59). A cottage could "assert itself sufficiently without being decked with tawdry ornaments, or the vanity of cupola or towers" (Fig. 60). Brunner pointedly marginalized plan-selling pattern book authors and their clientele by arguing against "ready-made houses," which implied both plan sales and pre-fabricated woodwork. Brunner separated himself from entrepreneurial pattern book authors and aligned himself with his fellow established East Coast architects by presenting the illustrated houses as examples of contemporary design, *but* they were not patterns for a builder to copy. Nor were his plans available for purchase. The chapters and drawings prepared the client for hiring an architect's services.[4]

William Tuthill, whose work was illustrated in Brunner's book, contributed to the polemic against the spread of undisciplined house designs and sales of plans. He asserted in *The Suburban Cottage* (1885), "All good designs should be characterized by unity and directness, with truth and breadth of expression," which was much in contrast to "recent building, notably so in suburban and seaside cottages."[5] Criticism of such seaside holiday cottages was common among his peers because their inventive designs were often associated with

Fig. 59. As complexly silhouetted and decorated homes became more popular, architects who aligned themselves with the American Architect's *arguments for simplicity produced pattern books with colonial-inspired shingle-house designs. (Brunner,* Cottages, or Hints on Economical Home Building, *1884)*

Fig. 60. A.W. Brunner argued that a cottage could "assert itself sufficiently without being decked with tawdry ornaments, or the vanity of cupola or towers." However, six years later, a home was built in Bellingham, Wash., following Brunner's design but with the addition of a tower. (By F. White in Brunner, Cottages, or Hints on Economical Home Building, *1884)*

professional estimations of the Queen Anne genre as frivolous. From Florida in 1887, the architectural firm of Carrere and Hastings bemoaned the condition of resort architecture at St. Augustine, claiming, "Specimens of this exotic architecture have obtruded themselves on our stroll in the shape of smart little Queen Anne villas, with an impudent gable here and a meaningless turret there, strongly suggesting that Queen Anne has gone mad and has attired herself like a dude on Easter day."[6] Language was used to mark a distinct separation. Images of truth and harmony were pitted against impudence and affectation. Again, we cannot ignore the use of the feminine to make the criticisms more expressive and the fashion less acceptable. When so-called Queen Anne was viewed favorably, the gendered pronoun was avoided.

Tuthill's readers were presented with houses reflecting gothicized Queen Anne, which retained meanings of domesticity for a broader public, but a simplified version without remarkable decoration. They were clapboard and shingle-sided houses with hipped tent roofs similar to those found in earlier issues of the *American Architect*. Their irregular massing, with gables, dormers, and oriels, was much in the vein of the modern genre concurrently developing in entrepreneurial pattern books, although the general silhouette was more substantial in appearance. Similar to shingle-house interpretations stemming from the 1870s, exterior wall expanses were broader and the appendages, such as turrets and bays, were weightier.

Although some authors unequivocally verbalized their positions on architectural discipline, the Queen Anne fashion, and unseemly entrepreneurship, most continued to negotiate between the stringent standards and current building practices. As the mantel of professionalism was taken up by architects and pattern book authors across the United States, these members of the building trades plied the exhortations for containment by fluidly crossing its borders. A typical example is Pierce & Dockstader of Elmira, New York, who published *Modern Buildings of Moderate Cost* (1886), a book of designs with chapters titled "Cheap Houses," "Houses of Medium Cost," and "Better Houses." The firm sold plans and specifications and ventured into offering photographs of houses constructed from their plans. By offering photographs, they gave prospective clients assurance that others found their houses appealing. Photographs were proof that their designs were indeed buildable, a selling point stressed by most entrepreneurial pattern book authors. Perhaps fitting their entrepreneurial business practices, Pierce & Dockstader houses most closely resembled the type stemming from gothicized Queen Anne and its popularized renditions (Fig. 61). Some were described as picturesque, some had turrets or very elaborate massing. The architects encouraged "variety of form" and ornamentation; decorative features that could not be seen well should be highlighted by painting them in a contrasting color. But they followed by complaining, ". . . the indiscriminate, barber-pole style of painting of our so-called Queen Anne houses is simply horrid."[7]

Manly Cutter and the New York Building Plan Company stepped more aggressively into the slowly developing market for middle-class colonial and shingle interpretations of domestic architecture. Such houses appeared to be sufficiently marketable for the

Fig. 61. The modern house fashion that developed from gothicized Queen Anne, with its suggestions of colonial, and early-nineteenth-century vernacular architecture, predominated in pattern books in the mid-1880s. (Pierce & Dockstader, Modern Buildings of Moderate Cost, *1886)*

sales of plans on the East Coast. Plans and specifications for contained floor plans for houses with gambrel roofs, gently canted gables, and arched doors and windows outnumbered examples of gothicized verticality in their book, *Designs for Modern Buildings* (1887; Fig. 62). But while restraint was exercised in fashion, it was not in business. The firm's approach to the pattern book business was among the most entrepreneurial, and Cutter covered all bases. Plans and specifications were thorough enough for the client "to take charge of his own building operations." But the prospective homeowner could now order all the building materials, furniture, and materials needed for interior decoration. If complete interior decoration was not desired, the firm could provide a schedule of furnishings in good taste provided by a "well-known metropolitan artist."[8] The company's legal department was the client's source for consultation concerning real estate transactions, building contracts, loans, and insurance. With the

Fig. 62. Other architects continued to propose colonial and shingle designs, which included Dutch antecedents as well as English. A gambrel-roof house. (Cutter, Designs for Modern Buildings, *1887)*

assurance of contemporary styles and modern business methods, the client, however, was given the comfort of tradition, which was also grounded in the modern Aesthetic Movement. John Ruskin, Owen Jones, and Lewis Day were cited as authorities, and the client was told, "Of modern ornament, the most perfect is that which is not modern." Citing E. W. Godwin, the English architect who designed the first home for the artistic suburb of Bedford Park, the company included a lengthy chapter on Anglo-Japanese interior decoration, but the interpretation did not promote simplicity in Japanese design. Ornate decorative patterns such as those found on vases and furniture panels were enlarged to cover complete wall surfaces (Fig. 63). The New York Building Plan Company attempted to meet the needs of a clientele who were diverse in their tastes.

At the close of the decade, more architects published books in which the colonial and classical tendencies predominated. Gambrel

Fig. 63. Manly Cutter was an entrepreneurial pattern book author who offered the latest in interior and architectural design fashions, building plans and specification, building materials, furniture, legal consultation, loans, and insurance. His illustrations of interiors using Japanese decorative patterns contrasted with the simplicity of the house exteriors in his pattern book. "Anglo-Japanese Room." (Cutter, Designs for Modern Buildings, *1887)*

roofs, salt box interpretations, the classic box, and enlarged volumes on shingle-style houses suggested a new vocabulary for the end of the century. Most of the authors were from the eastern states, but a number came from midwestern states. Yet, most publications directed to the nation's middle-class communities interpreted the nostalgia-produced colonial in terms of relatively unadorned vertical massing that developed from the eclectic heritage and picturesque silhouette of gothicized Queen Anne as it interbred with local building customs. For architect Louis H. Gibson and others, classicizing intentions associated with the colonial meant shingle-cladding and relatively unadorned surfaces in contrast with the "extravagant crudeness of so-called Queen Anne architecture." From their perspective, the Queen Anne fashion had become for a time all things to all architects, but it had served an important purpose. Gibson both criticized popular interpretations and proposed the colonial as the new fashion with, "The 'Queen Anne' architecture of a few years ago meant anything—particularly something that was pointed, erratic, and unusual. It, however, did a good work. It enabled the architects to get out of the old beaten paths. . . . the vehicle for the passage from an old conservatism, which had to do only with the commonplace, to something which was fresh and attractive."[9]

Pattern book authors did not align themselves into distinct positions—colonial fashions and simplicity vs. gothicized Queen Anne and elaboration. Nor did their clients. The architects who argued for the integrity and discipline of simplicity presented themselves as cultural authorities, but they could not impose their ideas on the larger public. It would be a mistake to regard their works as a seed planted for gradual spread from northeast to south and west without our recognizing the creative participation of the building public who made their own marks on new housing fashion. Pattern book authors took up the new fashions from abroad and from published designs in the *New York Sketch Book, American Architect, American Builder,* and other builders' periodicals and pattern books, then made them their own. As a result, there were many crossings back and forth over the boundaries of good design as they were set up by such architects as Van Brunt and Oakey.

Through the 1880s, the genre of design developed from gothicized Queen Anne and nineteenth-century vernacular architecture coalesced into the quintessential modern yet picturesque suburban house that signified a place called home. Robert Shoppell's selective visual history of housing design leading from the log cabin to the "modern" house demonstrated for his clientele the general appearance of the genre (see Fig. 2). He and others worked with many variations on the theme, but a recognizable type of house emerged, one that has been embraced in contemporary historical memory and reinvoked for revival in expanded interpretation in the late twentieth century. These houses have shown the fluid crossing between restraint and free latitude, for some were more colorful and ornate than others, but they all shared the eclectic architectural vocabulary that permitted inventive interpretation while sustaining a recognizable fashionable image (Fig. 64).

Fig. 64. The modern suburban style was a genre of design with an eclectic architectural vocabulary that permitted broad individual interpretation while sustaining a recognizable up-to-date fashionable image. Home in Bellingham, Wash. (Photograph by Barbara Plaskett)

Among the shared nineteenth-century characteristics are plans that are essentially rectangular but made complex with projections from first and second stories, such as short ells, bays, oriels, and towers. Roofs are often Holly's "tent" configuration and punctuated with prominent chimneys, gabled and eyebrow dormers, and finials. Windows are often sash, with a larger central pane surrounded by small square lights, a configuration shown in pattern books as "Queen Anne windows." Scroll-sawn decoration and pendants are applied to gable ends, porches, and verandas. Although many of these houses were built of brick, most of the houses are wood. Their cladding is clapboard, at times with a shingle-covered second story. Gable ends covered with scalloped shingle also are very common. Small one-story cottages often have patterned shingles and applied decoration to signify the new fashion. Both larger houses and small cottages frequently have chamfered bays (Fig. 65). This configuration was a marked feature of E. W. Godwin's house, number One, the Avenue, in Bedford Park, and it became a prominent sign of the new fashion in pattern books in the United States.

The popularization of this type over the horizontal and contained fashions occurred as the cultural authority desired by the professional architects was being recast by their entrepreneurial pattern book competitors, who targeted a more diverse audience of working and middle-class people living in new and growing communities across the United States. These pattern book authors, many of whom had successful practices independent of their publications, were defining themselves as professional authorities to rival the architects who aligned themselves with the American Institute of Architects. But the imprint of professionalism, desired by both pattern book authors and their middle-class clients, had to be mediated with the societal need for a display of status through symbolic consumerism. As the "professional" architects had feared, the new fashion called "Queen Anne" was transferred to the popular domain. Ownership of the name, and more significantly of the design genre that developed from the new fashion, was won by the pattern book authors, builders, carpenters, and homeowners of the working and middle classes to become manifest in increasingly colorful formulations through the 1890s. The pattern book public in the rapidly

Fig. 65. Chamfered bay. Home in Bellingham, Wash. (Photograph by Barbara Plaskett)

growing western and southern lands, especially, embraced and held tenaciously to the fashion. The many historic house surveys completed by communities a century after this period of pattern book publication clearly demonstrate that colonial and shingle houses did not become prominent selections among homeowners in the South, Midwest, and West until the turn of the century. The more popular interpretations of gothicized Queen Anne were first noted by name in entrepreneurial pattern books and, from newspaper accounts, by many of their clients. Later, the name was used less frequently and the houses were described with adjectives. Known by any name— and one author called it the "anonymous style"—many of the houses would have fulfilled the *American Architect* description of the nation's "native work" as "the natural thing for a people restless, inventive, restrained by no artistic scruples or diffidence, fond of positive and even startling effects and given to display."[10]

Explorations and mediation

The matter of house style was a national concern, and mediation with the fashions from the cultural leadership of the east coast was transnational. Some pattern book authors who did not live in that urban sphere of high culture negotiated between their clients' predilections and their own desire for approval. The *San Francisco Evening Bulletin* compiled a series of designs for small houses that had been published in issues of their newspaper from April 1880 to January 1882 and published them as *Cheap Dwellings*. Each of the designs was by local architect John C. Pelton and each was a line drawing accompanied by specifications and construction information, with some discussion concerning architectural fashion. The designs included small one-story houses appropriate for the local climate (Fig. 66), houses that would be appropriate for city or country lots, and new fashions from England via the eastern United States. Aware of new fashion as well as domestic design preferences where he lived, Pelton obviously wanted his clients to know that trend-setting East Coast designs were also available in the West. Houses built west of the Ohio valley were gaining a reputation for ill-advised design. The Palliser brothers, for example, offered one house as an antidote, a "model of

neatness and a great change from the stereotypical style of the buildings generally erected in Western towns."[11] John Pelton presented
himself as a leader in bringing good taste to the Pacific West public,
whom he considered "particularly slow" to take advantage of recent
directions in housing design. Adopting a stance that was familiar
among critics of American architecture, he lamented that people of
the United States—and especially on the Pacific coast—had paid too
much attention to "business pursuits and industrial development"
and too little to art.[12]

Providing an antidote, Pelton found an improving condition of
American domestic architecture from the hands of eastern architects,
and he offered his rendition in "A Seven Room Cottage." First turning to the recognized correlation between eighteenth-century Queen
Anne architecture and houses in early America, he observed that
subsequent changes had led to an American style. As had Elisha

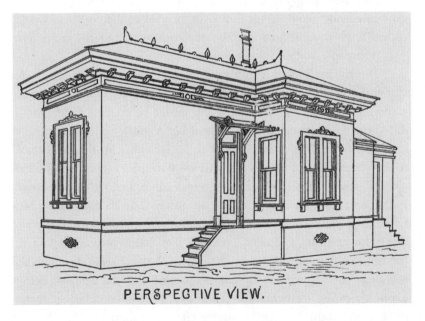

PERSPECTIVE VIEW.

*Fig. 66. California pattern book architect John Pelton interpreted East Coast fashions
for his clients but he also recognized local building customs and tastes. A small
California home. (Pelton,* Cheap Dwellings, 1882, *computer-generated
reproduction)*

Hussey, he gave special note to Swiss stylizations, and observed their merging with American houses to become a new "American style." Gleaning from his own house's description, he may have had in mind the "stick style" houses, for the beauty of the cottage was derived from "emphasizing the structural features of the building." He used this opportunity to argue against elaborate machine-made decoration by avoiding "any expensive surface ornamentation, or encumbering the house with unnecessary 'mill' work."[13]

The San Francisco architect again addressed the subject of mill work in a cottage with a more complex plan and exterior massing but without any "fanciful mill-work." This house was presented to his west coast readers as typical of modern "Eastern States" domestic architecture and much different from local custom. Pelton clarified his alliance with the nation's cultural leaders and used ethnic biases so common at the time to claim the unsuitability of extravagance, "Our California fanciful bird-cage imaginations (they can scarcely be called designs), though apparently admired here, are unknown in the Eastern States, and we doubt if in any other part of the civilized world, unless it be in China or the Eastern continent; the common term "gingerbread" can be oftener applied."[14]

But the architect's arguments for good taste did not deny exterior embellishment. As a practicing architect in San Francisco, where elaborated design was increasingly popular, he needed to accommodate local taste, too. Pelton assumed his readers' ignorance of new fashion and informed them about the colors now applied to houses in east coast cities and suburbs. All were in the range of colors considered appropriate to nature—"green, olive, yellow, sage, brown, Indian and Venetian red, crimson, salmon red, black, etc." Then, contradicting his stance on mill work, he encouraged such applied decoration on his "Eastlake Cottage." The Eastlake was popular in the far west, as attested to by articles in the *California Architect and Building News* as well as by extant examples of the houses. Pelton explicitly posed millwork for the heavy decorative detail as "ornamentation producing quite a pretty effect," and quite different than "somber roofs" on the heavier villa styles of the new fashion (Fig. 67).[15]

John Pelton's essays and designs suggest some confusion about what constituted the new fashions and ambivalence about his place

Fig. 67. Pelton spoke against the use of machine-made decoration; yet he designed houses that called for mill work. "Eastlake." (Pelton, Cheap Dwellings, *1882, computer-generated reproduction)*

in the professional architects' venture. He was not alone. Others were on the periphery of the debates on a suitable national domestic architecture, and not necessarily by geographic separation. Robert Shoppell produced his *How to Build, Furnish and Decorate* (1883) as a plan sales book of 126 house designs, with gothic, Italian, stick work, and French mansard stylizations, all fashions found in pattern books published ten years earlier. Few of the houses were given specific stylistic designation, but among the designs were eight houses identified as "Queen Anne." These houses did not incorporate many of the already established Queen Anne forms and features seen in the *American Architect* or in books such as William Comstock's, although a number of the houses appear to have resulted from attempts to integrate gothic and classic. Much of the former was drawn from the manner of vernacular gothic from several decades earlier, while the classic was represented with fragments of decorative detail, much as if their designer relied on verbal descriptions of the new fashion to spark his imagination rather than on visual models. One feature from classical antiquity often unconventionally appears on his houses—large molded or carved *akroteria* perched on gable peaks (Fig. 68).

The intervening year from his 1883 volume to *Modern, Low-Cost Houses* (1884) brought a striking change in the styles of houses offered by the Co-operative Building Plan Association, for most of the 40 house designs exhibited standard operative features of the genre developing from gothicized Queen Anne. Their audience was informed, too, of their being more current with the new fashion, for one-fourth of the house designs were identified as Queen Anne. Few others were given stylistic designations, although the classical tradition was remembered with an "Italian Villa" and a "Renaissance" house. The only "Gothic" building noted in the price list was a gesture to the mixture of styles associated with colonial and early American architecture. It was a gate lodge deemed appropriate for Thomas Jefferson's Monticello and described: "This beautiful and quaint looking little structure with its turreted bay window is in the sixteenth century Gothic style."[16] The Queen Anne houses in *Modern, Low-Cost Houses* were not as idiosyncratic as the 1883 designs. Many resembled designs earlier published in the *American Architect*, but

Shoppell's staff of architects re-interpreted the popular forms and features of Queen Anne with characteristic freedom.

In the same year, California architects Samuel and Joseph C. Newsom published the first of several books. The Newsom brothers were highly successful architects, having offices in Oakland and San Francisco. Their 1884 book, *Picturesque California Homes,* was a promotional advertisement for their work, without lengthy essays and without plan sales. However, the book's larger format allowed for larger drawings of the houses. The Newsom brothers, too, offered Queen Anne, but they also offered "modern," "picturesque," "suburban," and "city" homes. As we find in many pattern books, their denotation of Queen Anne did not mean a unique stylization among

Fig. 68. Robert Shoppell first interpreted the new fashion's integration of classical and medieval by adding akroteria to gable peaks. (Shoppell, How to Build, Furnish, and Decorate, *1883)*

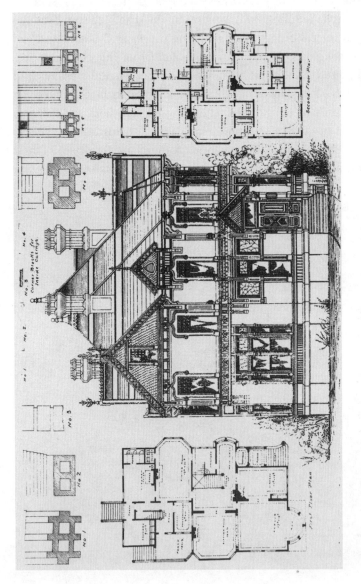

Fig. 69. The highly successful California team of architects, Samuel and Joseph Newsom, tended to ignore the mandates of simplicity published in the American Architect. "Queen Anne." (Newsom, Picturesque California Homes, 1884)

the other houses. It functioned more as one of several names circulating to form the conception of a modern suburban home. Overall, their built and published house designs contributed Pacific coast versions to the panoply of elaborated residential design (Fig. 69).[17] The architects applied the massing of volumetric forms common to the developing genre seen in pattern books up to this time, but their ornamentation was heavier and more exuberantly displayed, particularly on facades visible to the public. These houses with dressed up public faces accommodated narrow San Francisco city lots and drew attention away from the more economical plain side and rear facades (Fig. 70).

The Newsom brothers appear to have been less concerned with the east coast establishment's exhortations for discipline than their regional colleague, John Pelton, and their successful practice demonstrated that their course was well chosen. Not every architect opted for such independence. While Joseph and Samuel Newsom houses were built from northern to southern California, J. H. Kirby, whose practice in Syracuse, New York, was located closer to the urban leaders, published a small pamphlet of house designs that he designated as Queen Anne. The *American Architect* reviewed *Portfolio of Cottages* (c. 1885) with a harsh and rather lengthy criticism for such a small booklet:

> . . . conceived in what is spoken of by the unprofessional American as the "Queen Anne style," that is, designs which depart from the vernacular in that they are emphasized by scroll-work panels, pedimented window-heads, small-lighted windows, bargeboards, false half-timber work, overhanging gables, marvelously-shaped brackets and piazza posts, and windows of all sorts, shapes and sizes, in ordinary and untoward positions, most of these things wrought in wood. . . .[18]

Kirby responded by publishing a larger volume. He prepared *Modern Cottages*, with 125 illustrations, and all, he explained, were in the Queen Anne style. Compared within the range of current architectural elaboration, most of his more recent houses were designed with restraint. Kirby had acknowledge the fashion leadership of the *American Architect*. He introduced his book with an observation that contemporary architecture was "more quiet and less florid than it has been for several years past." Repudiating elaboration as a temporary inclination, he claimed his houses as timeless. They would carry well into the future because they were without "flimsy and trashy details," designed "more for repose and harmony and less for ostentatious

Fig. 70. A "city house" with an elaborate public face designed for narrow city lots found in San Francisco and other cities. (Newsom, Picturesque California Homes, *1884)*

display." Kirby sold his brand of the modern fashion as picturesque Queen Anne, but with understatement, describing it as "a style which is calculated to meet the wants of people who desire good, comfortable homes and yet something pleasing to the eye. The picturesque roof is the principal feature. . . ." (Fig. 71)[19]

Kirby was not so accommodating in his response to other criticisms from the *American Architect* reviewer. Although lacking mail-order plans and services, the book was an unmistakable entrepreneurial endeavor that functioned as an advertisement for Kirby's professional expertise and a means to enlarge his practice. Kirby unequivocally told his prospective clients that his book was published to improve his profits, and in this, he claimed, it deviated from the

Fig. 71. J. H. Kirby, Syracuse, N.Y., responded to harsh American Architect *criticism of an earlier pattern book by publishing a larger volume that clearly stated his intentions. His "Queen Anne" houses were "picturesque" and without "flimsy and trashy details." (Kirby,* Modern Cottages, *1886)*

"missionary" intent found in traditional publications. With his selection of words, Kirby countered the language of evangelistic ardor that
had been prevalent in the American Institute of Architects convention speeches heralding the advent of their "professional" journal. In
fact, the 1885 review in the journal had specifically criticized the work
as "advertisement" and the author as one whose "only interest lies
in the profit from its sale. . . ."[20]

D. S. Hopkins, in Grand Rapids, Michigan, was another architect who was a competitive businessman. He sold plans "at less than
one-half the price usually charged by Architects for new designs"
through his *Cottage Portfolio* (1886), a small book of twelve designs
for "[c]onvenient, comfortable and artistic low-cost homes." His
houses were in the picturesque and modern suburban picturesque
genre and he attested to its popularity. Design number two shared
these features and, he claimed, had been built "scores of times in the
United States and Canada within the past year." Design number ten
was "more suburban" and the most expensive, with its "ample sized
rooms" and "fine hall." A "new and different" house demonstrated
the growing interest in middle and far eastern decorative additions
to the fashion. Hopkins gave Design number five the requisite modern suburban silhouette but added a faceted onion dome atop a
turreted bay, which he called "a blending of the 'Moorish' which gives
many graceful lines to the exterior, and a design to be much admired
for its grace and dignified appearance"[21] (Fig.72).

The image of the modern suburban home was directed to rural
and frontier audiences by D. W. King in his "plain and practical aid,"
Homes for Home Builders (1886).[22] The houses were various interpretations of contemporary farmhouses and most had little ornamentation,
in tandem with the prevailing convention that held elaborate decoration as inappropriate for plain and sturdy farm homes. Nonetheless,
the architect included shingle and clapboard, tent-roofed and turreted
houses with the "Queen Anne" title, and his descriptions of these
houses, in contrast with his descriptions of the other houses, suggested
upward social mobility and suburban or country house living. Among
the designs, King unwittingly provided an example of the shift of
associations of name and style. One house was a Swiss cottage described as "quite in contrast to the so-called Queen Anne cottages."

Ironically, this "modified Swiss Cottage" had been previously published in the August 1885 issue of *Godey's Lady's Book* and titled "Modified Queen Anne Cottage."[23] King's 1886 Queen Anne was "for a family of means" (Figs. 73, 74).

Text and image in pattern books

Pattern books showing this fashion reached the rural, frontier, small-town, and suburban populations across the United States and Canada. Periodicals for the masses carried the news and countered the message of those directed to the upper middle classes. The transfer of superintendency over the character of the domestic landscape came

Fig. 72. Asian and Middle Eastern motifs were added to the compendium of forms. D. S. Hopkins added a "Moorish" onion dome to the modern house silhouette. (Hopkins, Cottage Portfolio, *1886)*

Fig. 73. Precise stylistic categorization was not the rule. This "modified Swiss cottage" had been published earlier in Godey's Lady's Book *as "Modified Queen Anne." (King,* Homes for Home Builders, *1886)*

Fig. 74. "Queen Anne Cottage." (King, Homes for Home Builders, *1886)*

with a greater sophistication in pattern book publication, especially among some of the more successful sellers of plans who combined visual and textual information to convey meanings of home ownership of a particular type. Their experimentation with pattern book format and content was a significant factor in selling individually owned houses to the late-nineteenth-century middle class public who lived in a time of phenomenal expansion in mass communication. They were participants in a developing print culture that contributed to shaping cultural symbols with mass appeal. Improved printing technology, lowered postal rates for books and periodicals, and increased rail service brought newspapers, books, and magazines in a heretofore unimagined quantity and variety at lower prices to a nationwide audience. By 1885, there were approximately 3,300 periodicals in the United States and by 1890 there were 4,400.[24] They were directed to men, women, children, families, occupations, and specific interest groups. The nineteenth century, more than any preceding time, was a period in which dominant beliefs were strengthened through their textual articulation in books, lengthy articles, instructional manuals, and printed tracts. Writing, as with so many endeavors in the late nineteenth century, was being defined as a professional activity, and text-based pattern books by professional architects shared the prestige of authoritative writing.

Among the devices used by authors to appeal to readers of informative books was to transform education into narrative. Eugene Gardner, an author of numerous books on architecture from the late 1870s to the early 1890s, wrote an entertaining book on house building titled *The House that Jill Built, after Jack's Had Proved a Failure* (1882). Frank L. Smith wrote his book, *A Cosy Home* (1887), as a dialogue between a client with a venerable colonial surname, "Mr. Charles Alden," and Smith, the architect. The dialogue demonstrated the mediation between the positions on fashion, but through the story's narrative Smith directed the reader to a conclusion that less elaboration was desirable. Although more houses in the book reflected the modern suburban genre, the climax of the story was a presentation of the most appropriate contemporary house—colonial. Smith asked his client, Mr. Alden, "Do you like the modern style of house usually termed 'Queen Anne'?" Alden answered, "Yes, and no. I am fond of ornament, but do not like architectural gymnastics, I want something more quiet, perhaps, than I commonly see, yet I do not want a 'boxy' house."[25] Smith's response to his client's preference was drawings for houses designed in the mode of unadorned modern suburban houses, with some modified slightly in the direction of shingle and Queen Anne integrations. Then the client who wished to be up-to-date was surprised with "something different," a house in the colonial style with more gently sloped broad eaves (Fig. 75).[26]

Smith and other authors relied heavily on textual exposition. But the persuasive power of visual representation was not lost in the accelerated print activity of the later nineteenth century. Pattern books, of course, contained images, for they were selling a visual cultural symbol. While some pattern books gave prominence to the visual by

Fig. 75. A cottage in the "colonial" style. (Smith, A Cosy Home, *1887)*

having drawings of houses and little or no text, other books balanced text and image, such as the Pallisers' 1878 publication that faced each house design with a page of description. We could assume that the readers of pattern books who contemplated building homes would be most interested in what the houses looked like as they perused the pattern books, but the number of pattern books having more space allotted to text than house designs shows that the authors were appealing to differing sensibilities of their clients. Some assumed a clientele who wished a broader education on the subject of house building more than a variety of house fashions from which to choose. However, the most often-used format was a balance of space dedicated to text and to illustration. The text in these pattern books typically consisted of a selected few phrases to connote desirable traits of the house and a lengthier portion explaining specifications and construction. They were essentially catalogues of house designs, and this was the format used by Sears, Roebuck and Company to sell prefabricated homes at the turn of the century.

House and text formed a dialogue between the illustration, made more evocative with brief description, and the pragmatic considerations of site, materials, and cost. But there were other subtle appeals that fed the home-building public's desires. While the actual houses were undeniably the objects of the consumer's interest in these books, the style of drawing in which the houses were illustrated contributed to forming the pattern book audience's notions of house and home. For the most part, the perspectives and elevations in the entrepreneurial pattern books were simple line drawings that clearly delineated the features of the houses. Perspective drawings typically included a small amount of landscape detail; often both perspectives and elevations were given dimensionality with shadows from projecting ells, verandas and gables (for example, see Fig. 76). These straightforward drawings were much different from the artistically rendered perspectives and elevations done in the Beaux-Arts manner presented to clients by academically trained architects. The visual presentations in the pattern books were drawn in what William Woollett, Fellow of the American Institute of Architects and producer of traditional pattern books, called preliminary studies from the drafting tables of his architectural firm.[27] This style of drawing was an expedient method of illustration and inexpensive to produce for the low-priced pattern books. That the drawings could function as working drawings for local builders was noted by authors, such as Bicknell and Comstock, who produced pattern books but did not sell plans. In the books selling architectural services and plans, the useful illustrations were more effective visual recommendations to builders, contractors, and their practical clients. Because the house designs were not obscured by artistic latitude, the method of drawing was an assurance that the illustrations were honest representations of the houses as they would appear when built.

Sophisticated techniques

Among the architects producing pattern books from 1880 to the end of the decade, several experimented with more persuasive uses of both text and image. Pictures and words worked together to convey a more convincing message. As seen earlier, their success in selling houses and promoting their social meanings was accomplished through their participation in the ongoing competition in developing marketing techniques, and from the 1880s they began to acknowledge changes in the print culture. At this time of increased mass production and nationally known name brands, advertising was also emerging as a more sophisticated business tactic. Earlier advertising, up until the mid-1870s, was typically text with little visual information, but during the last quarter of the century advertisers began to apply the persuasion of carefully selected evocative language to visual renditions of their products. Advertising, too, began to be taken into the hands of experts. Viewers of trade cards and readers of magazines were introduced to the wonders of Pears Soap, Gold Dust Washing Powder, Minton Tiles and Perry's Comedone and Pimple Remedy, the Infallible Skin Medicine in advertisements that united visual representations with laudatory verbal descriptions. Products were often endorsed by renowned Americans who added their prestige to the value of the product. Even the eminent theologian Henry Ward Beecher was paid to endorse a hernial truss and Pears' Soap.[28] This emphasis on celebrity authority and product name distanced the modern viewer from the local shopkeeper who was in danger of becoming an impersonal purveyor of goods. The vividly colored trade cards, which could be found in many homes collected and pasted in scrapbooks, expressly worked to create a relationship between the consumer and the product's manufacturer to supersede neighborly business exchanges.[29] Pattern books that sold plans did the same, albeit in modified form to accommodate building custom. Some successful pattern book authors provided the authority of architect-designed modern houses and contributed to their popularization by formulating connections between the meanings of the houses and the appearance of the houses in a manner that is familiar to us today as advertising strategies. These pattern book authors worked with a system of values in which words and patterns of language already had strong associative significance, and from this they formulated persuasive arguments for their houses and their services.

One of the notable correlations of language and illustration is found in Shoppell's 1884 publication, *Modern Low-Cost Houses.* As in other pattern books, the house designs were visually prominent in order to establish a dialogue with the text. The houses were factually described with sprinklings of vivid adjectives, again a customary approach, but for several houses, language was manipulated more expressively. Words describing the houses were particularly resonant for his audience of prospective suburban homeowners, and they were placed in brief text that was entertaining as well as instructive. Shoppell introduced the sales appeal of anecdotal imagery to portray a lifestyle that the houses ostensibly made possible. Several designs and their descriptions evoked visions of a safe haven for the busy man of the household, which, he suggested, benefitted the family, too. Design No. 140, "A $2800 Parsonage," featured a study for the minister for whom it was projected, but for a layman, the room could be a sewing room or "'growlery' . . . a room where the man of the house retires when he doesn't feel well, and look over his bills, &c, &c." Design No. 143, "A Delightful House, $2,000," was "A truly delightful country house," with "particularly comfortable features" to keep the men happily at home. "The men folks of a family do not 'go to lodge' so often when they live in a house like this," and following a list of amenities found in such a house—generous food, billiards, easy chairs and cigars on the veranda—"the men have about all the creature comforts they want." This type of description placed the house in a social context. Particular moments in daily life were selected and their activities could be visualized. Much as in advertising today, the meanings were not specific to the particular house but made a connection between a way of life and the product sold. Shoppell's "$6000 Queen Anne Villa," Design No. 163, was introduced with puffery that imaged family values and social mobility: "This beautiful design is one that meets the requirements of a large family of cultivated taste. The elevation is noble and dignified and yet home-like, suggesting the comfort and taste of the interior" (Fig. 76). Shoppell, like others who used the language of hegemonic American

Fig. 76. Much as in advertising, pattern book authors made verbal connections between a way of life and the illustrated house designs. This "$6,000 Queen Anne Villa" with its "noble and dignified yet home-like" exterior was for a "family of cultivated taste." (Shoppell, Modern Low-Cost Homes, 1884)

values, structured a relationship between the beliefs that were being forged as the norm for Americans and the types of house that represented the norm. The expensive villa was a variation on the theme of some contemporary shingled houses, but with complex massing.

Using Shoppell again as an example, the company's 1887 publication, *Modern Houses, Beautiful Homes*, contains experimentation with visual presentation. Most pattern books that showed houses in a physical context distorted proportions by enlarging the house. Fashionably dressed adults and playing children often were placed within scenes of lawn, shrubs, trees, and walk or drive, but they were drawn as small foreground figures, as if in reverse perspective. In a few drawings, Shoppell's illustrators slightly enlarged the figures to make the scenes more realistic. Proportional accuracy, however, was not adopted until photographed houses were included in pattern books. The 1887 book showed a concentration on developing an artistic presentation more than a realistic one. Its cover featured a large scene of domestic coziness enclosed in a circular frame superimposed over drawings of stylized nature (Fig. 77). Houses inside were placed in more complete scenes of nature, often with drawn sky. Several were framed visually with circles and other geometric shapes, and vignettes were superimposed to show plans and additional views.

S. B. Reed was not as creatively artistic but he presented a clean, organized format that called attention to his elaborate designs. Reed, who designed houses for a rural audience, had not embraced the new fashion when it was introduced by other pattern book authors. Following the popular response to his 1878 book of *American Agriculturalist* house designs, he published another in 1883. In each, the houses were examples of earlier prevailing styles and were drawn with rough, bold lines. When he produced a book for new suburban homeowners with *Dwellings for Village and Country* (1885), his house designs and the drawing style had become more polished. The new, fashionable houses were drawn with more delicate line. Each house was presented with a frontal view, side elevation, and floor plans on pages that were simply framed with a drawn line. The reader knew what to expect with each turn of the page: on the left page, a frontal view, the construction cost, a name for the house and a description; on the right, the elevation and plans and continued description.

The houses presented in this logical and unelaborated format ranged from simple two-story cottages to extremely elaborate houses that he called "free style." Most of his houses combined the forms and massing typical of the modern suburban genre, but the individual elements of decoration frequently were increased in size. On many, enlarged forms competed with one another for the viewer's attention and introduced a full-blown robustness for late-nineteenth-century domestic architecture. These would have been conspicuous even amid other homes built in the more elaborate interpretations of the fashion. His use of language followed a similar tact, with brevity bringing forward powerful words. The houses were not titled with names of

Fig. 77. Emphasis on domestic coziness for a pattern book cover. (Shoppell, Modern Houses, Beautiful Homes, *1887)*

styles or with generally used adjectives but were given names of suburbs. Each was directed to the new, more profitable market. Attractive and prosperous settings for his homes were communicated with community names known to his East Coast clientele, including New London, Montclair, Vineland, and Mamaroneck. His descriptive passages were not anecdotal but they combined in few sentences the key signifying words. His "Norwalk" house was "modern," "novel," "suburban," "domestic," "home-like," with "convenient" interior planning and designed to "befit choice situations" (Fig. 78). Those who read his concluding essay titled, "Home," (see page 59) were assured that these houses fulfilled their dreams of a home in nature and community.

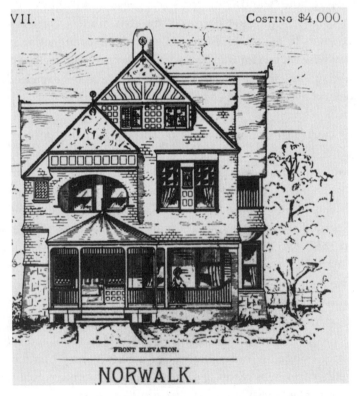

Fig. 78. Reed described his suburban homes as "modern," "novel," "domestic," and "home-like," with convenient interior planning. "Norwalk." (Reed, Dwellings for Village and Country, 1885)

Among the manipulations of text and image, few pattern books took advantage of color plates. Color reproduction was too costly, and their goal was to sell inexpensive volumes to large numbers of people. The *Scientific American Builder's Edition* and the *National Builder* were among the exceptions. Promotional brochures circulated by paint companies were another means for the house-building public to see house designs in full color. Their focus, however, was not solely the new house market. Much of their business was to convince owners of older houses to modernize them with new paint colors, and their brochures demonstrated the transition from out-of-date to timely. Seeley Brothers Paint transformed several of Elisha Hussey's 1876 houses with warm tones of brown and golden wheat, including his Swedo-gothic home. Aniline paints had made possible a transition from white houses and Downing's soft greys and beiges to deeper, richer tones.[30] The new paint colors also made it possible for homeowners to paint their homes in almost any combination of colors they wished, but for the most part, the house-building public did not take full advantage of them. Pattern book authors exercised discipline and avoided "barber-pole" color schemes.

Modern suburban homes to the end of the century

The entrepreneurial competition to sell modern suburban homes of the type characterized by today's umbrella term "Victorian" continued. Major players in the field were Robert Shoppell, the Pallisers, and George F. Barber, an architect working from Knoxville, Tennessee. In 1887, two of the more prolific entrepreneurial pattern book firms marketed new volumes. Robert Shoppell's Co-operative Building Plan Association published *Modern Houses, Beautiful Homes*, and the Palliser brothers published *New Cottage Homes and Details*. While architects who identified themselves with the direction taken by the professional architects were turning to colonial gambrel and saltbox roofs and bungalow horizontality for contemporary home building, neither firm was ready to embrace fully modern colonial. Their businesses relied on selling plans transcontinentally, and they offered choices for their customers. Shoppell even included plans for a house with a French mansard roof, disclaiming it with, "From an artistic

point of view, we do not admire the Mansard or French roof, yet it
has some advantages over other forms. . . ."[31] The majority of
Shoppell's designs tended to be shingle-house in appearance, but his
above-noted illustrated history of American houses criticized earlier
box-like houses with contained massing as "non descript" and scientifically validated the "modern" house in the popular suburban mode
as the current culmination of architectural evolution. Most of the
Pallisers' houses were unmistakably in the modern suburban mold,
although colonial houses were included. However, in the following
year, the Palliser Company published another new pattern book,
American Architecture—a compilation of two earlier publications,
American Cottage Homes (1877) and *Palliser's Model Homes* (1878)—in
which they evidently again judged their public unready for the colonial and classicizing fashions.

Neither of the companies emphasized style names but the
Palliser book used their houses to claim a national style for the United
States. Readers of *New Cottage Homes and Details* were informed that
the houses were not in any "well defined style," but they were
American, for the houses were peculiar to America, a land where
differing people and their needs required variety in domestic design.
The Palliser brothers echoed the nationalism fueled over a decade
earlier by the Centennial: "[T]here is springing up a National style
which is becoming more distinctive in character and unlike that of
any other nation, as the American climate, life, economy of time and
labor, requiring greater facility and conveniences, with snug and
comfortable quarters for Winter and shady porches and verandas for
Summer."[32] The house they considered most national in character was
their "modern American Renaissance . . . being of a decided classic
mould," but here again, the classical did not mean horizontality or
colonial shingle (see Fig. 12).[33] A small urn finial, classical swag
moldings, and a relatively judicious amount of elaboration denoted
classical in a familiar popular translation of the professional exhortations for simplicity. When compared to the colonial, bungalow, and
classic box houses built by the middle classes in the coming decades,
these houses were ornate, but the Pallisers argued differently. They
spoke against the "nonsensical," "gewgaws," and "eccentricities" to
define "American Vernacular" as "so-called Queen Anne" disciplined

by good taste (Fig. 79). Their cleaned-up Queen Anne was placed on the cover (see Fig. 31), and its communicative attributes were described with eloquence to draw associations of the paradigmatic businessman owner who required a retreat from the demands of his workday life,

> . . . a good sample of what the homes of many successful business men ought to be who appreciate their spare moments and desire to spend them in enjoyment and social intercourse with the family, free from the cares and restraints of the business world. Such homes as this are wanted all over our country, and it is the business men of fair means who can live in them, and who, by so doing, will educate the public taste to appreciate the sensible and artistic treatment

Fig. 79. *"American Vernacular." (Palliser,* New Cottage Homes, *1887)*

that is so satisfying and pleasing to the mind through the eye, cultivating the taste for something honest and simple in construction, and leading the desire away from that which is pernicious . . . made only to gratify the whims and caprices of the ignorant and uneducated. . . .[34]

At the beginning of the next decade, two architect-authors interpreted the public's demands for housing design differently than the authors described above, and perhaps they would have been categorized as ignorant by the Pallisers. George Garnsey and George F. Barber sold plans for embellished houses. The National Builder Publishing Company published a compilation of designs by Chicago architect George Garnsey as an *Album of Beautiful Homes* (1891).[35] The *National Builder* was a monthly building and interior decoration magazine that each month published colored drawings of a house and sold blueprints for the featured house at a cost of three dollars. The company substantiated its success by publishing letters of commendation received from Whatcom, Washington, Daytona, Florida, New York, New York, Cedar Rapids, Iowa, Waterloo, Ontario, even from the London, England, *Plumber and Decorator*. The book *Beautiful Homes* was a compilation of designs, with minimal text and only occasional reference to styles. Although some homes are not unusual, some of the houses defy description. The architect intermixed forms from the late-nineteenth-century compendium and invented new ones. On one small cottage a three-quarter circular bay was perched so precariously on a veranda roof that it would have frustrated any builder (Fig. 80). Several of the Garnsey houses rivaled and surpassed the ornate S. B. Reed and Newsom houses in their profuse decoration and multiple intersecting volumes. The inventive Garnsey was apparently so tempted by the feast of available architectural motifs that he promoted emancipation from stylistic constrictions and decorative restraint. Not only did he mix classical and medieval, but he applied motifs from the Asian east to the western structures. Plate 29, "The Connell & Dengler Cottage," was designed with the modern suburban irregular perimeter plan, a chamfered bay, multiple gables, and moderately pitched roof lines (Fig. 81). Its cladding was clapboard and shingle, and its silhouette was punctuated by finials and a massive

Fig. 80. One Chicago architect included designs that appeared to be unbuildable. "Bradley Cottage." (Garnsey, National Builders' Album, *1891)*

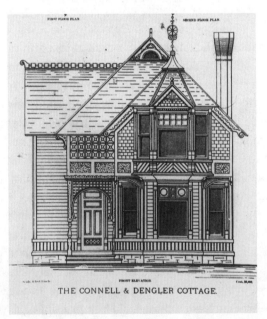

Fig. 81. "Connell & Dengler Cottage" displayed an inventive use of motifs on a small home. (Garnsey, National Builder's Album, *1891)*

chimney, while a small king post decoration and a band of delicate pseudo- half-timber decoration tended toward the medieval. To make it more Asian, motifs appear such as curved gable finials similar to illustrations of Japanese temples in popular magazine articles. Reticulation, formed by tile patterns reproduced in wood, and a moon, or horseshoe, window also suggested eastern designs. Garnsey kept these displays in check with rectangles formed by applied strips of wood, corner boards, and window moldings grooved with modern classical regularity. He applied this design strategy to his even more elaborate N. & G. Taylor Villa (Fig. 82).

George F. Barber, too, paid little attention to the strongly promoted classicizing tendencies. Barber has been described as "one of this country's most successful, late-nineteenth-century domestic architects," with houses built across the United States, its territories and Canada. Recently moved from DeKalb, Illinois, Barber entered the national market with *The Cottage Souvenir, No. 2 A Repository of Artistic Cottage Architecture and Miscellaneous Designs* from his new business location in Knoxville, Tennessee.[36] Barber typified the entrepreneurial, self-educated carpenter who established himself as an architect and sold plans by mail order. Advertisements for his pattern book in popular periodicals and trade journals caught the attention of the home-building public. By 1900, there were some fifty employees working for Barber's architectural firm.[37] He offered fully pre-fabricated homes, which would have been a feasible proposition in his new Tennessee location, a center of forestry and building materials manufacturing.

Barber's successful pattern book illustrated a series of houses in the modern suburban genre of design (Fig. 83). Page after page presented yet another rendition with forms and features drawn from British and European contemporary, classical and medieval, American colonial, and Asian sources. Shingle and bungalow house types were not in his repertoire. Verticality communicated the medieval foundations of the Queen Anne fashion and was emphasized with the frequent addition of towers and turrets. Barber wielded the late-nineteenth-century architect's artistic freedom wholeheartedly. The majority of the houses were more ornate than those designed by Kirby, Shoppell, and the Pallisers, and were occasionally as

Fig. 82. "N & G. Taylor Villa." (Garnsey, National Builder's Album, *1891)*

Fig. 83. From Knoxville, Tenn., an elaborate modern suburban home. (Barber, Cottage Souvenir, *No. 2, 1891)*

flamboyant as those designed by the Newsoms and Garnsey. At the same time, he convinced his public that the designs were built according to the laws of nature, stating that harmony would be achieved with color and with proportion accomplished by the correct relation of height, breadth, and length of the house and its parts. According to Barber, ornamentation was the most difficult aspect of composing a building, but properly done, it added "life, expression and dignity."[38] His houses and rhetoric both marketed and appropriated contemporary architectural theory, petitions for artistic taste in America, and popular taste. George F. Barber, among others, prolonged the life of the modern suburban genre to the end of the century, for his homes have been documented in states from the southeast to the northwest. Among the many extant Barber houses, an illustrious 1890s home in Jacksonville, Oregon, is claimed to have been shipped from Tennessee to the Pacific northwest as a kit ready to assemble.

NOTES

[1] See Woods, *The "American Architect and Building News" 1876–1907*, 1983.

[2] "American Vernacular Architecture.-4," p. 5.

[3] Mariana Griswold Van Rensselaer, "Recent Architecture in America. Public Buildings. I.," *Century Magazine* 28(May 1884): 61.

[4] Brunner, pp. 7, 8, and 26.

[5] William Burnet Tuthill, *The Suburban Cottage* (New York: William T. Comstock, 1885), p. 8.

[6] John Carrere and Thomas Hastings, *Florida, the American Riviera, St. Augustine the Winter Newport* (New York: Gliss Brothers and Turnure, the Art Age Press, 1887), n.p.

[7] Pierce & Dockstader, *Modern Buildings of Moderate Cost* (Elmira, N. Y.: By the Authors, 1886), p. 37.

[8] Manly Cutter, *Designs for Modern Buildings* (New York: New York Building Plan Co., 1887), Prospectus.

[9] Louis H. Gibson, *Convenient Houses with Fifty Plans for the Housekeeper* (New York: Thomas Y. Crowell & Co., 1889), pp. 104–05.

[10] "American Architecture—With Precedent and Without," *American Architect* 3(October 26, 1878): 139.

[11] Palliser, *Model Homes*, 1878, p. 52.

[12] John C. Pelton, Jr., *Cheap Dwellings* (San Francisco: The San Francisco Bulletin Company, 1882).

[13] Ibid., pp. 23, 24.

[14] Ibid., p. 50.

15 Ibid., p. 43.

16 The company numbered their house plans consecutively through the years. *Modern Low-Cost Houses* were numbered 127–67.

17 Samuel and Joseph C. Newsom, *Picturesque California Homes* (San Francisco: By the Authors, 1884; reprint ed., Los Angeles: Hennessey & Ingalls, Inc., 1978).

18 "Books," *American Architect* 18(August 29, 1885): 104.

19 J. H. Kirby, *Modern Cottages* (Syracuse, New York: By the Author, 1886), p. 8.

20 Ibid., pp. 8 and 9.

21 David S. Hopkins, *Cottage Portfolio* (New York: Fred A. Hodgson, Pub.., 1886), Preface.

22 David Woodbury King, *Homes for Home Builders or Practical Designs for Country, Farm and Village* (New York: Orange Judd Co., 1886).

23 Ibid., p. 69. Four "Queen Anne Cottage" illustrations by King were published in *Godey's* in 1885.

24 Frank Luther Mott, *A History of American Magazines 1885–1905* (Cambridge: The Belknap Press of Harvard University Press, 1957), p. 11.

25 Smith, 1887, p. 8.

26 Ibid., description of Des. D.

27 Woollett, *Villas and Cottages*, preface.

28 Bledstein, pp. 65–75.

29 Ellen Garvey examines trade cards and the developing culture of consumption in *The Adman in The Parlor: Magazines and the Gendering of Consumer Culture, 1880s to 1910s.* (New York: Oxford University Press, 1996).

30 Roger Moss, *Century of Color: Exterior Decoration for American Buildings—1820–1920* (Watkins Glen: The American Life Foundation, 1981).

31 Robert Shoppell, *Modern Houses, Beautiful Homes* (New York: Co-operative Building Plan Association, 1887), Des. 307, p. 106.

32 Palliser, *New Cottage Homes*, "Introductory," n.p.

33 Ibid., Plate 6.

34 Ibid., Plate 1.

35 George Garnsey, *The National Builder's Album of Beautiful Homes* (Chicago: The National Builder Publishing Co., 1891).

36 George F. Barber, *Cottage Souvenir, No. 2* (Knoxville, Tenn.: S.B. Newman & Co., 1891).

37 Michael A. Tomlan, intro., *Toward the Growth of an Artistic Taste* (Watkins Glen: American Life Foundation, 1982), passim; reprint ed., Barber, *Cottage Souvenir.*

38 Barber, *Cottage Souvenir*, n.p.

◢ Epilogue: ◣

One Town in the Pacific Northwest

There have been many variations on pattern book business practices since the close of the nineteenth century. Through the 1920s, especially, catalogue-sold, mass-produced houses were immensely popular among prospective homeowners across the North American continent. A multitude of brochures from local lumber companies and builders joined catalogues from such large companies as Sears Roebuck and the Michigan-based Aladdin Company to sell both homes and the conception of home ownership as integral to American identity.[1] Today, too, books and magazines with house designs participate in a larger media culture to assert the self-owned home surrounded by lawn as a cultural symbol for the "American dream," a narrative of American life in which hard work is followed by financial success, and moral and domestic security. As in the late nineteenth century, contemporary economic constraints often make it difficult for people to buy homes, but the notion of owning a single-family, detached dwelling has been accomplished as a nationally accepted right of citizenship in the United States. Even while communities struggle with the consequences of this dream—long commutes to jobs, suburban sprawl, and environmental consideration—it is difficult for most to accept alternative solutions to housing and community planning. The union of discourses on nationalism and home ownership in the late nineteenth century so convincingly accomplished the spatialization of this condition of American identity that it is largely unquestioned. Living in a duplex, condominium, or row house is still perceived as a temporary measure. Perhaps looking back with nostalgia to the mythologized past today is an act of finding reassurance that the dream can be realized.

Admiration of nineteenth century "Victorian" houses is central to imagining the past, but amid the search for and preservation of these houses, more attention has been paid to owners, to the

architects, or to the "craftsmanship" than to the means of their popularization. The documentation of pattern book houses has been treated
sparingly, due either to the limited circulation of primary sources or
the lack of interest in such a mundane matter, for pattern books are
items of the everyday more than of celebrity. Nonetheless, when
authors and local historians do look for Palliser, Barber, Shoppell, and
other pattern book homes, they find many examples. As I noted earlier, houses from pattern books and house fashions that were
circulated in pattern books can be found in most communities that
experienced dramatic population growth in the last quarter of the
nineteenth century. Many of these towns and cities were located in
the Southeast and western half of the country, but late-century
architectural fashions were built by the middle classes in the Northeast as well.

This book is concerned with a national scope, but as I concluded
the project, I was curious about local interpretations. I again questioned just how prevalent pattern book houses were and to what
extent communities and individuals played their parts in producing
the hegemonic meanings of national, community, and personal identity. My own community, Bellingham, Washington, seemed a good
place to start. It was an example of a late-nineteenth-century boom
town in which many large, elaborate houses in the modern suburban
fashions, as well as their more modest counterparts, were built. Of
these, many have been destroyed or modernized, but a surprising
number have remained relatively intact. Interestingly, until my study,
none had been recorded as pattern book houses in written or oral
history, for greater pride was taken in the work of the town's architects. But a cursory look immediately revealed the popular use of
architectural fashions that may be associated with the spread of pattern book designs. Of course, these houses were situated on spacious
lots, and in the practice of suburban planning, they were distanced
from the commercial center.

Bellingham, Washington

At the close of the nineteenth century a new home was raised in a
small but growing community in the far northwestern corner of the

United States between Vancouver, British Columbia, and Seattle, Washington (see Fig. 1). Built on a hillside edging the Pacific Ocean's Bellingham Bay, the house held a commanding view of busy logging and fishing operations and nature's colorful sunsets over the forest-covered San Juan Islands. Seen from below, the house was an imposing sight. Its high, irregular silhouette formed by a hipped roof and gabled ells echoed a backdrop of undulating mountain foothills. A gabled entrance porch with elaborately turned posts and scroll-cut moldings supported a balcony on the house's right front facade, and an octagonal "Moorish" turret decorated with rows of scalloped shingles and panels of incised and painted decoration added a touch of the exotic. Extending the eastern theme, a moon window, of the type often considered "Chinese," opened the house to the scene below. On the left of the facade, a windowed chamfered bay with multiple gables, button barge-board molding, carved pendants, lattice work, scalloped shingles and a large sunflower motif, gave an asymmetrical picturesque cast to the home's intricate compositional balance. Above it all, a tall, flared, red brick chimney signaled a warm fire to ward off the chilling fogs of the bay.

When the owners of the home, Mr. and Mrs. Robert Morse, determined in 1897 to build a new home appropriate to their social standing in the community, they did not hire a local carpenter. Instead, they consulted Alfred Lee, a local architect who had been commissioned earlier to build a new city hall for Bellingham, a neighboring community less than a mile away. Alfred Lee was highly respected and would remain one of Bellingham's leading architects in actual practice and in memory. That fact notwithstanding, his status as a professional architect would have been questionable according to American Institute of Architects standards. He was not formally trained, but was a wagon maker who had moved from Oregon to make his fortune farther north. And when Lee built the Morse home, he did not produce an original design. He used the plans for a house found in George Barber's 1891 pattern book (Fig. 84).

The Morse family living in Bellingham today does not know whether Mr. and Mrs. Robert Morse were aware of the source for their home's design. Certainly Barber's pattern books were familiar to people in the northwest. He advertised regularly in the *Ladies Home*

Journal and, as noted earlier, a Barber home was built in Jacksonville, Oregon. But family records give no indication that anyone other than Alfred Lee was the architect. However, it may have been important that someone with the professional appellation "architect" be hired. Robert Morse was a consummate businessman at a time when the label "businessman" was highly esteemed, as it signified a man who by his own hard work had attained financial and social success. A businessman's home was both a product and a sign of that success. Morse's story, later written and published by his family, fulfilled the

Fig. 84. Pattern book model for Morse home, 1897. Original design for Chas. J. Burton, Gloversville, N.Y. (Barber, Cottage Souvenir, *No. 2, 1891)*

promises of the American dream. Robert Morse had moved to the Pacific west from Maine and arrived in San Francisco in 1875, at the age of seventeen, with only "sugarbowl" savings in hand. Nine years later, he, his wife and son moved to the far northwest to open a hardware store. While the communities along Bellingham Bay experienced periods of economic growth countered by recession and the Panic of 1893, Morse's business grew. Within twelve years, he had become a pillar of the community and began to make plans to build one of the town's more illustrious homes. Passing over shingle houses, gambrel-roof colonial houses, Richardsonian Romanesque derivations, and the new boxy colonial-classical forms, Mr. and Mrs. Morse elected to build in the picturesque, modern suburban genre.[2] This fashion was clearly the most popular among the small communities in Bellingham Bay, for many in this genre had been built in the years from 1890 to 1892. By following a precedent set by affluent families a half-decade earlier, the Morses established themselves as mainstream community members.

The George Barber house was built when the region was coming back to life after the crash of 1893. Bellingham Bay's short-lived boom time had begun about 1888. The three villages of Fairhaven, Sehome, and Whatcom that lined the edge of the bay comprised a population of 400 people in 1888, but within a year they had grown by ten times.[3] Building businesses began in earnest. Commercial lots were selling in Fairhaven for $2,500, $1,500 and $1,000, and though the streets were rutted with water-filled potholes, the grand Hotel Fairhaven, which was projected at a cost of $80,000, and an opera house costing $150,000 were planned. One of the local newspapers hailed the "splendid moral effect" of the new buildings and assured its readers that the edifices would "immensely increase real estate values"[4] As in so many western towns, civic leaders of Fairhaven envisioned the community as a city of the future. The editor of the *Herald* exhorted: "Fairhaven is to be the Pittsburgh of the west, so far as the matter of working iron of course. In the matter of culture, it will be the Boston of the west; in brotherly love it will be the Philadelphia of the west; in commercial push and enterprise, it will be the Chicago of the west; as a shipping point, it will be the New York of the west." It is no surprise, then, that the Hotel Fairhaven was not designed by local builders but by Boston transplants, architects Longstaff and Black, who interpreted the Queen Anne style of masonry commercial buildings found in their East Coast hometown. Once opened with great fanfare, the hotel was reported to have entertained visitors from the East Coast who considered Hotel Fairhaven to have the best interiors and dining in the state. In 1891, railroad track connected Bellingham Bay with New Westminster, British Columbia, and the future seemed assured.

Despite the rhetoric of promotion, the towns of Bellingham Bay were far removed from today's idealized notion of the late nineteenth century. Instead, words describing the social and architectural condition of the United States expressed in an *American Architect* article on the vernacular is more fitting: "Our boundless heritage has its dangers, no doubt; we have not learned how to classify and how to use it with discretion and true respect, how to adjust it to our new materials and conditions of life. We are yet sowing our wild oats with a fruitless expenditure of resources."[5] The forests of the bay had been clear-cut and tree stumps impeded traffic on some streets and marred the lots prepared for building. The fishing, shipping, and logging industries located on the bay were active with noise, dirt, and odors. The newspapers bemoaned the crime rate. One daring young man read about a diamond robbery in the *San Francisco Examiner* and copied every detail in order to successfully rob a local firm of its jewels. Worse, shootings "in cold blood without provocation" were too common.

Nonetheless, new residents appeared from 1888 to 1891 at such a rate that houses could not be built fast enough. While tents sheltered those who could not afford the hotel rates that from demand were even higher than in the east, houses were built steadily. Shanties, cottages, and mansions began to dot the streets of the three towns. Each town was laid out in the same grid pattern of development found in the other growing communities. The only complication to the urban grid system, however, came from the fact that each of the communities aligned its grid with its own respective edge of the curving bay rather than with the points of the compass. As the towns grew together into one larger community, the grids joined with a disorienting confusion of angles and curves that continues to perplex today's newcomers to Bellingham. But platting towns with orientation to the bay was common in coastal communities. In this way, residential development could be directed to views of the water and the houses could sustain spatial order by having their front facades face the street. Then, as now, houses with views had higher real estate value.

The towns' residents worked to bring "civilization" to the bay in the familiar social pattern found across the United States. Fourth of July celebrations included yacht races, sack races, balls, and parades. One parade featured a float with a Goddess of Liberty and forty-four young women dressed in white to represent the states of the union. Patriotic speeches stirred national pride that was built on beliefs about the dominant culture of northern European descendants that were common throughout the nineteenth century. At the Hotel Fairhaven celebration in the same year, the guests were entertained with a poem that began, "And let us hope the pattern set by Anglo-Saxon sires, who lit for all humanity sweet Freedom's altar fires, May win 'till all the nations shall stand beside us here. . . ." From 1890 to the end of the century, men and women who settled in the community joined a variety of social and church-affiliated organizations. In 1896, the mayor of Fairhaven proclaimed the town's participation in Arbor Day and local philanthropists donated money to plant nearly three hundred trees to replace those cut down some years earlier. Each street was to be planted with a different kind of tree and there was to be a tree every twenty-five feet. Women in neighboring Whatcom planned to follow this example. Such enthusiasm for village improvement continued well into the twentieth century.

The homes built by these residents of Bellingham Bay included a broad range of fashions stemming from Queen Anne. Most were similar in massing to Shoppell's "modern house," (see Fig. 2) and all stood on lots ready for planting with lawn, trees, and shrubs. Unfortunately, many have been destroyed through the years. Among those remaining, the importance of pattern books to local home builders is readily apparent, for several are from pattern books or are pattern-book inspired. A large Robert Shoppell pattern book house was built on the corner of Garden and Chestnut Streets in 1890 (Fig. 85). This house, about which little historical information has been found, does

Fig. 85. House in Bellingham, Wash., 1890, from Shoppell's Artistic Modern Houses, *ca. 1887. (Photograph by Barbara Plaskett)*

Fig. 86. "Wardner's Castle," Bellingham, Wash., 1890, in the shingle style by Boston transplants, Longstaff and Black. (Photograph by Barbara Plaskett)

not have the elaborate decoration embraced by owners of many of the houses that were torn down. It was one of Shoppell's recent integrations of shingle and modern suburban, complete with bell candle turret, bays, and porches. The Longstaff and Black team designed "Wardner's Castle" in 1890 for real estate promoter James F. Wardner, who was reported to have made sixty thousand dollars through investments in two months (Fig. 86). The house is a massive three-story, sixteen room home similar to shingled summer homes for the Boston wealthy. The two architects built a slightly smaller home in the vertically massed shingle fashion for themselves a few blocks down the hill from the Wardner home (Fig. 87). Investigation of the home's structure by the current owner finds that they built it as a

Fig. 87. Shingle style residence of Longstaff and Black families, Bellingham, Wash., 1890. (Photograph courtesy of Madge Gleeson)

double house with an external appearance as one large home. Roland Gamwell, a former Bostonian himself, hired Longstaff and Black, too, but the architects and their client took full advantage of the eclectic exuberance so criticized by proponents of colonial and shingle simplicity (Fig. 88). Even in this dramatic house with its plethora of decorative detail and brilliant stained glass windows, the Gamwells shunned the use of mass-produced interior woodwork. Several German-born craftsmen who could not find enough work in a now-struggling Tacoma were hired to finish the stair hall (Fig. 89). In the meantime, the James Bolster family built an uncommon home in this

Fig. 88. Gamwell house by Longstaff and Black, Bellingham, Wash., 1890–1892. (Photograph courtesy of Ken and Marcia Culver)

land of old growth forests. It was a red brick home in the prevailing modern suburban genre (Fig. 90). Bolster owned a brick manufacturing company, and the house was an advertisement for his product. The Bateman family built a house with a squared, compact plan, but with all of the decorative features excoriated by the architects who argued for discipline in architectural design (Fig. 91). The Clark home, begun in 1889 and voted the most beautiful example of residential architecture in Fairhaven in 1890, was more elaborate than any of the houses noted above. It would have sent A. F. Oakey into paroxysms of horror (Fig. 92). But in the years that the *Craftsman* published its

Fig. 89. Gamwell house stair hall completed by German immigrant craftsmen, 1892. (Photograph courtesy of Ken and Marcia Culver)

harsh criticisms of nineteenth-century taste, which were quoted in the introduction, the Clark house was remodeled into a stately Tudor home (Fig. 93).[6] Oddly, in 1892, the treasurer of New Whatcom chose a house design from a much earlier pattern book. The design for the Isensee house was introduced in A. J. Bicknell's *Cottage and Construc-*

Fig. 90. A brick home in the modern fashion built by a local brick manufacturer. Bolster house, Bellingham, Wash., 1891. (Photograph by Barbara Plaskett)

tive Architecture (1873), although the Isensee family may have seen it in the book's 1886 edition (Fig. 94). Perhaps a house that demonstrated enduring fashion held some importance for an owner who was convicted of embezzling $50,000 from the city before he could move into it! With a very different perspective on fashion, Mr. and Mrs. A. W. Atkins built a small home in the very latest shingle fashion and very similar to F. White's design in Brunner's 1884 pattern book, but with a turret.

Other late-nineteenth-century homes with and without pattern book house silhouettes and details remain in contempoary Bellingham, and the city is now capitalizing on its history for housing design, tourism, and business development. Maps guide visitors through the streets of Fairhaven and other areas of Bellingham containing turn-of-the-century houses. Several of the houses have become bed and breakfast lodgings. One is a so-called Queen Anne revival built in the 1970s that prompts tourists to take photographs for their record of "Victorian Bellingham." Vestiges of the old are popular in new houses for local residents, too. Recently built

Fig. 91. Bateman house, Bellingham, Wash., 1891. (Photograph by Barbara Plaskett)

housing developments are filled with houses that are unmistakably (post)modern, but they have multi-paned windows, bays, gabled dormers, eyebrow dormers, turrets, and complex silhouettes.

The community is growing and changing rapidly once again. The mythical image of the Northwest as a land of opportunity, beautiful nature, and small, safe communities again lures new residents from the east and south. The commercial center of Bellingham struggles, however, because a new, enclosed mall has moved in, and the downtown has quickly deteriorated. Consumers seek both the variety of goods and the protection from weather the mall has to offer. Feeling a loss of business and community identity a decade later, a large group of citizens has been organized to revitalize the heart of

Fig. 92. Clark house, Bellingham, Wash., 1889, voted the most beautiful home in the community of Fairhaven, 1891. (Photograph courtesy of Angela Cuevas)

this formerly small town. One plan that is taking hold in the citizens' minds is a beautification program that will add planters of flower, old-fashioned street lights, and rehabilitated old buildings. Buses disguised as trolleys are already in operation. In this proposal, the central street will be closed off to make a community common space—especially for downtown shopping. Meanwhile, at a suburban edge of Bellingham, an open-air shopping center specifically designed as a small-town Main Street holds festivals and other activities to foster a sense of community for the suburban residents who are moving into a new development that sprawls over hills above. The streetlights emulate nineteenth-century designs and the building facades are recognizably old-fashioned as well as new. A bandstand gazebo and a fountain are its crowning touches. In Bellingham and in many other cities it seems that many contemporary "Americans" have chosen to make use of nineteenth-century notions about a model way of life. The social conditions are very different at the close of this century, but important questions about reconstructing a nostalgic past are raised as we look closely at the formations of national, community,

Fig. 93. Clark house as it was remodeled ca. 1904. (Photograph by Barbara Plaskett)

Fig. 94. Isensee house, Bellingham, Wash., 1892, after a design in Bicknell's Cottage and Constructive Architecture, 1873. *(Photograph by Barbara Plaskett)*

and social identity from the late nineteenth century. The processes of forming a relationship between American identity and suburban home ownership should prompt us to ask, whose memory is being proposed today as a normative vision for the future? And whose identity is being affirmed or dislocated as citizens and civic leaders work toward community?

NOTES

1 See Alan Gowans, *The Comfortable House: North American Suburban Architecture 1890–1930* (Cambridge and London: MIT Press, 1986).

2 From Ramon Heller, *Sell 'em Low — Send and Get More, A Centennial History of Morse Hardware Company* (Bellingham, Wash.: Morse Hardware Company, 1984); Washington State Archives, Western Washington University, and Morse family archives, Bellingham, Wash.

3 There were also a New Whatcom and an Old Bellingham in the chronicle of changing names for the bay communities.

4 *The Fairhaven Herald*, December 29, 1890, editorial page. Additional quotations and Bellingham history are drawn from E. Rosamonde Ellis Van Miert, *The Fairhaven Hotel Journal 1889–1956* (Bellingham, Wash.: By the Author, 1993). Other sources used are Lottie Roeder Roth, ed., *History of Whatcom County. Vol. I* (Chicago: Pioneer Historical Publishing Company, 1926), and Daniel E. Turbeville III, *An Illustrated Inventory of Historic Bellingham Buildings 1852–1915* (Bellingham, Wash.: Bellingham Municipal Arts Commission, 1977). Special thanks to Richard Vanderway, Director of Education, Whatcom Museum of History and Art for his observations.

5 V. B. (Van Brunt?), "Archaeology and the Vernacular Architect," *American Architect* 4(October 26, 1878): 143.

6 "Clark Mansion,"*Fairhaven Gazette* 5(Winter 1990): 1–2.

◿ Bibliography ◺

Primary sources

Allen, Frank P. *Artistic Dwellings*. Grand Rapids, Michigan: By the Author, 1891.
American Architect and Building News 1(May 13, 1876): 154; 3(January 26, 1878): 25–26; 3(April 20, 1878): 134; 3(August 10, 1878): 47.
"American Architecture—Past." *American Architect* 2(July 29, 1876): 242–44.
"American Architecture—Present." *American Architect* 1(August 5, 1876): 251.
"American Architecture—with Precedent and without." *American Architect* 4(October 26, 1878): 138–40.
American Builder 11(November 1875): 262; 23(September 1887): 223.
"American Institute of Architects. Boston Chapter." *American Architect* 2(February 17, 1877): 53–54.
"American Vernacular Architecture." *American Architect* 2(September 1, 1877): 280; "American Vernacular Architecture. II." 3(May 25, 1878): 182; "American Vernacular Architecture. III." 3(June 8, 1878): 198–99; "American Vernacular Architecture. IV." 3(July 6, 1878): 5; "American Vernacular Architecture. V." 3(September 21, 1878): 101.
"An Apt Reply." *American Architect* 1(August 12, 1876): 264.
"Archaeology and American Architecture." *American Architect* 1(July 1, 1876): 243.
"Art." *Atlantic Monthly* 33(January 1874): 119–23; 39(May 1877): 641–44.
Atwood, Daniel Topping. *Atwood's Country and Suburban Houses*. New York: Orange Judd & Company, 1871.
Atwood, Daniel Topping. *Atwood's Rules of Proportion*. New York: By the Author, 1867.
"'Balloon-built Buildings'—How False Statements Gather Strength." *California Architect and Building News* 2(February 1881): 16.
Barber, George F. *Cottage Souvenir, No. 2: A Repository of Artistic Cottage Architecture and Miscellaneous Designs*. Knoxville, Tenn.: S. B. Newman & Company, 1891.
"Bedford Park, London." *Chamber's Journal* 31(December 1881): 41.
Beecher, Catherine E. "A Woman's Profession Dishonored." *Harper's New Monthly Magazine* 29(November 1864): 76.
Beecher, Catherine E., and Harriet Beecher Stowe. *American Woman's Home, or, Principles of Domestic Science*. New York: J. B. Ford & Co., 1876.
Beers, Henry A. *A Suburban Pastoral And Other Tales*. New York: Henry Holt and Company, 1894.
"Better Times Coming." *Quarterly Architectural Review* 1(January 1879): 20.
Bicknell, Amos Jackson. *Cottage and Villa Architecture*. New York: A. J. Bicknell & Co., 1878.
———. *Detail and Cottage Constructive Architecture*. New York: A. J. Bicknell & Co., 1873.

————. *Specimen Book of One Hundred Architectural Designs*. New York: A. J. Bicknell & Co., 1878.

————. *Supplement to Bicknell's Village Builder*, 5th ed. New York: A. J. Bicknell & Co., 1878.

————. *Village Builder*. Troy, N.Y. and Springfield, Ill.: By the Author, 1870.

Bloor, A. J. "Annual Address." Tenth Annual Convention, Phila-delphia. *American Architect and Building News* 2(March 24, 1877): Supplement.

Bolles, Albert C. *Industrial History of the United States*. 3rd. ed., reprint ed. New York: August M. Kelley, 1966 (1881).

"Books." *American Architect* 18(August 29, 1885): 104.

Boston Society of Architects. Minutes, 2 February 1877; 8 February 1878.

Brunner, Arnold William. *Cottages, or Hints on Economical Building*. New York: William T. Comstock, 1884.

Brydon, John McKean. "A Few More Words About 'Queen Anne.'" *American Architect* 2(October 6, 1877): 320–22.

"Builders' Book Keeping." *American Builder* 14(November 1878): 4.

"Building in New Haven." *American Architect* 1(November 25, 1876): 380–81.

Burnet, William T. *The Suburban Cottage*. William T. Comstock, 1885.

C___. "The 'Queen Anne' Style." *American Architect* 7(February 21, 1880): 73.

C___., W___. S___. "Mr. Holly's Modern Dwellings." *American Architect* 3(June 15, 1878): 212.

Cady, Cleveland J. "Some Features of the Dutch Farm-Houses of New Jersey." *American Architect* 2(December 1877): 401–02.

Campbell, Helen. *The Problem of the Poor: A Record of Quiet Work in Unquiet Places*. New York: Fords, Howard and Hulbert, 1882.

————. *Darkness and Daylight: Lights and Shadows of New York Life*. Hartford: The Hartford Publishing Company, 1895.

Carpenter, James H. *The Complete Housebuilder*. Chicago: Donohue, Henneberry & Co., 1890.

Carrere, John, and Thomas Hastings. *Florida, the American Riviera, St. Augustine the Winter Newport*. New York: Gliss Brothers and Turnure, the Art Age Press, 1887.

"Centennial Architecture." *American Architect* 1(June 3, 1876): 178; "Centennial Architecture. II." 1(June 10, 1876): 186.

"Centennial Morbidity." *The Mobile Daily Register*, 19 January 1876, p. 2.

"Centennial Notes." *Arthur's Illustrated Home Magazine* 43(November 1875): 689.

"Characteristics of the International Fair. I." *Atlantic Monthly* 38(July 1876): 85–91; "Characteristics of the International Fair. II." 38(August 1876): 233–39; "Characteristics of the International Fair. III." 38(September 1876): 350–59; "Characteristics of the International Fair. IV." 38(October 1876): 492–501; "Char-acteristics of the International Fair. V." 38(November 1876): 737–38.

Clark, Alfred C. *The Architect, Decorator and Furnisher*. Chicago: Cowdrey, Clark & Co., 1884.

Clarke, Thomas Curtis. "Rapid Transit in Cities. I.—The Problem." *Scribner's Magazine* 11(January–June 1892): 566–78.

Comstock, William T. *Modern Architectural Designs and Details*. New York: William T. Comstock, Architectural Publisher, 1881.

Conway, Moncure. "Bedford Park." *Harper's New Monthly Magazine* 62(March 1881): 481–91.

————. *Travels in South Kensington*. New York: Harper & Brothers, 1882.

Cook, Clarence. "Beds and Tables, Stools and Candlesticks." *Scribner's Monthly Magazine* 10(June 1875): 169–82; "II." 11(January 1876): 342–57; "III." 11(February 1876): 488–503; "IV." 12(April 1876): 809–22; "V." 13(June 1876): 168–75; "VI." 13(October 1876): 796–807; "VII." 13(November 1876): 86–95; "VIII." 13(January 1877): 318–28; "IX." 13(March 1877): 656–66; "X." 13(April 1877): 816-820; "XI." 14(May 1877): 1–8.

————. *The House Beautiful* New York: Scribner, Armstrong and Company, 1878.

"Correspondence." *American Architect* 1(April 1, 1876): 110.

"Correspondence: An Architectural Year." *American Architect* 2(February 14, 1877): 60–61.

"Correspondence: Styles of Architecture." *Carpentry and Building* 5(February 1883): 36.

"Country Building." *American Builder* 15(March 1879): 59.

"Crazy Quilt Architecture." *American Architect* 18(July 11, 1885): 20.

Croff, Gilbert Bostwick. *Model Suburban Architecture*. New York: By the Author, 1871.

————. *Progressive American Architecture*. New York: Orange Judd Company, 1875.

Crosby, Ernest. "The Century of Ugliness." *Craftsman* 6(July 1904): 409–10.

Cummings, Marcus Fayette, and Charles Crosby Miller. *Architecture: Designs for Street Fronts, Suburban Houses, and Cottages*. Troy, N.Y.: Young & Benson, 1865.

Custer, George A. "Battling with the Sioux on the Yellowstone." *Galaxy* 22(July 1876): 91–102.

Cutter, Manly. *Designs for Modern Buildings*. New York: New York Building Plan Co., 1887.

Darwin, Charles. *On the Origin of Species*, reprint ed. New York: Heritage Press, 1963 (1859).

Davis, Alexander Jackson. *Rural Residences*. New York: By the Author, 1837.

Downing, Andrew Jackson. *The Architecture of Country Houses*. New York: D. Appleton & Co., 1850; reprint ed., New York: Dover Publications, 1980.

————. *Cottage Residences*. New York and London: Wiley & Putnam, 1842.

————. *Cottage Residences*, new ed. New York: John Wiley & Son, 1873.

Eastlake, Charles Locke. *Hints on Household Taste*, 4th ed. London: Longmans, Green and Company, 1878; reprint ed., New York: Dover Publications, 1969.

————. "From Mr. Charles L. Eastlake." *California Architect and Building News* 3(April 1881): 1.

"Eclecticism in Architecture." *American Architect* 1(January 15, 1876): 18–19.

Eidlitz, Leopold. *The Nature and Function of Art, More Especially of Architecture*. New York: A.C. Armstrong, 1881.

Eidlitz, Leopold. "The Qualifying of Architects." *The American Architect* 3(May 25, 1878): 185–86.

Elliot, Charles W. "Pottery at the Centennial." *Atlantic Monthly* 38(November 1876): 575–76.

Elsing, William T. "Life in New York Tenement-Houses." *Scribner's Magazine* 11(January–June 1892): 697–721.

"English Architecture at the Exhibition." *American Builder* 12(April 1876): 81–82.

Fergusson, James. *A History of Architecture in All Countries from the Earliest Times to the Present Day*. London: John Murray, 1874.

Ferree, Barr. "An 'American Style' of Architcture." *Architectural Record* 1(July–September 1891): 39–45.

Flagg, Wilson. "Rural Architecture." *Atlantic Monthly* 37(April 1876): 428–43.

Fletcher, Henry J. "The Doom of the Small Town." *Forum* 19(April 1895): 214–23.

"Foreign Buildings at the Centennial." *American Architect* 1(March 25, 1876): 101–02.

Garnsey, George. *The National Builders' Album of Beautiful Homes*. Chicago: The National Builder Publishing Co., 1891.

Gibson, Louis Henry. *Convenient Houses with Fifty Plans for the Housekeeper*. New York: Thomas Y. Crowell & Co., 1889.

Graphites. "The 'Queen Anne' Style." *American Architect* 7(February 21, 1880): 73.

Hamilton, Walter. *The Aesthetic Movement in England*. 3rd. ed. rev. London: Reeves and Turner, 1882.

Hamlin, A. D. F. "The Battle of Styles." *Architectural Record* 1(January–March 1892): 265–75.

———. *A Text-book of the History of Architecture*. New York: Longmans, Green, and Co., 1897.

"Handsome Brick Cottages." *American Builder* 15(October 1879): 232.

Hartshorne, Henry. *Our Homes*. Philadelphia: Presley Blakiston, 1880.

Harvey, Turlington W. "Letter to a Friend." 17 November 1888. From the Harvey File, Moody Bible Institute Library, Chicago, Illinois. In James Gilbert. *Perfect Cities: Chicago's Utopias of 1893*. Chicago: University of Chicago Press, 1991.

Hobbs, Isaac and Son. *Hobbs's Architecture*. 2nd. ed. rev. and enl. Philadelphia: J. B. Lippincott & Co., 1876.

Holly, Henry Hudson. "The American Style." *American Architect* 2(August 18, 1877): 267.

———. *Modern Dwellings in Town and County Adapted to American Wants and Climate with a Treatise on Furniture Decoration*. New York: Harper & Brothers, Publishers, 1878.

———. "Modern Dwellings: Their Construction, Decoration, and Furniture. I. Construction." *Harper's New Monthly Magazine* 52(May 1876): 855–67; "II. Color Decoration." 53(June 1876): 49–64; "III. Furniture." 53(July 1876): 217–26; "IV. Furniture." 53(August 1876): 354–63.

"A Home Costing about $1,200." *Scientific American Architects and Builders Edition* 2(September 1886): 53.

Hopkins, David S. *Cottage Portfolio*. New York: Fred A. Hodgson, Pub., 1886.

———. *Houses and Cottages*. Grand Rapids, Mich.: By the Author, 1889.

———. *Houses and Cottages*. Book No. 4. Grand Rapids, Mich.: By the Author, 1891.

Horton, Caroline W. *Architecture for General Students*. New York: Hurd and Houghton, 1874.

"Household Furnishing: The Queen Anne Style." *Harper's Bazaar* 9(October 1, 1876): 674–75.

Howells, William Dean. "A Sennight at the Centennial." *Atlantic Monthly* 38(July 1876): 92–107.

Hoyt, Charles S. "The Causes of Pauperism." *Tenth Annual Report of the State Board of Charities*. New York, 1877.

Hussey, Elisha Charles. *Hussey's National Cottage Architecture or Homes for Everyone*. New York: George E. Woodward, 1874.

———. *Home Building*. New York: By the Author, 1876.

"Important New Buildings." *American Builder* 15(March 1879): 59.

"Industrial Education." *American Builder* 14(December 1878): 272.

Ingram, J. S. *The Centennial Exposition*. Philadelphia: Hubbard Bros., 1876.

"In Search of a Style." *American Architect* 1(August 12, 1876): 259–60.

King, David Woodbury. *Homes for Home Builders or Practical Designs for Country Farm and Village*. New York: Orange Judd Co., 1886.

Kirby, J. H. *Kirby's Domestic Architecture*. Philadelphia: By the Author, 1874.

———. *Modern Cottages*. Syracuse, N.Y.: By the Author, 1886.

Lakey, Charles. *Lakey's Village and Country Houses* (New York: American Builder Publishing Co., 1875.

Leicht, Alfred F. *A Few Sketches of Picturesque Suburban Homes*. New York: By the Author, 1892.

Longfellow, W. P. P. "The Course of American Architecture." *The New Princeton Review* 3(March 1887): 200–11.

Manning, Warren H. "The History of Village Improvement in the United States." *Craftsman* 5(February 1904): 423–32.

Mason, George C., Jr. "Colonial Architecture.—I." *American Architect* 10(August 13, 1881): 71–74; "Colonial Architecture.—II." 10(August 20, 1881): 83–85.

Mason, George C., Jr. *The Old House Altered*. New York: G.P. Putnam's Sons, 1878.

———. "Queen Anne or Free Classic Architecture." *Lippincotts Magazine* o.s. 36, n.s. 10(November 1885): 454.

McCabe, James D. *The Pictorial History of the United States*. Phila-delphia: The National Publishing Co., 1877.

"Miscellaneous Notes." *American Builder* 15(July 1879): 169.

Mitchell, Donald G. "In and About the Fair." *Scribner's Monthly Magazine* 12(September 1876): 742–49.

Morse, Edward S. *Japanese Homes and Their Surroundings*. Boston: Ticknor and Company, 1886.

Narjoux, Felix M. "Journey of an Architect in the North-West of Europe. III: How Corners are Treated at Hanover." *American Architect* 2(February 3, 1877): 39–40; VII." 2(March 17, 1877): 87–88.

National Building Plan Association. *Artistic Homes*. Detroit: National Building Plan Association, 1888.

"Nebulae." *The Galaxy* 21(March 1876): 431–36; 21(April 1876): 580–83; 21(May 1876): 721–23.

"The Necessity of Individual Research." *American Architect* 1(April 8, 1876): 119–20.

"The Need of Unity." *American Architect* 1(January 1, 1876): 2–3.

Nelson, Richard. *Suburban Homes for Business Men, on the Line of the Maretta Railroad*. Cincinnati: Nelson & Bolles, Land Agents and Note Brokers, n.d.

"New Books." *American Architect* 1(September 16, 1876): 303.
"A New Profession." *American Architect* 1(April 1, 1876): 109–10.
"New Publications." *American Builder* 12(August 1876): 192–93; 13(September 1877): 208; 14(February 1878): 44–45; 14(July 1878): 162; 14(November 1878): 258; 15(March 1879): 59.
Newsom, Samuel and Joseph C. *Picturesque California Homes.* San Francisco: By the Authors, 1884; reprint ed., Los Angeles: Hennessey & Ingalls, Inc., 1978.
Northrup, Birdsey Grant, "The World of Village-Improvement Societies." *Forum* 19(March 1895): 95–104.
"Notes and Clippings: New Jersey and the Centennial Exhibition." *American Architect* 1(February 19, 1876): 64.
"Notes and Clippings: Queen Anne." *American Architect* 1(October 21, 1876): 344.
"Notes on Current Topics." *American Builder* 12(January 1876): 5.
Oakey, Alexander F. "Architect and Client." *American Architect* 1(August 26, 1876): 275–77.
———. *Building a Home.* New York: D. Appleton and Company, 1881.
Palliser, George. *Model Homes for the People.* Bridgeport, Conn.: By the Author, 1876; reprint ed., Watkins Glen: American Life Foundation, 1978.
Palliser, Palliser and Co. *American Architecture; or Every Man a Complete Builder.* New York: J. S. Ogilvie, Publisher, 1888.
———. *Miscellaneous Architectural Designs and Details.* New York: J. S. Ogilvie, Publisher, 1891.
———. *Modern Dwellings: A Book on Building for Industrial Americans.* New York: J. S. Ogilvie, Publisher, 1892.
———. *New Cottage Homes and Their Details.* New York: Palliser, Palliser and Co., 1887.
———. *Palliser's Model Homes.* Bridgeport, Conn: Palliser, Palliser and Co., 1878.
———. *Useful Details.* Bridgeport, Conn.: Palliser, Palliser and Co., 1881.
Peabody, Robert S. "A Talk about 'Queen Anne.'" *American Architect* 2(April 28, 1877): 133–34.
———. "Georgian Houses of New England." *American Architect* 2(October 20, 1877): 338–39.
Pelton, John C., Jr. *Cheap Dwellings.* San Francisco: The San Francisco Bulletin Company, 1882.
Pennell, Elizabeth Robins. "Cycling." *St. Nicholas* 17(July 1890): 733–39.
"The Point of View." *Scribner's Magazine* 9(January–June 1891): 393–96.
Pierce & Dockstader. *Modern Buildings of Moderate Cost.* Elmira, N.Y.: By the Authors, 1886.
Price, Bruce. "The Suburban House." *Scribners Magazine* 8(July 1890): 3–19.
"Publisher's Circular." *American Builder* 12(December 1876): 283.
Quackenbos, John D. *Physical Geography.* Appleton's American Standard Geographies. New York: D. Appleton and Co., 1887.
"The Qualifying of Architects." *American Architect* 3(April 20, 1878): 135; "The Qualifying of Architects. II." 3(April 27, 1878): 142.
"Queen Anne." *American Architect* 7(April 7, 1880): 168.

R___. "Correspondence. So-Called Queen Anne Work.—Mr. Burges's House." *American Architect* 3(November 2, 1878): 148.

Reed, Samuel Burrage. *Cottage Houses for Village and Country Homes*. New York: Orange Judd Company, 1883.

———. *Dwellings for Village and Country*. New York: Orange Judd Company, 1885.

———. *House Plans for Everybody*. New York: Orange Judd Company, 1878.

Rehman, Antoinette. "The Modern House Beautiful: An Exhortation." *Craftsman* 7(February 1905): 567–70.

"Report of Meetings: The Baltimore Chapter." *American Architect* 1(February 19, 1876): 63.

Richards, C. J. *House-Building from a Cottage to a Mansion*. New York: G. P. Putnam's Sons, 1873.

Rideing, William H. "Life on Broadway." *Harper's New Monthly Magazine* 56(December 1877–1878): 229–39.

Riis, Jacob A. "How the Other Half Lives." *Scribner's Magazine* 6(December 1889): 643–62.

Robbins, Mary Caroline. "Village Improvement Societies." *Atlantic Monthly* 79(1897): 212–22.

Ruskin, John. *Sesame and Lilies*. Boston: Dana Estes and Company, 1900 (essays written 1864–1869).

———. *The Seven Lamps of Architecture*. New York: John Wiley, 1849; reprint ed., New York: Noonday Press, 1961.

Schuyler, Montgomery. "Concerning Queen Anne." *American Architect*. 1(December 16, 1876): 404–05.

———. "Recent Building in New York." *Harper's New Monthly Magazine* 67(September 1883): 557–78.

———. "What Constitutes Queen Anne?" *American Architect* 2(October 20, 1877): 339.

Scientific American Architects and Builders Edition 2(September 1886): 53.

Scott, Frank J. *The Art of Beautifying Suburban Home Grounds*. New York: D. Appleton & Co., 1870.

Shoppell, Robert W. *Artistic Modern Houses at Low Cost*. New York: The Co-operative Building Plan Association, ca. 1887.

———. *Building Plans for Modern Low-Cost Houses*. New York: The Co-operative Building Plan Association, 1884.

———. *How to Build a House*. New York: Co-operative Building Plan Association, ca. 1883.

———. *How to Build, Furnish, and Decorate*. New York: The Co-operative Building Plan Association, 1883.

———. *Modern Houses*. New York: The Co-operative Building Plan Association, ca. 1887.

———. *Modern Houses, Beautiful Homes*. New York: The Co-operative Building Plan Association, 1887.

Sloan, Samuel. *City Homes, Country Houses and Church Architecture, or the American Builders' Journal*. Philadelphia: Claxton, Remsun & Heffelfinger, 1871.

———. *The Model Architect*. Philadelphia: E.G. Jones & Co., 1852.

Smith, Frank L. *A Cosy Home: How It Was Built*. Boston: Press of T. O. Metcalf & Co., 1887.

————. *Suburban Homes; or, Examples of Moderate Cost Houses for Wollaston Park.* Boston: Wood, Harmon, & Co., 1890.

Smith, George T., and Charles M. Robinson. *Art in House Building.* Pittsburgh: By the Authors, 1890.

Smith, Oliver P. *The Domestic Architect.* Buffalo: Phinney & Co., 1854.

Smithmeyer, John L. *Our Architecture, and Its Defects.* Washington, D.C.: By the Author, 1880.

————. *Strictures on the Queen Anne Style of Architecture.* Washington, D.C.: By the Author, 1881.

Spofford, Harriet. *Art Decoration Applied to Furniture.* New York: Harper & Brothers, 1878.

Stevens, John Calvin, and Albert Winslow Cobb. *Examples of American Domestic Architecture.* New York: William T. Comstock, 1889.

Stevenson, John J. "Gothic Architecture." *Harper's New Monthly Magazine* 52(January 1876): 234–41.

Steward, Ira. "Poverty." *Massachusetts Statistics of Labor, House Document 173.* Boston: Wright and Potter, 1873.

Strong, Josiah. *Our Country: Its Possible Future and Its Present Crisis.* New York: Baker & Taylor, 1885.

Sturgis, Russell, Jr. "Modern Architecture." *North American Review* 112(January 1871): 160–77.

"Sub-contracts." *American Architect* 1(April 8, 1876): 120.

"Summary." *American Architect* 1(February 12, 1876): 50.

Sumner, William Graham. *What Social Classes Owe to Each Other.* New York: Harper & Brothers, 1883.

Swinton, William. *Elementary Course in Geography.* New York: Ivison, Blakeman, Taylor and Co., 1875.

"A Talk about Queen Anne." *American Architect* 2(April 28, 1877): 134.

Thompson, Robert Ellis. *The Development of the House: Annals of the Wharton School.* Philadelphia: Wharton School of Finance, University of Pennsylvania, 1885.

Todd, Sereno Edwards. *Todd's Country Homes and How to Save Money.* Hartford: Hartford Publishing Company, 1870.

"Too Much High Education." *American Builder* 15(May 1879): 114.

Trowbridge, John. "Imaginary Dialogue on Decorative Art." *Atlantic Monthly* 40(June 1878): 693–97.

Tuthill, William Burnet. *The Suburban Cottage.* New York: William T. Comstock, 1885.

"Unoccupied Houses in San Francisco." *Quarterly Architectural Review* 1(January 1879): 20.

V___. B___. "Archaeology and the Vernacular Architecture." *American Architect* 4(October 26, 1878): 143.

Van Brunt, Henry. "Architecture in the West." *Atlantic Monthly* 64(December 1889): 772–84.

————. Introduction to *Discourses on Architecture* by Eugene Emmanuel Viollet-le-Duc. Boston: James R. Osgood, 1875.

————. "On the Present Condition and Prospects of Architecture." *Atlantic Monthly* 57(March 1886): 374–84.

————. "Opening Address before the American Institute of Architects." *American Architect* 1(January 29, 1876): 35.

Van Rensselaer, Mariana Griswold. "American Country Dwellings. I." *Century Magazine* 32(May 1886): 3–20.

————. "Recent Architecture in America. Public Buildings. I." *Century Magazine* 28(May 1884): 323–38.

Varney, Almon C. *Our Homes and Their Adornments*. Detroit: J. C. Chilton & Co., Publishers, 1882.

Vaux, Calvert. *Villas and Cottages*, 2d. ed. New York: Harper & Brothers, 1864.

Walker, Charles Howard. "The Use of Architectural Styles." *American Architect* 9(April 16, 1881): 184–85.

Walker, Hobart A. "Cottages." *The Art Interchange* 34(August 1895): 50.

"What Constitutes Queen Anne?" *American Architect* 2(October 20, 1877): 339.

Wheeler, Gervaise. *Homes for the People in Suburb and Country*. New York: Charles Scribner, 1855.

Woodward, George Evertson. *Woodward's Country Homes*. New York: By the Author, 1865.

————. *Woodward's National Architect*. New York: By the Author, 1874–1877.

Woollett, William M. *Old Homes Made New*. New York: A. J. Bicknell & Co., 1878.

————. *Villas and Cottages, or Homes for All*. New York: A. J. Bicknell & Co., 1876.

"A Word with Clients.—I." *American Architect* 1(July 8, 1876): 222–23; "A Word with Clients.—III." 1(September 2, 1876): 284–85.

"The Workman Again." *American Architect* 1(February 19, 1876): 50–51.

Youmans, Edward L. *Herbert Spencer on the Americans and the Americans on Herbert Spencer*. New York: D. Appleton and Company, 1883; reprint ed., New York: Arno Press, 1976.

Secondary Sources

Anderson, Benedict. *Imagined Communities: Reflections on the Origin and Spread of Nationalism*. New York: Verso, 1983.

Andreski, Sanislav. *Herbert Spencer: Structure, Function and Evolution*. London: Michael Joseph, 1881.

Atherton, Lewis. *Main Street on the Middle Border*. Bloomington: University of Indiana Press, 1954.

Baer, Morley, Elizabeth Pomada, and Michael Larson. *Painted Ladies: The Art of San Francisco's Painted Victorian Houses*. New York: E. P. Dutton, 1978.

Bailey, Barbara Ruth. *Main Street Northeastern Oregon: The Founding and Development of Small Towns*. Portland: Oregon Historical Society, 1982.

Bakhtin, Mikhail M. *Speech Genres and Other Late Essays*. Trans. Vern W. McGee. Austin: University of Texas Press, 1986.

Barrows, Robert G. "Beyond the Tenement: Patterns of American Urban Housing, 1870–1930." *Journal of Urban History* 9(August 1983): 395–420.

Bassett, Donald. "Queen Anne and France." *Architectural History* 24(January 1981): 83–91.

Bledstein, Burton J. *The Culture of Professionalism: The Middle Class and the Development of Higher Education in America*. New York: W. W. Norton and Company, 1976.

Bloomfield, Anne. "The Real Estate Associates: A Land and Housing Developer of the 1870s in San Francisco." In Thomas Carter, ed. *Images of an American Land*. Albuquerque: University of New Mexico Press, 1997.

Blumin, Stuart M. "Black Coats to White Collars: Economic Change, Nonmanual Work, and the Social Structure of Industrializing America." In Stuart W. Bruchey, ed. *Small Business in American Life*. New York: Columbia University Press, 1980.

————. *The Emergence of the Middle Class: Social Experience in the American City, 1760–1900*. Cambridge, New York and Melbourne: Cambridge University Press, 1989.

Boyer, Paul. *Urban Masses and Moral Order in America, 1820–1920*. Cambridge: Harvard University Press, 1978.

Brendell-Pandich, Susanne. "From Cottages to Castles: the Country House Designs of Alexander Jackson Davis." In Peck, Amelia, ed. *Alexander Jackson Davis: American Architect 1803–1892*. New York: Metropolitan Museum/Rizzoli, 1992.

Brown, Dona. *Inventing New England: Regional Tourism in the Nineteenth Century*. Washington and London: Smithsonian Institution Press, 1995.

Chambers, S. Allen, Jr. *Lynchburg: An Architectural History*. Char-lottesville: University Press of Virginia, 1981.

Chudacoff, Howard P. *Mobile Americans: Residential and Social Mobility in Omaha 1880–1920*. New York: Oxford University Press, 1972.

Clark, Clifford Edward, Jr. *The American Family Home, 1800–1960*. Chapel Hill: University of North Carolina, 1986.

"Clark Mansion." *Fairhaven Gazette* 5(Winter 1990): 1–2.

Coles, William, ed. *Architecture and Society: Selected Essays of Henry Van Brunt*. Cambridge: Belknap Press of Harvard University Press, 1969.

Cooledge, Harold N., Jr. *Samuel Sloan: Architect of Philadelphia 1815–1884*. Philadelphia: University of Pennsylvania Press, 1986.

Cowan, Ruth Schwartz. *More Work for Mother: The Ironies of Housework Technology*. New York: Basix Books, 1983.

Culbertson, Margaret, comp. *American House Designs: An Index to Popular and Trade Periodicals, 1850–1915*. Westport: Greenwood Press, 1994.

Damon-Moore, Helen. *Magazines for the Millions: Gender and Commerce in the* Ladies Home Journal *and the* Saturday Evening Post, *1880–1910*. Albany: State University of New York, 1994.

Davies, Jane B. "Introduction." In Amelia Peck, ed. *Alexander Jackson Davis: American Architect 1803–1892*. New York: Metropolitan Museum/Rizzoli, 1992.

de Certeau, Michel. *The Practice of Everyday Life*. Trans. Steven Rendall. (Berkeley, Los Angeles and London: University of California Press, 1988.

Decker, Peter R. *Fortunes and Failures: White-Collar Mobility in Nineteenth-Century San Francisco*. Cambridge: Harvard Uni-versity Press, 1978.

Doucet, Michael J., and John C. Weaver. "Material Culture and the North American House: The Era of the Common Man, 1870–1920." *Journal of American History* 72(December 1985): 560–87.

Ebner, Michael H. *Creating Chicago's North Shore: A Suburban History*. Chicago: University of Chicago Press, 1988.

Edwards, Alba M. *Population: Comparative Occupation Statistics for the United States, 1870–1940. Sixteenth Census of the United States, 1940*. Washington, D.C.: U.S. Government Printing Office, 1943.

Elsen, Ruth M. *Guardians of Tradition*. Lincoln: University of Nebraska Press, 1964.

Ewen, Stuart. *All Consuming Images: The Politics of Style in Contemporary Culture*. New York: Basic Books, 1988.

Foner, Eric. *Reconstruction: America's Unfinished Revolution 1863–1877*. New York: Harper & Row, 1988.

Foner, Philip S. *The Great Labor Uprising of 1877*. New York: Monad Press, 1977.

Francaviglia, Richard V. *Main Street Revisited: Time, Space, and Image Building in Small-Town America*. Iowa City: University of Iowa Press, 1996.

Garvey, Ellen Graber. *The Adman in the Parlor: Magazines and the Gendering of Consumer Culture, 1880s–1910s*. Oxford: Oxford University Press, 1996.

Garvin, James L. "Mail-Order House Plans and American Victorian Architecture." *Winterthur Portfolio* 16(Winter 1981): 309–34.

Gilbert, James. *Perfect Cities: Chicago's Utopias of 1893*. Chicago: University of Chicago Press, 1991.

Girouard, Mark. *Sweetness and Light: The "Queen Anne" Movement 1860–1900*. Oxford: At the Clarendon Press, 1977.

Goody, Marvin, and Robert P. Walsh, eds. *Boston Society of Architects: The First Hundred Years, 1867–1967*. Boston: Boston Society of Architects, 1967.

Gowans, Alan. *The Comfortable House: North American Suburban Architecture 1890–1930*. Cambridge and London: MIT Press, 1986.

Greenfield, Richard R. "The 'Journey-to-Work': an Empirical Investigation of Work, Residence and Transportation, Philadelphia, 1850 and 1880." In Theodore Hershberg, ed. *Philadelphia: Work, Space, Family, and Group Experience in the Nineteenth Century*. New York: Oxford University Press, 1981.

Gutman, Herbert G. *Work, Culture, and Society in Industrializing America: Essays in American Working-Class and Social History*. New York: Alfred A. Knopf, 1976.

Hamer, David. *New Towns in the New World: Images and Perceptions of the Nineteenth-Century Urban Frontier*. New York: Columbia University Press, 1990.

Hamilton, Nancy. Interview. Bellingham, Wash., May 1998.

Handlin, David. *The American Home: Architecture and Society, 1815–1915*. Boston and Toronto: Little, Brown and Company, 1979.

Harris, Neil. "Museums, Merchandising, and Popular Taste: The Struggle for Influence." In Ian M.G. Quimby, *Material Culture and the Study of American Life*. New York: W. W. Norton and Company, 1978.

Hart, Arthur, A. "M. A. Disbrow & Company: Catalogue Archi-tecture." *Palimpsest* 56, 4(1975): 98–119.

———. "Sheet Iron Elegance: Mail Order Architecture in Montana." *Montana Historical Society* 40(Autumn 1990): 26–31.

Haywood, C. Robert. *Victorian West: Class and Culture in Kansas Cattle Towns*. Lawrence: University Press of Kansas, 1991.

Heller, Ramon. *Sell 'em Low—Send and Get More, A Centennial History of Morse Hardware Company.* Bellingham, Wash.: Morse Hardware Company, 1985.

Hersey, George L. "Godey's Choice." *Journal of the Society of Architectural Historians* 18(October 1959): 104–11.

Hitchcock, Henry Russell. *American Architectural Books.* New York: DaCapo Press, 1976.

———. "Ruskin and American Architecture, or Regeneration Long Delayed." In John Summerson, ed. *Concerning Architecture: Essays on Architectural Writers and Writing Presented to Nikolaus Pevsner.* London: Allen Lane, the Penguin Press, 1968.

Hofstader, Richard. *Social Darwinism in American Thought.* rev. ed. New York: George Braziller, 1959.

Hogan, David John. *Class and Reform, School and Society in Chicago, 1880–1930.* Philadelphia: University of Pennsylvania Press, 1985.

Holden, Wheaton A. "The Peabody Touch: Peabody and Stearns of Boston, 1870–1917." *Journal of the Society of Architectural Historians* 32(May 1973): 114–31.

Holquist, Michael. "Answering as Authoring: Mikhail Bakhtin's Trans-Linguistics." *Critical Inquiry* 10(December 1983): 307–19.

Hovinen, Gary R. "Suburbanization in Greater Philadelphia 1880–1941." *Journal of Historical Geography* 11, 2(1985): 174–95.

Horowitz, Daniel. *The Morality of Spending: Attitudes toward Consumer Society in America 1875–1940.* Baltimore: Johns Hopkins University Press, 1985.

Huseas, Marion M. "Entertainment on the Western Frontier." *Gateway Heritage* 3, 1(1982): 22–33.

Jackson, John Brinckerhoff. *American Space: The Centennial Years 1865–1876.* New York: W. W. Norton & Company, 1972.

Jackson, Kenneth T. *Crabgrass Frontier: The Suburbanization of the United States.* New York: Oxford University Press, 1985.

Kane, Kevin David, and Thomas L. Bell. "Suburbs for a Labor elite." *Geographical Review* 75, 3(1985): 319–34.

Katz, Michael B. *Poverty and Policy in American History.* New York: Academic Press, 1983.

Keyssar, Alexander. "Unemployment and the Labor Movement in Massachusetts, 1870–1916." In Herbert G. Gutman and Donald Bell, eds. *The New England Working Class and the New Labor History.* Urbana and Chicago: University of Illinois Press, 1987.

Kornwolf, James. "American Architecture and the Aesthetic Movement." In Metropolitan Museum of Art. *In Pursuit of Beauty: Americans and the Aesthetic Movement.* New York: Rizzoli, 1987.

Lagumina, Salvatore, J. *From Steerage to Suburbs.* New York: Center for Migration Studies, 1988.

Larsen, Lawrence H. *The Urban West at the End of the Frontier.* Lawrence, Kan.: Regents Press of Kansas, 1978.

Leach, William R. *Land of Desire: Merchants, Power, and the Rise of a New American Culture.* New York: Pantheon Books, 1993.

Lears, T. J. Jackson. "The Concept of Cultural Hegemony: Problems and Possibilities." *American Historical Review* 90(June 1985): 567–93.

————. *No Place of Grace: Antimodernism and the Transformation of American Culture 1880–1920*. New York: Pantheon Books, 1981.

Leavitt, Thomas W. "Creating the Past: The Record of the Stevens Family of North Andover." *Essex Institute Historical Collections* 106, 2(1970): 63–87.

Leonard, Carol, Isidor Williamson, and Wayne Rohrer. "Groups and Social Organizations in Frontier Cattle Towns in Kansas." *Kansas Quarterly* 12, 2(1980): 59–63.

Lloyd, William J. "Understanding Late Nineteenth-Century American Cities." *Geographical Review* 71, 4(1981): 460–71.

Maass, John. *The Glorious Enterprise: The Centennial Exhibition of 1876 and H. J. Schwarzmann, Architect-in-Chief*. Watkins Glen: American Life Foundation, 1973.

Marsh, Margaret. "Suburban Men and Masculine Domesticity 1870–1915." *American Quarterly* 40, 2(1988): 165–86.

McClaugherty, Martha Crabill. "Household Art: Creating the Artistic Home, 1868–1893." *Winterthur Portfolio* 18(Spring 1983): 1–26.

McGuire, Robert. "Economic Causes of Agrarian Unrest." *Journal of Economic History* 41(December 1981): 835–45.

McMurray, Sally. *Families and Farmhouses in Nineteenth-Century America: Vernacular Design and Social Change*. New York and Oxford: Oxford University Press, 1988.

Metropolitan Museum of Art. *In Pursuit of Beauty: Americans and the Aesthetic Movement*. New York: Rizzoli, 1987.

Mitchell, Eugene. *American Victorian*. New York: Van Nostrand Reinhold Company, 1979.

Morgan, Murray. *Puget's Sound: A Narrative of Early Tacoma and the Southern Sound*. Seattle: University of Washington Press, 1979.

Mosier, Richard D. *Making the American Mind: Social and Moral Ideas in the McGuffy's Readers*. New York: King's Crown Press, Columbia University, 1947.

Moss, Roger W. *Century of Color: Exterior Decoration for American Buildings, 1820–1920*. Watkins Glen: American Life Foundation, 1981.

Mott, Frank Luther. *A History of American Magazines 1885–1905*. Cambridge: The Belknap Press of Harvard University Press, 1957.

Noel, Thomas J. *Buildings of Colorado*. New York and Oxford: Oxford University Press, 1997.

Ohman, Richard. *Selling Culture: Magazines, Markets, and Class at the Turn of the Century*. London and New York: Verso, 1996.

Omoto, Sadayoshi. "The Queen Anne Style and Architectural Criticism." *Journal of the Society of Architectural Historians* 23(March 1964): 29–37.

Purser, Margaret. "Keeping House: Women, Domesticity, and the Use of Domestic Space in Nineteenth-Century Nevada." In Thomas Carter, ed. *Images of an American Land*. Albuquerque: University of New Mexico Press, 1997.

Reps, John W. *The Forgotten Frontier: Urban Planning in the American West before 1890*. Columbia and London: University of Missouri Press, 1981.

Rifkind, Carole. *Main Street: The Face of Urban America*. New York: Harper & Row, 1977.

Ripley, Thomas Emerson. *Green Timber: On the Flood Tide to Fortune in the Great Northwest.* Palo Alto: American West Publishing Company, 1968.

Roth, Leland M. *McKim, Mead & White Architects.* New York: Harper & Row, 1983.

Roth, Lottie Roeder, ed. *History of Whatcom County. Vol. I.* Chicago: Pioneer Historical Publishing Company, 1926.

Rowe, Peter G. *Making a Middle Landscape.* Cambridge: MIT Press, 1991.

Rydell, Robert. *All the World's a Fair: Vision of Empire at American International Expositions, 1876–1916.* Chicago: University of Chicago Press, 1984.

Saint, Andrew. *Richard Norman Shaw.* New Haven and London: Paul Mellon Centre for Studies in British Art Ltd. and Yale University Press, 1976.

Schlereth, Thomas J. *Artifacts and the American Past.* Nashville: American Association for State and Local History, 1980.

———. *Victorian America: Transformations in Everyday Life 1876–1915.* New York: HarperCollins Publishers, 1991.

Schuyler, David. *The New Urban Landscape: The Redefinition of City Form in Nineteenth-Century America.* Baltimore: Johns Hopkins, 1986.

Scully, Vincent J., Jr. *The Shingle Style and the Stick Style.* rev. ed. New Haven and London: Yale University Press, 1971.

Sharp, Joanne P. "Gendering Nationhood." In Nancy Duncan, ed. *Bodyspace: Destabilizing Geographies of Gender and Sexuality.* London and New York: Routledge, 1996.

Short, John Rennie. *Imagined Country: Environment, Culture and Society.* London and New York: Routledge, 1991.

Slotkin, Richard. *The Fatal Environment: The Myth of the Frontier in the Age of Industrialization 1800–1890.* New York: Atheneum, 1985.

Smeins, Linda E. "National Rhetoric, Public Discourse, and Spatialization: Middle Class America and the Pattern Book House." *Nineteenth-Century Contexts* 16(Spring 1992): 135–64.

Stein, Roger B. "Artifact as Ideology: The Aesthetic Movement in Its American Cultural Context." In Metropolitan Museum of Art. *In Pursuit of Beauty: Americans and the Aesthetic Movement.* New York: Rizzoli, 1986.

Stilgoe, John R. *Borderland: Origins of the American Suburb, 1820–1939.* New Haven and London: Yale University Press, 1988.

Stone, May N. "The Plumbing Paradox: American Attitudes toward Late Nineteenth-Century Domestic Sanitary Arrangements." *Winterthur Portfolio* 14(Autumn 1979): 283–309.

Strasser, Susan. *Never Done: A History of American Housework.* New York: Pantheon Books, 1982.

Stratton, Joanna L. *Pioneer Women: Voices from the Kansas Frontier.* New York: Touchstone, Simon and Schuster, 1981.

Teaford, Jon C. *Cities of the Heartland: The Rise and Fall of the Industrial Midwest.* Bloomington: Indiana University Press, 1993.

Thernstrom, Stephan. *Poverty and Progress: Social Mobility in a Nineteenth Century City.* Cambridge: Harvard University Press, 1964.

Thernstrom, Stephan, and Peter R. Knight. "Men in Motion: Some Data and Speculations about Urban Population Mobility in Nineteenth-Century America." In Tamara K. Hareven, ed. *Anonymous Americans: Explorations in Nineteenth-Century Social History.* Englewood Cliffs: Prentice Hall, 1971.

Tomlan, Michael A. Introduction to reprint ed., *Model Homes for the People* by George Palliser. Watkins Glen: American Life Foundation, 1978.
————. Introduction to *Toward the Growth of an Artistic Taste*, in reprint ed., *Cottage Souvenir No. 2* by George F. Barber. Watkins Glen: American Life Foundation, 1982.
Townsend, Gavin. "Airborne Toxins and the American House, 1865–1895." *Winterthur Portfolio* 24(Spring 1989): 29–42.
Turbeville, Daniel E. *An Illustrated Inventory of Historic Bellingham Buildings 1852–1915*. Bellingham, Wash.: Bellingham Municipal Arts Commission, 1977.
Underwood, Kathleen. *Town Building on the Colorado Frontier*. Albuquerque: University of New Mexico Press, 1987.
United States Bureau of the Census. *Historical Statistics of the United States: Colonial Times to 1970, Bicentennial Edition*. Washington, D.C.: U.S. Government Printing Office, 1975.
————. *Historical Statistics of the United States: Colonial Times to 1957*. Washington, D.C.: U.S. Government Printing Office, 1960.
Upton, Dell. *America's Architectural Roots: Ethnic Groups that Built America*. Washington, D.C.: The Preservation Press, 1986.
Upton, Dell. "Pattern Books and Professionalism: Aspects of the Transformation of Domestic Architecture in America, 1800–1860." *Winterthur Portfolio* 19(Summer/Autumn 1984): 107–50.
Van Miert, E. Rosamonde Ellis. *The Fairhaven Hotel Journal 1889–1956*. Bellingham, Wash.: By the Author, 1993.
Ward, David. *Poverty, Ethnicity, and the American City, 1840–1925*. New York: Cambridge University Press, 1989.
Warner, Sam Bass, Jr. *Streetcar Suburbs: The Process of Growth in Boston (1870–1900)*. Cambridge and London: Harvard University Press, 1978 [1962].
Wiebe, Robert H. *The Search for Order 1877–1920*. New York: Hill and Wang, 1967.
Williams, Raymond. *Problems in Materialism and Culture*. London: Verso Editions and NLB, 1980.
Wilson, Christopher P. "The Rhetoric of Consumption: Mass-Market Magazines and the Demise of the Gentle Reader, 1880–1920." In Richard Wightman Fox and T. J. Jackson Lears, eds. *The Culture of Consumption: Critical Essays in American History, 1880–1980*. New York: Pantheon Books, 1983.
Wilson, Julie. "'Kansas Uber Alles!': The Geography and Ideology of Conquest, 1870–1900." *Western Historical Quarterly* 27(Summer 1996): 171–87.
Wilson, Richard Guy. "American Architecture and the Search for a National Style in the 1870s." *Nineteenth Century* 3(Autumn 1977): 74–80.
————. "'The Decoration of Houses' and Scientific Eclecticism." *Nineteenth Century* 8, 3/4(1982): 193–204.
————. *McKim, Mead & White Architects*. New York: Rizzoli International Publications, 1983.
Wiltshire, David. *The Social and Political Thought of Herbert Spencer*. London: Oxford University Press, 1978.

Wood, Joseph P. "The New England Village as an American Vernacular Form." In, Camille Wells, ed. *Perspectives in Vernacular Architecture, II.* Columbia: University of Missouri Press, 1986.

Wood, J. S. and Steinitz, M. "A World We Have Gained: House, Common and Village in New England." *Journal of Historical Geography* 18, 1(1992): 105–20.

Woods, Mary. *The "American Architect and Building News" 1876–1907.* Dissertation, Columbia University, 1983.

Wright, Gwendolyn. *Building the Dream: A Social History of Housing in America.* New York: Pantheon Books, 1981.

———. *Moralism and the Model Home: Domestic Architecture and Cultural Conflict in Chicago 1873–1913.* Chicago: University of Chicago Press, 1980.

Zunz, Oliver. *The Changing Face of Inequality: Urbanization, Industrial Development, and Immigrants in Detroit, 1880–1920.* Chicago: University of Chicago Press, 1982.

⩗ Index ⩘

⟋ *About the Author* ⟍

Linda E. Smeins received her Ph.D. in 1989 from the Fine Arts Department at the University of British Columbia, with a specialization in North American Architecture. Smeins is currently a professor in the Department of Art at Western Washington University. Her teaching and research interests include the history of architecture and visual culture, with emphasis on North America. She has recently collaborated with two sociologists to co-author a book on the North American honeymoon (Bulcroft, Smeins, Bulcroft, *Romancing the Honeymoon*, working title, forthcoming from Sage Publications), in which she analyzes the cultural and architectural spaces of romantic tourism.

Other publications include a study of 1950s suburbs, "Stopovers in the Flight of Time," in Barbara Johns, ed., *Jetstreams* (exhibition catalogue, University of Washington Press/Tacoma Art Museum, 1994). Smeins has also examined pattern book houses in an article entitled "National Rhetoric, Public Discourse, and Spatialization: Middle Class America and the Pattern Book House," (*Nineteenth Century Contexts* 16 [Fall 1992]).